FRACTURE

FRACTURE

Barack Obama, the Clintons,
and the Racial Divide

❖

JOY-ANN REID

wm

WILLIAM MORROW
An Imprint of HarperCollins*Publishers*

HarperCollins books may be purchased for educational, business, or sales promotional use. For information please e-mail the Special Markets Department at SPsales@harpercollins.com.

FIRST EDITION

Library of Congress Cataloging-in-Publication Data has been applied for.

ISBN 978-0-06-230525-1

15 16 17 18 19   OV/RRD   10 9 8 7 6 5 4 3 2 1

For Philomena

CONTENTS

INTRODUCTION

IF YOU WERE A BLACK KID GROWING UP IN THE UNITED STATES in the 1970s and '80s—and you lived in a house like the one I grew up in, where we read the newspaper every morning, watched the evening news and *Nightline,* and rarely missed the Sunday talk shows—you knew that when you were old enough to vote, you would be a Democrat. The Democrats were "our party." The Republicans were "their party."

Sure, occasionally you heard about black Republicans here and there. But they were the exception: the stuffy business types with the perfectly symmetrical corporate Afros; the old southerners who liked to go on and on about the party of Abraham Lincoln; or Republican "wannabes," like my Congolese father, who didn't live in the United States and so only knew the political parties as an abstraction. For most black Americans, being political meant being a Democrat. Or in my Guyanese-immigrant, single mother's parlance, this was the party of Shirley Chisholm and Jack Kennedy, Lyndon Johnson and civil rights, "Run Jesse Run" and "Where's the beef?"—the hilarious Wendy's TV-commercial slogan appropriated by doomed presidential candidate Walter

Mondale. (My mother didn't care that he had no chance of beating Ronald Reagan. She loved that line.) The message that We Are Democrats was all but piped into my ideological DNA.

When Reagan beat Jimmy Carter in 1980, my sister and I burst out crying. She was in seventh grade and I was in sixth. (We didn't bother crying over Mondale; it was clear early on that his cause was lost.) The first vote I cast in a presidential primary was for Jesse Jackson, and my first vote for a presidential candidate was for Michael Dukakis. My sister canvassed for Gary Hart after school. I started working in the TV news business in 1998 and briefly left it in 2004 to work for the election of a Democratic president. I did so again in 2008. But the party that seemed almost organically to be my natural political home wasn't always so.

THE DEMOCRATIC PARTY'S TRANSFORMATION—FROM REPRE-senting the antebellum South, known for its "massive resistance" to integration and literal terrorism against black citizens; to the party that represented the vast majority of black Americans, whether descended from the enslaved or newly minted as U.S. citizens; and ultimately to the party that produced the nation's first black president—was one of the most dramatic turnabouts in American political history. It came through the crucible of a white, southern president, Lyndon Johnson, whose civil rights triumphs were quickly overwhelmed by a war that split him from the very coalition that had brought about such veritable miracles of civil rights and civic justice.

And it came at a cost.

After Johnson—and the tumult of the 1968 election, which saw the assassinations of Robert Kennedy and Martin Luther King Jr., and ultimately the election of Richard Nixon—the Democratic Party spent decades wrangling with his legacy, often disowning it, as the party struggled to regain favor with increasingly resentful white voters up north, and to stem the flight of white voters down south, as it continued to pursue the elusive White House.

As Republicans essentially took over as the party of southern conservatives, Democrats struggled to reconcile their newly robust multiracial character with the changing politics of the country. From Richard Nixon to Ronald Reagan, Republican presidential candidates nurtured and profited from the white working class's growing sense of grievance over those Johnson-era programs that attempted to add economic stability to the cadre of basic rights secured for African Americans (and poor whites). For Democrats, race would be both an elevator under their feet, growing their voter rolls particularly in the southern states and putting presidential elections within closer reach, and an anchor around their necks, shrinking their popularity with white working-class voters for a generation.

By the time Barack Obama and Hillary Clinton fought for the Democratic nomination in 2008, the party had largely ceded the southern states to the Republicans, even though the Democrats had sent two more white southerners to the White House after LBJ: Jimmy Carter and Bill Clinton. Clinton in particular struggled both during and after his presidency to reconcile the thorny issues of race and politics in American life. In 1992, he faced down Jesse Jackson, who in a scant twenty years had gone from bête noire of the Martin Luther King Jr. coterie to the pre-eminent force in black political life, and Clinton deftly emerged from his various showdowns, with Jackson and other black leaders who spoke out about Clinton's dramatic policy shifts to the right, to claim the symbolic mantle of "first black president."

But the Democratic Party in its present form—racially mixed in the north and west and nearly all black "down south"—wasn't completed before the ascent of the real first black president. Barack Obama's elevation to the White House in January 2009 was the symbolic coup de grâce that finally brought about that transformation. And President Obama's brief forays into the cultural thicket of race—speaking out on the shooting deaths of two young black men, Trayvon Martin and Michael Brown, and on the police's treatment of Harvard professor Henry Louis Gates—set off ideological grenades that by 2014 had tested his own party's tolerance for a "national conversation on race" and for a president who by his very being couldn't help but avoid the subject. The racial polarization of the Obama era helped push the Democratic Party into becoming precisely what conservatives in 1964 had wryly predicted it would: a party of ethnic minorities and liberal, northern whites, with almost no white presence south of the Mason-Dixon Line.

This book traces the Democratic Party's turbulent racial history, and the rocky road Democratic candidates and elected presidents have trod on their way to reconciling their party and their country's racist past with its increasingly diverse future. In many ways, the Democrats' evolution mirrors America's. Its internal struggle to balance the needs and aspirations of a multiracial citizenry offers a microcosm of the national imperative to do the same. With increased diversity, our national will to confront both the past and present conditions of a shrinking white majority and an ascending multiracial minority is increasingly being tested, over issues of immigration, voting rights, gay rights, policing, and more.

If the modern Republican Party represents the part of America that in fundamental ways is pulling backward toward a distant and irretrievable past, the current iteration of the Democratic Party represents the possibilities and challenges of a multiracial future. It doesn't always get the alchemy right, and if it ultimately fails, party loyalties and demographic compositions could one day be scrambled again. But for the time being, and for the foreseeable future, particularly for African Americans, the

Democrats are the only ball game, and with pressing issues of economic, health, and educational disparities, and with voting rights hanging in the balance, failure is not an option.

As Barack Obama prepares to end his presidency after two terms, the Democratic Party is poised to turn once again to the Clintons, with Hillary Clinton—the former Young Republican and onetime First Lady who remade herself into a United States senator and Obama's secretary of state—poised to inherit the mantle of leadership, and with it the job of managing and shaping the party's demographic future.

I wrote this book because if the Democrats can't get it right— and they haven't yet—it's hard to see how the country can.

FRACTURE

CHAPTER 1

1964

Negroes are continuously making progress here in this country. The progress in many areas is not as fast as it should be but they are making progress and we will continue to make progress. There is prejudice now, there's no reason that in the near and the foreseeable future that a Negro could also be president of the United States.

—Attorney General Robert F. Kennedy in a Voice of America broadcast, May 23, 1961

"They keep saying I have all this trouble in the Negro community, and I've never heard a Negro say that," Lyndon Johnson told Whitney Young, head of the National Urban League, during a brief telephone conversation on January 6, 1964.

The country was still reeling from the assassination of President John F. Kennedy, who had been cut down in LBJ's Texas just two months earlier. Racial strife rippled across the South, where black and white college students in carefully pressed and starched shirts and horn-rimmed glasses sat down at Woolworth's lunch counters; weathered women and men with sun-drawn faces lined up to register to vote; and young pastors and children with old souls met the whip and the hose and the stone wall of white resistance and hardened fealty to segregation.

In two days Johnson would be giving his first State of the Union address, and he was making a flurry of phone calls to gain support for a host of items. He was worrying over everything from a budget bill he was sending to the House to the elections later that year, when he would have to stand for president in his own right.

Johnson also had to deal with his fellow southerners in Congress who had signed the so-called Southern Manifesto, which was conceived in 1956 by Richard Russell of Georgia and Strom Thurmond of South Carolina and condemned the Supreme Court's ruling in *Brown v. Board of Education,* and which pledged to resist the desegregation of southern schools by "all lawful means." It had been signed by nineteen southern Democrats—all but the Tennessee delegation of Albert Gore Sr. and Estes Kefauver—and seventy-seven members of the House of Representatives. Johnson thought these lawmakers were being bullheaded in the face of history's headwinds. He had watched as his predecessors Dwight Eisenhower and John Kennedy were drawn reluctantly into defending civic justice for black Americans, but he saw in this issue a legacy he could build for himself.

The hardscrabble Texan had an uneasy relationship with the specter of the fallen president, in whose shadow he'd labored since 1960. And he was incensed that even as he contemplated a pair of recess appointments that would place two black men, Spottswood Robinson III and Aloysius Leon Higginbotham Jr., on the federal bench, *Jet* magazine was questioning his commitment to the cause.

Jet, the weekly bible of black news since its founding in Chicago in 1951, was where African Americans saw the gruesome pictures from the open casket containing the remains of lynched fourteen-year-old Emmett Till in 1955 and learned that a disturbed black woman named Izola Ware stabbed Martin Luther King Jr. with a letter opener in a Harlem department store in 1958. Now *Jet* readers were learning that Johnson had not been photographed with any black leaders since assuming the presidency.

"I want to appoint these judges," Johnson growled through the Oval Office telephone to Young. "[But] I don't want to do it unless the whole Negro community knows that *I'm* doing it and the *Democrats* are doing it, and this damned *Jet* and the rest of 'em quit cutting us up and saying that I hate the '*Nigroes.*'"

Young, along with other civil rights and labor leaders, including Roy Wilkins, the president of the National Association for the Advancement of Colored People (NAACP); Rev. Martin Luther King Jr.; James Farmer of the Congress of Racial Equality; and A. Philip Randolph, had spent three years lobbying, cajoling, and negotiating with the Kennedy administration for a civil rights bill that would put teeth into the Fourteenth and Fifteenth Amendments, and bring the South into full compliance with federal law and civilized modernity. Before that, in 1957, they'd pushed President Dwight Eisenhower to sign a civil rights bill—the first since Reconstruction—to bring federal power to bear to protect the voting rights of African Americans in the South, and which established a civil rights commission and a civil rights division at the Department of Justice.

"[The] strategy is as simple as it is profound," journalist Theodore H. White wrote in 1956. "It is to alter totally the patterns of Southern custom and life. 'It does no good,' the leaders of the NAACP say almost to a man, 'to send a rescue party South or mourn a colored man murdered in Mississippi. But if the federal government guarantees the Negro the right to vote down South, everything changes. No outsider can do anything about a Negro-hating sheriff in Tallahatchie County, but if Negroes vote they can change the sheriff. Arguing about segregation up North does little good—but if Negroes sit on school boards down South, they can act for themselves.'"

That fight had been long, arduous, and bloody. By 1964 just 4 in 10 African American adults in the South were registered to vote, and the situation was far worse in Alabama, where just 23 percent were registered, and in Mississippi, where the figure was only 6 percent. But with scathing front-page newspaper stories landing on the doorsteps of white American households up north, King's visible public image, and the nightly television broadcasts focused on the American South, civil rights groups had leveraged the 1963 March on Washington, and the firebombing of the 16th Street Baptist Church in Birmingham two weeks afterward—following months of marches, beatings, buses set on fire, dogs and fire hoses trained on men, women, and children in the city that blacks wryly nicknamed "Bombingham"—to push the Democratic-controlled Congress to advance the Civil Rights Act of 1963.

Johnson now carried the burden of seeing the civil rights bill through Congress while keeping his party from being torn in two. He wanted help from labor and civil rights leaders to shake loose the Republican votes the bill needed to defeat a filibuster by southern Democrats.

"They say I'm an arm twister," Johnson told Roy Wilkins during a January 22 call. "But I'm not a magician. . . . I can't make a southerner change his spots any more than I can make a leopard change his spots." Johnson's advice to Wilkins and his fellow civil rights leaders was paradoxical for the titular head of the Democratic Party. He urged them to work Republican senator Everett Dirksen of Illinois, and even to dangle the potential for black voter support for Dirksen's reelection, to solicit his help on the bill.

On February 10, the Civil Rights Act of 1964 emerged from

the grip of Howard W. Smith, the powerful Democratic chairman of the House Rules Committee and a hardened Virginia segregationist, and passed overwhelmingly in the full House by 290 votes to 130.

The vote came as America's cultural evolution was accelerating. The night before, the Beatles captivated 73 million Sunday night television viewers of *The Ed Sullivan Show*. Two weeks later, on February 25, a twenty-two-year-old boxer and 1960 Olympic gold medal winner from Louisville, Kentucky, named Cassius Clay beat Sonny Liston in a landmark bout in Miami Beach, at a time when neither man was permitted to try on clothes at the downtown Miami department stores, and when even Joe Louis, the retired champ, had to sleep in private homes in Miami's downtown black district, called Overtown. In victory, Clay announced that his name was now Muhammad Ali, and he would soon test the country's patience for a black superstar who shed Christianity for the Nation of Islam, and the dignified acceptance of secondary citizenship for an unabashed and defiant demand to speak loudly, and as an equal.

In the Senate, the civil rights bill rested in the hands of the Democratic majority leader, Mike Mansfield of Montana, who used a procedural maneuver to bypass the Judiciary Committee, led by James Eastland, a pugnacious Mississippi Democrat known as the "Voice of the White South." In 1957 Eastland had insisted in a rambling television interview with journalist Mike Wallace, just over a month before passage of the first Civil Rights Act, that 99 percent of "Nigras" in the South *preferred* segregation.

"The races segregate *themselves* on buses," Eastland said, adding that it had been "found, throughout the years, you have more harmony and the races can make more progress under a system of separate."

The bill would outlast a record fifty-four-day filibuster led by Russell, the Georgia Democrat, who declared that the southern bloc would "resist to the bitter end any measure or any movement which would have a tendency to bring about social equality and intermingling and amalgamation of the races in our states." He was joined by Thurmond of South Carolina and Robert Byrd of West Virginia. Those two, along with a handful of Republicans including Barry Goldwater, who happened to be running for president, launched a fourteen-hour filibuster of their own. But on June 19, 1964, the bill passed in the Senate, 73 votes to 27. It was a triumph for Lyndon Johnson, whose arm-twisting proved quite potent indeed. In the end, 46 Democrats and 27 Republicans voted in favor, while 21 southern Democrats and 6 Republicans voted "nay."

Two days after the Senate vote, on Father's Day, three civil rights workers—James Chaney, twenty-one, a local black man, and two young Jewish men from New York City, Michael "Mickey" Schwerner, twenty-four, and Andrew Goodman, twenty—disappeared in the heart of Neshoba County, deep in the Mississippi Delta, The three men had been part of the Student Nonviolent Coordinating Committee's "Mississippi summer project," which would later be dubbed "Freedom Summer," an attempt to send an integrated northern army of volunteers to strengthen the resolve of terrorized black would-be voters.

News of the men's disappearance, their faces peering out from an FBI flyer urging public help, quickly became a national and an international sensation, increasing the urgency for their representatives in Washington to act, because now white lives were also on the line.

When the Civil Rights Act went back to the House for final passage on July 2, it received overwhelming affirmation again: 289 to 126. The bill had split the Democratic Party straight down the Mason-Dixon Line, with the all-Democratic caucuses of Mississippi, Alabama, Louisiana, Arkansas, and North and South Carolina voting unanimously against it, while the tiny, all-Democratic delegations in Oregon, Rhode Island, Delaware, Hawaii, and Idaho were solid "ayes."

Senator Hubert Humphrey hailed the act as "the greatest piece of social legislation of our generation." President Johnson signed it into law hours after final passage, two days before Independence Day. But southern Democrats were crying "tyranny" and condemning the forces they blamed for it: the clergy, the media, and even labor unions, long a core component of the Democratic election apparatus.

Though he had taken a first, historic step toward history, and toward finishing what Kennedy, prodded by a broad and insistent civil rights movement, had started, Johnson could see the dam of political realignment massing inside his party's southern stronghold. The alienation of the South from the labor movement, and the sense of siege across the former Confederate states, particularly regarding the press, would be lasting.

One month after Johnson signed the Civil Rights Act, on August 4, the bodies of Goodman, Chaney, and Schwerner were found. They had been shot, beaten, and buried in an earthen dam in Philadelphia, Mississippi.

A month after that, on September 16, Strom Thurmond quit the Democratic Party for good, pledging his support, his South Carolina political machine, and his counsel to Goldwater. Thurmond accused his former party of "leading the evolution of our nation into a socialist dictatorship"; Democrats, he said, had "forsaken the people to become the party of minority groups, power-hungry union leaders, political bosses, and big businessmen looking for government contracts and favors."

"The Democratic Party has encouraged lawlessness, civil unrest, and mob actions," Thurmond ranted. "The Democratic Party . . . has sent our youth into combat in Vietnam, refusing to call it war. The Democratic Party now worships at the throne of power and materialism."

Thurmond was the first of the "Dixiecrats" to go. He wouldn't be the last. And his view of his former party would come to be the dominant view of a majority of white southern voters.

OUTSIDE THE SOUTH, NATIONAL DEMOCRATS, INCLUDING THE president, quickly began to view the newly liberated and growing black vote as their reward for a job well done on the Civil Rights Act. Johnson believed he'd earned the loyalty of the civil rights establishment and the black body politic, a belief that would be severely tested as the country became increasingly involved in Vietnam. Just one month after he signed the landmark civil rights bill, activists from Mississippi disrupted the Democratic National Convention in Atlantic City, New Jersey, with round-the-clock protests on the boardwalk. At the convention, activist Fannie Lou Hamer gave dramatic testimony, broadcast by the three televisions networks, about the brutality she and other would-be registrants endured inside a Mississippi jail. Johnson wanted Hamer off TV, fearing that the spectacle had the potential to cast him and his Democratic Party as villains in yet another racial conflagration.

African Americans had always seen their relationship with the two political parties as a means to an end. Constant agitation and pushing presidents from both parties were simply part of the process, and King had long warned the movement about becoming entangled in partisan affairs, telling a February 11, 1958, gathering at Bennett College in Greensboro, North Carolina: "I'm not inextricably bound to either party. I'm not concerned about telling you what party to vote for. But what I'm saying is this: that we must gain the ballot and use it wisely."

After Abraham Lincoln, black voters, when they could access the ballot box, had been strongly Republican, and after Franklin Roosevelt, increasingly Democratic.

Even in 1936, when black voters lent 71 percent of their

ballots to reelect Roosevelt, only 44 percent of African Americans identified themselves as Democrats, though by this time fewer than 40 percent continued to call themselves Republicans. When Roosevelt was elected to a fourth term in 1944, black party identification had *fallen* by 4 points, and FDR's share of the black electorate was down to 68 percent, with 21 percent calling themselves independents.

While the party often failed to address segregation, and in some cases, like housing, served to entrench it, the New Deal had been the first tranche of federal policy since Reconstruction to lift large swaths of African Americans out of despair. And with FDR's vice president, Harry Truman, up for election in 1948, facing Republican Thomas Dewey and "Dixiecrat" Strom Thurmond, who was running on a segregation line, black voters clung to the Democrats all the more, boosting their party identification by 16 points, and the share of their votes to 77 percent.

Theodore White, in a much-circulated column in *Collier's* magazine in August 1956, titled "The Negro Voter: Can He Elect a President?" wrote: "By 1948, when Truman squeezed out his hair's-breadth win over Dewey, carrying Illinois by 33,612 votes, California by 17,865 votes, Ohio by 7,107 votes, no practicing politician could ignore the fact that the Negro vote in these states was one of the vital margins by which the Presidency of the United States had been won."

Democrats held their overwhelming share of the black vote in 1952, as Adlai Stevenson, the liberal Illinois governor, received 76 percent as he faced war hero Dwight D. Eisenhower in the general election. But when Eisenhower faced Stevenson again four years later, two years after the Supreme Court's landmark school desegregation ruling in *Brown v. Board of Education of Topeka, Kansas,* Stevenson's share of the black vote dropped to 61 percent, Eisenhower's climbed from 24 to 39 percent, and just 56 percent of black Americans called themselves Democrats.

Eisenhower's reluctance to openly confront southern segregationists, his lack of public support for the *Brown* decision, and his reticence in using federal power to further the cause of civil rights may have encouraged southern resistance, and white citizens' councils sprang up across the southern states to resist the Supreme Court's desegregation ruling. But southern vehemence helped to doom the Democratic ticket with black voters. The Southern Manifesto debuted in the thick of the reelection campaign in March 1956, and among the signers was Stevenson's 1952 running mate, segregationist Alabama senator John Sparkman. And though Stevenson was now running with moderate Estes Kefauver, Stevenson's studious, "cautious disagreement" with the declaration of resistance worked to his disfavor as the news spread in black newspapers.

Stevenson, though mellifluous on the stump, was notoriously bland on civil rights, and at pains not to alienate his party's southern wing, whose consent had delivered him the nomination, including over Texas senator Lyndon Johnson. And Eisenhower, despite his silence on even the Emmett Till lynching, was a man with a growing record: on desegregating military bases and the District of Columbia, on increased federal hiring of black Americans, and on judicial appointments, where he put pro-desegregation moderates on the bench. Even Adam Clayton Powell Jr., the flamboyant Harlem congressman and the country's most visible black political leader, with a celebrity status in black households that was akin to a Hollywood star, took pains to point to Eisenhower as a man he could work with. Powell skipped the 1956 Democratic convention and even endorsed the president's reelection in October, forming "Independent Democrats for Eisenhower" (and earning the kind of scorn from the Democratic establishment the Dixiecrat apostates rarely faced).

By November 1956, Eisenhower, the Texas-born but Kansas-raised military man, and his Californian running mate, Richard

Nixon, seemed like a good deal for many black voters compared to a middling Democrat and a southerner.

It wasn't until 1964, with Johnson facing Goldwater, the outspoken foe of the Civil Rights Act, that the Democratic Party claimed the near-total support of black voters at 94 percent, with 82 percent of African Americans identifying as Democrats, a height from which they would barely look back.

Goldwater's victory over New York governor and billionaire Nelson Rockefeller for the Republican nomination ensured overwhelming black adherence to the Democratic ticket. And Goldwater's candidacy horrified prominent black Republicans, like groundbreaking baseball star (and Rockefeller supporter) Jackie Robinson, and Edward Brooke, then Massachusetts's pioneering black attorney general, who refused to give Goldwater his endorsement, later saying "you can't say the Negro left the Republican Party; the Negro feels he was evicted from the Republican Party."

National Review publisher William Rusher predicted the rise of the New Right the previous December, telling the Harvard Young Republican Club two days after Pearl Harbor Day that given Rockefeller's liberalism and Johnson's likely "swing over, rather sharply to the left" in a bid to "comfort and mollify" his party's liberals after Kennedy's assassination, "the hard-core South" was "once again up for grabs."

Indeed it was.

Goldwater also appealed to young conservatives outside the South, who were drawn to his message of individualism, and his challenge of the staid, hierarchical system of the Grand Old Party with its patrician northern and western elites. These young conservatives included Hillary Rodham, who, as the drama over the civil rights bill played out in Washington in the summer of 1964, canvassed her neighborhood in the Chicago suburbs for the Goldwater campaign.

The promising high school student came from a family of

rock-ribbed conservatives. Her father, Hugh Rodham, a western Pennsylvania native who owned a drapery business, raised Hillary and her two younger brothers on his strict Republican views. Hillary devoured Goldwater's book *Conscience of a Conservative* at the suggestion of a ninth-grade teacher. She was a member of the Young Republican National Federation, which since the Hoover administration had operated chapters nationwide, focused on nurturing conservatives under the age of forty. Four years earlier, Hillary had canvassed the South Side of Chicago for Richard Nixon in his razor-thin losing effort against Jack Kennedy.

But this "Goldwater girl" from Illinois, still a year off from her first term at Wellesley College, was also just the kind of rising white idealist that Democrats would build their future on, and whom they would doggedly pursue long after they'd lost white southerners and stopped worrying about the "black vote."

Hillary's worldview was being shaped by the convulsions of the 1960s—and by an April 1962 trip with her youth minister, Don Jones, who took a group from her conservative congregation at Park Ridge Methodist Church, to hear Martin Luther King Jr. deliver a speech titled "Remaining Awake Through a Revolution" at the Chicago Sunday Evening Club. Clinton would later write in her memoir that the speech "challenged [the] indifference" of her generation of young, white Americans, which in some ways was insulated from the trench warfare being fought by young men and women not much older than them, in states like Alabama and Mississippi, where the simple act of registering to vote invited sometimes violent resistance and the threat of economic disenfranchisement, ostracism, or even death.

That trajectory away from indifference and toward direct confrontation would lead Hillary Rodham, during her freshman year at Wellesley, to shock the all-white congregation at Park

Ridge by bringing a black classmate to service, and it would lead her, as president of the Wellesley College Young Republicans, to support Ed Brooke's history-making Senate campaign as a liberal Republican in 1966. But in 1964, Hillary was a Goldwater Girl.

With Goldwater on the ballot, American voter identification with the Democratic Party peaked at 51 percent in 1964—higher even than in 1942, at the height of U.S. involvement in World War II. The party of southern segregation had become the party of American modernism, while its southern appendage clung to Goldwater, who declared that "extremism in the defense of liberty is no vice," as he sank his party to a low ebb.

For black voters, 1964 was a watershed. With weeks to go before the election, the NAACP announced that 5.5 million African Americans had registered to vote across thirty-four states and the nation's capital, and that overall black voter turnout could reach 12 million—7 million more than the number thought to have voted in 1960.

On election day, they were proven right, as 58.5 percent of eligible African Americans went to the polls—72 percent in the northern states and 44 percent in the still restrictive South—a feat that would not be repeated for forty-four years.

The 1964 election saw the highest total voter turnout ever measured, before or since, with 69 percent of American adults pulling the lever nationwide and delivering a rebuke to Goldwater so complete that a month later, when Martin Luther King Jr. was asked if he could envision a Negro being elected president of the United States, he replied: "I have seen certain changes in the United States over the last two years that surprise me. I have seen levels of compliance with the civil rights bill, and changes that have been most surprising so on the basis of this, I think we may be able to get a Negro president in *less* than 40 years. I would think that this could come in 25 years or less."

Johnson and his party would have little time to celebrate the triumphs of the civil rights era as the president increasingly turned his attention toward the war in Vietnam.

THE U.S. TROOP PRESENCE IN VIETNAM WOULD GROW FROM 16,000 in 1965 to more than half a million in 1968. The nightly newscasts were teeming with images of Americans fighting and dying in a far-off conflict few Americans understood, but whose grasp able-bodied men lacking means or connections could scarcely avoid. Unrest among young Americans was spreading, across cities and college campuses nationwide, in some cases provoking violent clashes with police. The January 1968 Tet Offensive, which set U.S. troops on their heels, sapped the last hope that the war could be won.

By March, Johnson's approval ratings had fallen from an 80 percent peak in March 1964 to just 36 percent the week after a devastating February 27 broadcast in which CBS newsman Walter Cronkite, America's most trusted man, returned from Vietnam and all but declared the war unwinnable. After the telecast, Johnson was said to have remarked, "If I've lost Cronkite, I've lost America."

It was a swift and sudden reversal for the president who had, just a few short years before, shepherded not only the Civil Rights Act of 1964 but the Voting Rights Act of 1965. Now those achievements, along with the extension of the Social Security Act to include Medicare and Medicaid, plus an ambitious program to end poverty among poor black and white Americans, seemed a distant memory. And the president who'd marshaled it all was now seen by his party, and his country, as a relentless man of war.

The war also split Johnson from Martin Luther King Jr., who in April 1967 delivered a withering speech before a crowd of three thousand at New York's Riverside Church denouncing U.S. involvement in Vietnam and the concurrent defunding of

Great Society programs. King accused the war, and by extension, the Johnson administration, of "doing far more than devastating the hopes of the poor at home.

"It was sending their sons and their brothers and their husbands to fight and to die in extraordinarily high proportions relative to the rest of the population. We were taking the black young men who had been crippled by our society and sending them eight thousand miles away to guarantee liberties in Southeast Asia which they had not found in southwest Georgia and East Harlem. So we have been repeatedly faced with the cruel irony of watching Negro and white boys on TV screens as they kill and die together for a nation that has been unable to seat them together in the same schools. So we watch them in brutal solidarity burning the huts of a poor village, but we realize that they would hardly live on the same block in Chicago. I could not be silent in the face of such cruel manipulation of the poor."

Newspaper editorial pages, including the *New York Times* and the *Washington Post,* and even the NAACP, declared that King's speech had conflated unlike crises to the detriment of the core cause of black uplift. The major civil rights organizations had an investment in Lyndon Johnson, and they feared that King was throwing it away.

There had long been tension among black leaders over how best to interact with presidential power: whether as negotiators or agitators. King had, during the March on Washington and the Selma marches, played the role of negotiator, siding with the White House and other major civil rights groups to moderate the more radical members of the movement like John Lewis and Stokely Carmichael of the Student Nonviolent Coordinating Committee, or SNCC. Now he was squarely on the side of the radicals.

King had always sparked deep divisions in public opinion; making Gallup's list of "most admired Americans" twice, in fourth place in 1964, the year he won the Nobel Prize, and in sixth place in 1965. But his favorable ratings among the American public never exceeded 45 percent. By 1966, Americans' disapproval was overwhelming, at 63 versus 32 percent. By 1967, Alabama segregationist George Wallace was ranked among America's most admired men, and King, the antiwar agitator, was not. Meanwhile, King's break with Johnson was total—he would not be asked back to the White House.

Three weeks after King's Riverside address, on April 28, heavyweight champion Muhammad Ali publicly refused to report for induction into the army, prompting the World Boxing Association to strip him of his title and triggering a trial, set for June 20.

With Malcolm X gone—assassinated in February 1965 in Harlem—Ali was the most prominent Black Muslim in the country, and an idol to young African Americans for the bravado he expressed in his utter indifference to the strictures of racial comportment imposed on black men. He said his faith was the reason he refused to be drafted, but he also offered a withering critique of the war itself and the plight of African Americans at home.

"Why should they ask me to put on a uniform and go 10,000 miles from home and drop bombs and bullets on Brown people in Vietnam while so-called Negro people in Louisville are treated like dogs and denied simple human rights?" he told a Louisville reporter on May 4, as he and Dr. King, with whom he had quietly nurtured a growing friendship, came together to march for open housing. Ali was even blunter with Gil Noble, host of *Like It Is,* a popular public affairs show devoted to African American themes. "My conscience won't let me go shoot my brother, or some darker people, or some poor hungry people in the mud for big powerful America. And shoot them for what? They never called me nigger, they never lynched me, they didn't put no dogs on me, they didn't rob me of my nationality, rape and kill my mother and father. . . . Shoot them for what? . . . How can I shoot them poor people? Just take me to jail."

Ali's broadsides against the war shocked the country to an even greater degree than King's. But other nationally prominent black athletes came to his defense. Former football great Jim Brown, recently retired, and whose business interests included a piece of Ali's boxing contract, organized a June 4 meeting in Cleveland, Ohio, in which a group of black basketball and football greats—Brown, Lew Alcindor (the future Kareem Abdul-Jabbar), Boston Celtics star Bill Russell, who'd suffered his share of racial indignities as an NBA star, and NFL standouts Jim Shorter, Willie Davis, John Wooten, Bobby Mitchell, Sid Williams, Curtis McClinton, and Walter Beach, along with Ohio state representative and soon-to-be Cleveland mayor Carl Stokes—quizzed Ali extensively on his reasons for refusing the draft. After the two-hour session the group, some of whom had served in the military themselves, held a dramatic press conference in which they publicly backed the Champ.

Weeks later, an all-white jury convicted Ali of draft evasion, and the judge sentenced him to five years in prison, plus a ten-thousand-dollar fine. Banned from boxing for three years but free on bail, he embarked on a series of paid college speaking engagements, debating and expounding on his war stance. King vigorously supported Ali, praising his stand from the pulpit of Ebenezer Baptist Church in Atlanta, and urging other draft-eligible young men to follow his lead. But the revered athletes Joe Louis and Jackie Robinson opposed him, with Robinson accusing Ali of "harming the morale of a lot of young Negro soldiers over in Vietnam," and calling it a "tragedy" that in his words, "Cassius has made millions of dollars off of the American public, and now he's not willing to show his appreciation to a country that is giving him, in my view, a fantastic opportunity . . . [it] hurts a great number of people."

Robinson held a special place of respect in black and white

households, as the athlete who integrated Major League Baseball in 1947, the first black man inducted into the Baseball Hall of Fame. He'd been a guest on the platform at the March on Washington and until a very public falling-out with its leadership in 1967, a board member of the NAACP. Robinson had achieved a level of transracial notoriety reserved for a handful of black Americans, even starring in a 1950 movie about his life, opposite actress Ruby Dee. But Robinson was also a military veteran, having served in a segregated army unit in 1942 and exiting three years later as a second lieutenant after being acquitted in a general court-martial for refusing to sit at the back of an army bus in Fort Hood, Texas. Since 1957 he'd been a vice president of Chock Full O'Nuts, the New York–based coffee company, and was among a group of promising African Americans recruited by corporations who were aggressively looking to showcase "Negro" talent in diversity roles, including the Coca-Cola Company and even Woolworth's, whose lunch counters had become almost synonymous with southern segregation.

Robinson was a fervent patriot who in 1963 clashed, in a series of fierce public letters, with Malcolm X, whom he denounced as "racist" and who in turn derided Robinson's "White Boss" in Major League Baseball and beyond, the boss who "sent you to Washington to assure all the worried white folks that Negroes were still thankful to the Great White Father for bringing us to America, that Negroes were grateful to America (despite our not being treated as full citizens), and that Negroes would still lay down our lives to defend this white country (though this same white government wasn't ready nor willing to defend Negroes)."

In May 1967, one month after King participated in an antiwar march in New York City that drew Dr. Benjamin Spock, actor Harry Belafonte, and Stokely Carmichael (the former SNCC leader who coined the term "Black Power"), and weeks after King's praise of Ali from the pulpit, Robinson published an emotional "open letter" to King in Harlem's *Amsterdam News,* asking whether it was "fair" of his friend "to place all the burden of the blame on America and none on the Communist forces we're fighting?"—saying he believed the president was making valiant efforts to achieve peace, and adding: "I am confused, Martin. I am confused because I respect you deeply. But I also love this imperfect country."

Robinson, Ali, and King reflected the growing dichotomy between what was viewed as the "bourgeois" goals of the integrationist civil rights movement proper, like university admissions and jobs in Woolworth's management, and the urgent aims of a younger column of black activists like Carmichael: namely, addressing the economic inequities of class and racial prejudice that locked black Americans in urban ghettos, with few job prospects and often tense or even violent interactions with police, compounded by the invisible chains dragging spiraling numbers of already hopeless young men to Vietnam, often by way of all-white draft boards. (It was a convergence that would manifest itself a year later in Mexico City in the 1968 Summer Olympic Games, when a pair of track and field athletes, bronze medalist John Carlos and gold medalist Tommie Smith, raised their black-gloved fists in the universally understood gesture of Black Power.) King himself had begun to gravitate toward those causes, to the dismay of old friends like Robinson.

Black enlistees accounted for one in five combat deaths between 1961 and 1966—a quarter of the dead in 1965—despite making up less than 10 percent of the U.S. Army ranks and 13 percent of the American population. Moreover, few black citizens were able to take advantage of the draft exemptions offered to collegians, and increasing numbers were subject to relaxed draft standards that essentially punished black men already barred from decent educations by easing their path to Vietnam. And so African Americans were increasingly siding with the antiwar movement.

The furious attacks on Ali in particular, from the sports media and the mainstream press, made him the leading voice of black dissent on the war, praised as a "rugged individualist" in the pages of the *Amsterdam News,* where black New Yorkers interviewed by the paper's reporters in the spring of 1968 said they'd oppose Ali when white celebrities marched off to Vietnam.

For the first time since becoming president, Lyndon Johnson faced the possibility of a broad backlash against his leadership, from the very community he'd thought would be exceptionally and eternally loyal.

As the 1968 election approached, Johnson faced challengers for his party's nomination, in particular an antiwar candidate, Senator Eugene McCarthy of Minnesota, who shocked the sitting president by winning 42 percent of the vote in the March 12 New Hampshire primary. (Hillary Rodham, then a junior at Wellesley, had resigned from the Young Republicans and was driving to New Hampshire on weekends to stuff envelopes for the McCarthy campaign.)

And when Robert Kennedy, his late brother's attorney general and by this time a senator from New York, saw how well McCarthy was doing, he too entered the race, ensuring that Johnson continued to face the seemingly ever-present ghosts of Camelot.

Robert Kennedy appealed to young, liberal, white voters who were passionately against the Vietnam War. Unlike McCarthy, he also had a natural appeal to black voters as the man who had carried out his brother's aims with regard to civil rights at the Justice Department, and who together with Jack Kennedy had telephoned Coretta Scott King when her husband languished in a Birmingham jail. The number of black voters had swollen to more than 3 million across the South—topping a hundred thousand even in Mississippi—triple the total eight years before.

On March 31, Johnson announced he would not seek reelection, saying he was withdrawing his name in the interests of national unity. It was a stunning development for a president so recently at the height of his power.

On April 4, the Senate was debating the Civil Rights Act of 1968. It was the last in the trio of bills Johnson planned as the crowning achievements of his presidency. Commonly known as the Fair Housing Act, the bill sought to end discrimination in the sale, rental, and financing of housing. King had marched in Chicago the previous summer for open housing, even moving part-time into a housing development in a run-down section on the city's West Side to dramatize the "Daley brand" of segregation plaguing northern cities, which since 1950 were home to accelerating millions of migrating black families.

White Americans up north, along with the northern media, had no trouble shaking their heads at the retrograde southern policeman or the cartoonish segregationist, but it wasn't so easy to recognize discrimination in their own backyards. Passing open housing laws was, in fundamental ways, a longer reach even than voting rights.

In the Senate, Ed Brooke, the body's lone black member and a studiously temperate, liberal Republican, rose to tell of his own experience, coming home from fighting in World War II, only to be turned away from the homes of his choice because he was black. Brooke had introduced the Fair Housing Amendments in February, alongside Minnesota's Walter Mondale, and he'd sat on a federal commission, the Kerner Commission, which proclaimed housing segregation as among the causes of the urban unrest that had overtaken the country for four years of long, hot summers. Everett Dirksen, whose negotiating skills had been so crucial to passage of the Civil Rights Act of 1964, beat back yet another filibuster by southern Democrats, and the bill was passed.

By 6:05 that evening, Martin Luther King Jr. lay bleeding on the balcony outside room 306 at the Lorraine Motel in Memphis, Tennessee.

King's murder sparked riots in more than a hundred cities, including Chicago, where nine black men died during two nights of mayhem, and where ten days after the unrest on the city's West Side, Mayor Richard J. Daley infamously told reporters he'd issued orders to his police superintendent, "to shoot to kill any arsonist or anyone with a Molotov cocktail in his hand in Chicago because they're potential murderers, and to issue a police order to shoot to maim or cripple any arsonists and looters—arsonists to kill and looters to maim and detain."

Among the few major cities spared the chaos was Boston, where Hillary Rodham was among the thousands who gathered in peaceful protest downtown, and where James Brown forged ahead with a planned concert at the Boston Garden. In a deal between the singer's team and city officials, the concert was broadcast live on the local public television station, WGBH, keeping many young Bostonians at home.

In New York City, Robert Kennedy spoke in mourning for the slain civil rights leader. But just two months later, just after midnight on June 5, Kennedy—by then the likely Democratic nominee—would also be felled by an assassin's bullet, as he campaigned in California.

The scenes of urban rioting on the nightly television news broadcasts and on newspaper front pages stoked resentment among white working-class residents in northern and Rust Belt cities who were already rebelling against Johnson's Great Society. For white families, keeping their suburbs white meant they had to fight federally mandated housing laws, busing that sought to forcibly integrate suburban schools, and increasingly, Johnson's Democratic Party.

Republican nominee Richard Nixon and his team were more than willing to use it all. His campaign commercials featured jarring images from Vietnam that pointed to Johnson's mistakes at war and Nixon's vow to bring the conflict to "an honorable end."

The ads were tagged with the ominous caption: "This time, vote, like your whole world depended on it."

The Nixon campaign also focused on a white southern backlash against the civil rights legislation passed in 1964 and 1965, and in a precursor to the "southern strategy" Nixon would deploy four years later, flipped the Party of Lincoln, all but banished from the southern states after Reconstruction, on its head.

"Who needs Manhattan when we can get the electoral votes of eleven Southern states?" explained Kevin Phillips, a young lawyer who would put his operating principles for the Nixon campaign on paper in a 1969 book called *The Emerging Republican Majority*. "Put those together with the Farm Belt and the Rocky Mountains, and we don't need the big cities. We don't even want them. Sure, Hubert [Humphrey] will carry Riverside Drive in November. La-de-dah. What will he do in Oklahoma?"

Phillips foresaw a day when, in the words of Warren Weaver Jr., in a September 1969 review of Phillips's book for the *New York Times,* the Democratic Party "will consist largely of treacherous Yankees who forsook the Republican Party over the past 30 years, Negroes, Jews, some stubborn Scandinavians and the liberal establishment," broadly defined as a "privileged elite, blind to the needs and interests of the large national majority."

In late August, the Democrats opened their convention in Chicago amid antiwar demonstrations outside the convention hall and Mayor Daley's brutal deployment of the police to put them down by any available means.

Johnson and Daley doubted that McCarthy stood a chance against Nixon's "law and order" message. Daley hoped to see Ted Kennedy, the last surviving brother of the late president, be the nominee, but instead Johnson conspired with Democratic bosses to unseat McCarthy, using the party's arcane nominating rules to install Humphrey, his beleaguered vice president and former senator from Minnesota. McCarthy's backers, including those who had supported Robert Kennedy, could only watch in despair as Johnson and Humphrey did to the antiwar liberals what they had done to the Mississippi Freedom Democrats in 1964.

As the nomination was announced, antiwar protests outside grew into full-blown riots in the "Battle of Michigan Avenue" between stink-bomb-throwing protesters and tear-gas-firing police, who arrested nearly six hundred people including liberal activist Abbie Hoffman and Black Panthers cofounder Bobby Seale. Inside the hall liberal delegates marched around singing "We Shall Overcome," the civil rights anthem Johnson had borrowed in announcing the Voting Rights Act before a joint session of Congress in 1965, as Martin Luther King Jr. watched the president's speech on television, from the living room of Dr. Sullivan and Richie Jean Jackson's home in Selma, Alabama, and silently wept.

Johnson, in his final act as the leader of his party, planted the seeds of its further fragmentation by consenting to a demand by Senator George McGovern, leader of the liberal wing, for a commission that would change the way the party's nominee was chosen in future conventions. The new rules would make every primary and caucus binding, limiting the votes of party insiders and thus their power to impose a nominee. The commission challenged the makeup of convention delegates, requiring that the percentage of female, minority, and young delegates mirror the proportions of those groups in the states.

The changes set the stage for a more inclusive party, where outsider candidates would have a fighting chance; McGovern himself would be the first beneficiary in 1972. But they would also force the party into a bitter inner conflict, between the emerging constituencies empowered by this new paradigm and the increasingly alienated Democratic Center-Right.

Nixon won the general election narrowly, by just over 812,000 out of 76 million votes, but in an electoral rout, 301 to 191, with George Wallace winning 10 million votes and five southern states: Arkansas, Mississippi, Louisiana, Georgia, and his home state of Alabama, on a third-party ticket. On election night, with the vote counting in Illinois dragging on for more than fifteen hours, Wallace's forty-six electoral votes even briefly threatened to throw the contest to the House of Representatives.

Nixon had performed poorly in big cities like New York, Philadelphia, and Detroit, with their large black populations. But he'd swept the Midwest, the Rust Belt, and much of the "Sun Belt," which his operatives prized, including Florida and his home state of California. In a poignant turnabout for the candidate who'd narrowly lost the White House in 1960 to the superior Daley machine, Nixon's final margin of victory came just after midnight when he won Illinois.

Humphrey, for his part, had managed to turn out what the *Washington Post* called the "Roosevelt Coalition: organized labor, Negroes, Mexican-Americans and Jews." But that collection, Phillips's politically incorrect amalgam of "treacherous Yankees, Negroes," and liberals, wasn't enough to put a Democrat back in the White House.

Going forward, Democratic leaders would wonder whether their party had fundamentally erred by allowing itself to become too liberal on issues of law and order, too tentative in matters of war, and too beholden to those who were determined to push the country to its ideological limits on questions of race. Those questions would become the defining inner struggle for modern Democrats.

CHAPTER 2

All in the Family

*Archie Bunker: Now, no prejudice intended, but, you know, I
always check with the Bible on these here things. I think that,
I mean if God had meant for us to be together, he'd-a put us
together. But look what he done. He put you over in Africa, and
put the rest of us in all the white countries.*
*Sammy Davis Jr.: Well, he must've told 'em where we were because
somebody came and got us.*

—*All in the Family,* "Sammy's Visit," 1972

THE DEMOCRATIC PARTY THAT EMERGED FROM THE 1968
election was fundamentally different from the one that entered the civil rights battles of 1963 and 1964. Since the time
of FDR, the party had balanced the power of its southern
wing against the pragmatism of northern elites who, while occasionally pricking the Dixiecrats on civil rights, more often
tried to accommodate them in order to maintain the party's
near-constant congressional majority.

But without such outsize figures as Franklin Roosevelt, Harry

Truman, John Kennedy, and Lyndon Johnson, the party seemed moribund and adrift. Johnson had pushed the party further than it had ever gone on civil rights and as a result alienated the southern Democrats. Even in his overwhelming victory in 1964, he had failed to carry the band of southern states that stretched east from Louisiana to North Carolina, all of which, with the exception of Mississippi, Kennedy had carried in 1960, with LBJ on the ticket. Humphrey, though he lost by fewer than 1 million votes, had failed to carry much at all.

And though Strom Thurmond's exit from the party didn't immediately begin an avalanche, it signaled a shift that would soon inspire a rising class of southern Democratic politicians, including future United States senators Trent Lott of Mississippi, Jesse Helms of North Carolina, Phil Gramm of Texas, Lauch Faircloth of North Carolina, and Richard Shelby of Alabama, along with eventual national political figures like Elizabeth Dole, Condoleezza Rice, Alabama chief justice Roy Moore, and future Texas governor Rick Perry, to exit the party and join the formidable political architecture of an increasingly solid Republican South.

By 1972, the Democrats had a choice: They could become the party of racial advancement and social change and risk alienating white southern voters and northern blue collar voters, too; or they could gently push aside their liberal and African American factions and subordinate their pressing demands to increase the party's chances on election day. The Vietnam War had taken that choice away from Johnson and shelved his opportunity to make manifest his and his party's legacy to the growing number of Americans who, while reaping the rewards of Medicare and food stamps, federal housing assistance and guaranteed college loans, increasingly resented those very programs. And Republicans were, with increasing success, portraying those programs as giveaways to a lawless "entitlement class" consisting mainly of minorities and "illegal immigrants" who refused to support themselves with work, and whose liberal benefactors were bent on using federal welfare programs as both a cradle and a cudgel, to infantilize the poor and punish white, traditional middle-class Americans for the sins of the country's past.

Lyndon Johnson had been a towering force who successfully pressed Congress to make good on the promises of the Fourteenth and Fifteenth Amendments, and sold the War on Poverty as being just as much about saving Appalachia as it was reviving the inner cities. But without his voice, and that of Martin Luther King Jr.—the embodiment of the civil rights movement—there were few left to articulate the case for progressive change. Johnson had left no strong successor. The media had rushed to crown a young King associate, Rev. Jesse Jackson, but he lacked the trust of the broad civil rights leadership, who saw him as too eager to capitalize on King's memory.

And Ted Kennedy, the articulate young senator on whom the mantle of national leadership seemed destined to fall, had been involved in a scandal in 1969 in which a young woman, Mary Jo Kopechne, died in a car he was driving after it went off a bridge and sank to the bottom of a deep tidal pool on Chappaquiddick Island, in his home state of Massachusetts. Kennedy pleaded guilty to leaving the scene of an accident.

These were chaotic times for the Democratic Party, and that was reflected in the culture around it. The number-one television program in the country was *All in the Family*, which debuted in January 1971 and would be a runaway hit for five years. Carroll O'Connor played the Queens native, sardonically racist Archie Bunker. With his earnest wife, Edith, and their liberal daughter and son-in-law, Archie struggles to adjust to an increasingly multicultural world.

The Bunkers were more than a sitcom family. They embodied white America's quiet anxieties about race, integration and neighborhood change, gender, sex, and the war. For the Democratic

Party, Archie represented the Americans they were losing, and not just in the South, but also in the Rust Belt and the Northeast, who like their southern counterparts, resented the federal housing mandates and busing to end school segregation in the suburbs of cities like Boston, Philadelphia, Chicago, and New York.

Black leaders, meanwhile, viewed the 1972 presidential election as a golden opportunity to organize, and to address their lack of broad political power despite African Americans' determination to register and vote and despite the tremendous sacrifices and martyrdom of civil rights workers and leaders, black and white, up to and including King.

Only a handful of African Americans had been elected to Congress in the twentieth century, beginning with Oscar De Priest of Chicago in 1928. They had hailed from northern urban districts that were overwhelmingly black. And unlike their post-Reconstruction predecessors, they were overwhelmingly Democrats, with notable exceptions like Edward Brooke. The lawmakers, including Brooke, Adam Clayton Powell of New York, and Augustus Freeman Hawkins of California, both elected in 1963, endured a segregated Capitol and a House of Representatives in which their party remained divided between southerners hostile to African American interests and northerners with other fish to fry, leaving the handful of black House members with little legislative influence.

The Voting Rights Act had led many of the young ground troops of the civil rights movement to run for state and federal office. In January 1969, newly elected black congressmen including William Clay of Missouri, Louis Stokes of Ohio, and Shirley Chisholm of Brooklyn, the first black woman elected to the House, formed a Democratic Select Committee, chaired by Michigan congressman Charles Diggs, which two years later would be formalized as the Congressional Black Caucus, with thirteen founding members. Among them were Chisholm, Clay,

Ronald Dellums of California, John Conyers of Michigan, and Charles Rangel, who entered the House that session having defeated the flamboyant but famously (and fiscally) troubled Powell by two hundred votes in the Democratic primary in Harlem.

Both inside and outside Washington, black leaders were seeking ways to consolidate and build meaningful political power, and to create a coherent national agenda for black America.

In March 1972, some eight thousand delegates, including the Black Caucus members, descended on Westside High School in Gary, Indiana, for the National Black Political Convention. The conclave, a culmination of a year of meetings in cities like New York and Chicago, was presided over by the newly elected mayor, Richard Hatcher, a leading civil rights figure and one of the first black mayors of a major American city, along with Carl Stokes of Cleveland. The three-day event attracted the widows of King and Malcolm X; poet and author Amiri Baraka, who was a co-organizer; John Johnson, publisher of *Ebony* and *Jet* magazines; and rising civil rights leaders including Rev. Jesse Jackson, now head of the Southern Christian Leadership Conference's Operation Breadbasket in Chicago. Included on the eclectic program were Black Panther Party cofounder Bobby Seale, Nation of Islam cleric Louis Farrakhan, Texas state senator Barbara Jordan, former SNCC national communications director Julian Bond, Motown singer Kim Weston, and actor Richard Roundtree.

Organizers had hoped to craft a unified political strategy heading into the November elections, and the convention produced an ambitious platform that called for a network of national community health centers, a guaranteed minimum wage, the outlawing of capital punishment, and the establishment of a "system of national health insurance."

The "Gary Declaration" offered a stark assessment of black America in the post-Johnson era. Its central tension: whether to continue to work within the existing political system, or to walk away from politics and into the arms of black nationalism.

"We come to Gary in an hour of great crisis and tremendous promise for Black America," the declaration read, bleakly reporting that "[e]conomic, cultural, and spiritual depression stalk Black America, and the price for survival often appears to be more than we are able to pay. On every side, in every area of our lives, the American institutions in which we have placed our trust are unable to cope with the crises they have created by their single-minded dedication to profits for some and white supremacy above all."

The organizers in Gary were calling for nothing less than "radical political change." And they declared emphatically that when it came to politics, "[b]oth parties have betrayed us whenever their interests conflicted with ours (which was most of the time), and whenever our forces were unorganized and dependent, quiescent and compliant."

But the reality was that black power had indeed become both concentrated and dependent on the Democrats, who dominated both the South, where most African Americans continued to reside, and the major urban centers in the Rust Belt and the Northeast, where those drawn north by the Great Migration had settled. Black Republicans had been especially marginalized by Goldwater's candidacy, which rendered the Grand Old Party culturally unacceptable to a growing number of black voters. Despite the rank racism of the southern Democratic Party, blacks increasingly saw the party as the surest route to political participation. Black Republicans, who withdrew from the scene in Goldwater's wake, reemerged to support Richard Nixon in 1972, but Goldwater's lingering shadow made it all but impossible for black Republicans to make their case to the general body of black Americans. For better or worse, black Americans were casting their lot with the Democrats.

The Gary Declaration asserted that the delegates had "come to Gary confronted with a choice . . . not the old convention question of which candidate shall we support; the pointless question of who is to preside over a decaying and unsalvageable system," and posited that "the only real choice for us is . . . whether we will move to organize independently" toward "social transformation or social destruction." However, the reality was that the choice had already been made. For the vast majority of black voters, it was the Democrats or bust.

On the dais, Rev. Jackson gamely thundered to the delegates, "We are grown! We ain't taking it no more! No more *yes boss*. No more bowing or scrapping. We are twenty-five million strong. Cut us in or cut it out. It is a new ball game!" But few in the hall believed there was a game at all. Both parties were not vying equally for the African American vote. In fact, Nixon was angling for blue-collar white Democrats, using the specter of "urban" lawlessness as a wedge.

Before the convention in Gary, the organizers had hoped to launch an African American candidate for president, ahead of the July Democratic convention in Miami Beach. It was to be a bold stroke, just four years after King's assassination, and they had settled on Carl Stokes. But the plan never made it to Gary, having been upended in January by Shirley Chisholm's announcement from the pulpit of Concord Baptist Church in Brooklyn, in which she declared: "I am not the candidate of black America, although I am black and proud. . . . I am not the candidate of the women's movement of America, although I am a woman, and am equally proud of that. I am not the candidate of any political bosses or fat cats or special interests."

Chisholm made it clear she saw no prospect of getting the Democratic nomination. Instead she was calling for a "bloodless revolution at the Democratic National Convention," led by "blacks, women, young [and] Spanish-speaking peoples," who she proposed could "get together a ticket that is reflective of all different segments that make up this great land called America." She had been contemplating the idea since the previous July but had not discussed her intentions with her fellow Black Caucus members. In Gary, her run was greeted as an irritant and a move that undermined their daring agenda.

The rejection disappointed Chisholm's ardent supporters, including her New York youth organizer, a young preacher named Al Sharpton, who left the three-day conference incensed that so many leaders of the black political class were dismissing the daughter of a Guyanese burlap bag factory worker and a Barbadian seamstress, as a candidate of greater interest to women than to African Americans. For Sharpton and other Chisholm supporters, it was a sign of sexism, pure and simple, running like a rampant infection through the movement.

In the end, for black political organizers, Gary was a thrill, albeit an empty one that put the fragmentation of the black political movement since King's death on display. There was no overarching strategy for black political advancement, and certainly no appetite to marry it to the cause of women's rights. For all the declaration's fire and fury, at the Democratic convention the leaders defaulted to pragmatism and threw their support behind George McGovern, who was running on a populist liberal agenda that included a full withdrawal of U.S. forces from Vietnam, a blanket amnesty for those who had evaded the draft, and dramatic defense cuts to fund increased spending on domestic programs.

McGovern emerged from the Democratic convention on July 13 with 57 percent of the delegates, defeating Henry "Scoop" Jackson, the indefatigable George Wallace, and Chisholm, who placed fourth in the delegate count. But the nominating process produced a public spectacle that included failed entreaties by McGovern to Hubert Humphrey, Edmund Muskie, Walter Mondale, and McGovern's preferred choice, Senator Ted Kennedy, to serve as his running mate, as well as clashes with the National Women's Political Caucus, including Chisholm, Bella Abzug, Gloria Steinem, and Betty Friedan, over the inclusion of a plank supporting a woman's right to choose an abortion (which McGovern and his aides worked to quash) and the endorsement of an Equal Rights Amendment. Even the selection of Missouri senator Thomas Eagleton as McGovern's running mate descended into farce, as the voting dragged on into the wee hours, producing mock ballots for CBS newsman Roger Mudd, Mao Zedong, and even one for Archie Bunker.

The convention seemed to underscore the party's diminished state.

Nixon, meanwhile, was carrying overwhelming advantages into the general election, including the Twenty-Sixth Amendment, which lowered the voting age from twenty-one to eighteen; he'd signed it in 1970, and Congress affirmed it the following year. It instantly added more than 10 million new voters heading into November, ironically giving the famously uncharismatic president, who'd lampooned himself in 1968 in a "sock it to me" cameo on *Rowan and Martin's Laugh In,* a reason to tout himself to the young and hip.

Despite revelations in October in the *Washington Post* about a June break-in by political "burglars" at the Democratic National Committee's headquarters at the Watergate hotel and office complex in Washington, D.C., Nixon was decisively reelected.

Even the war had turned into his strength. The Weather Underground bombings, controversial testimony by former soldiers, and even officers like John Forbes Kerry, at the Fulbright hearings, the lore of "Hanoi Jane," and images of police subduing college protesters on elite campuses like the University of California, Berkeley and Columbia University—and outside the Republican

National Convention in Miami Beach—made the antiwar movement as unpopular as the war itself; while the ongoing clashes between black citizens and police in major cities, and even a prison riot at Attica prison in upstate New York in 1971, played to the Nixon campaign's "law and order" appeals. With more than 55 percent of newly eligible young voters going to the polls, Nixon won 18- to 29-year-olds by a margin of 52 percent to 46 percent.

For African Americans, the outcome of the election was grim. Despite gains in congressional seats and in state and local offices, fewer than 50 percent of black voters had participated in the election, with the African American vote underperforming the national electorate by 11 to 14 points, depending on the measure. "The most pervasive factors affecting the black vote," researchers at the newly formed Joint Center for Political and Economic Studies wrote, "appear to have been apathy, lack of interest in either candidate and a feeling that the result was a foregone conclusion."

When Johnson passed away on January 22, 1973, two days after Nixon's second inaugural, his party was left to grapple with his dual legacy, which spanned the heights of progress on civil rights, and the depths of despair over Vietnam. The party's leaders seemed decidedly uncertain of how to square what Johnson had given them and the country with what they'd lost.

By forcing his party, and particularly his fellow southerners, to reckon with the country's ongoing racial strife, Johnson had thrown open the doors to a growing and increasingly loyal liberal and African American base. But he had also driven scores of white Democrats into the arms of the Republican Party and a growing conservative movement that was quickly organizing around opposition to all that his administration had stood for. The rapidly changing culture was a long-term boon to the party of liberal social progress, but a short-term nightmare. And the question of whether Johnson had pushed too far and too fast, and been too easily swayed by the pressure from the Left and from civil rights leaders, or whether his ambitious social project had simply been devoured by an ill-conceived war, would linger over the Democratic Party for a generation.

JIMMY CARTER SAT IN THE GOVERNOR'S MANSION IN ATLANTA, Georgia, watching his party stray far afield of what he saw as the core values of a majority of Americans. He'd been elected governor in 1970 on a careful mix of the old and new South. He had refused to join a White Citizens' Council as a local businessman, but he kept an eye on the rural white voters who remained uncomfortable with the galloping tide of integration. He believed he understood what ailed the national Democrats, and he sensed an opportunity.

In March 1974, writing in *The Atlantic Monthly,* columnist David S. Broder diagnosed the psychic ills that were tearing the party apart. These were illustrated by the clashes between the old guard of LBJ and Mayor Daley versus the antiwar iconoclasts at the 1968 convention, and versus the "long-haired youths, blacks, Chicanos, and activist women" in 1972 who in the eyes of party regulars "had, by their action, consigned their own candidate, McGovern, to defeat." In the end, Broder wrote, and many Democrats believed, there wasn't enough room in the party for the old guard and the liberal irregulars.

Carter had taken sides in that fight and came down squarely on the side of the traditionalists. But he was, in some ways, a typical southern politician. Carter was as eager as any to profit from the anger of the real-life Archie Bunkers who resented the patchwork of civil rights and housing laws, busing and affirmative action, which they saw as giving an unfair leg up to agitating minorities at their expense, but he was always cognizant of the requirement to keep the growing ranks of black voters in the Democratic fold.

When he ran for governor, Carter wooed rural white primary voters by striking an obliquely genial tone toward George
Wallace, but once in office, he announced that segregation was
finished in Georgia, which angered many of the voters who'd
pulled the lever for him. By 1974, Carter had been named chairman of the Democratic Governor's Campaign Committee and
campaign chairman of the DNC, two key posts that put him in
national play.

Carter entered a crowded field in 1976 armed with key allies
among Georgia's black civil rights establishment, most especially
the "MLK block," which included the father and the widow of
the late Dr. King; Andrew Young, who had bailed King out of
various jails; and a young civil rights attorney named Vernon
Jordan, who had succeeded Whitney Young as president of the
National Urban League and had served as Georgia's NAACP
field secretary at the same time his friend Medgar Evers was
struggling mightily to register terrified black would-be voters
in Mississippi.

Carter made a major misstep in April 1976 during a question-
and-answer session in Philadelphia, when he said there's "nothing
wrong with city neighborhoods trying to maintain their ethnic
purity," referring to white ethnic areas, as well as predominantly
black parts of the city. It was a classic Carter two-step: one eye on
disgruntled white voters, the other on black Democrats.

One of his primary opponents, Arizona congressman Morris
"Mo" Udall, immediately mused to the media, "I think Americans, particularly our minorities, should ask him just who does
he want to wall out?" NBC News reported that "seventeen black
members of Congress . . . sent Carter a telegram protesting his
remarks."

Vernon Jordan, too, was called on to respond: "I think you
have to assume that if he in fact said these words I think these
words connote a philosophy," he said. "The problem is, is that

these words seem to be in contradiction to his record in Georgia and the whole area of open housing. He desegregated the real estate commission, he came out for open housing in Georgia and then to get to South Bend, Indiana, and to use these words and to espouse this philosophy apparently . . . is one of confusion for the black community and I think that we who have national responsibility of leadership in the black community have to call the governor on this issue."

An apology from Carter seemed to put the episode aside, but he still had Wallace and hawkish Senator Henry "Scoop" Jackson to his right; to the left were Udall, the pro–civil rights liberal, Idaho senator Frank Church, and Jerry Brown, who had succeeded Ronald Reagan as governor of California. The path to the Democratic nomination was narrow for Carter, and he was triangulating out of necessity.

Liberals formed an "ABC" coalition—"Anybody But Carter"—but once he defeated Wallace in the South Carolina primary, there was little they could do to stop him. In a play for the old New Dealers of the Rust Belt and Northeast, Carter selected as his running mate Senator Walter Mondale of Minnesota, who had helped steer the compromise with the Mississippi Freedom Democrats in 1964. And for the first time, the coveted keynote speech at the Democratic convention was delivered by a black woman: Barbara Jordan, the former state senator from Texas and the first black congresswoman from the Deep South, whose dramatic "yes!" vote to impeach Richard Nixon had earned her national attention.

Carter presented a new version of the Democratic Party: overtly religious but modest in its social piety, and opposed to both the emphatic liberalism of the McGovernites and the social crusading of LBJ. Even Wallace eventually endorsed him.

In the closing days of the general election, Plains Baptist Church, where Carter was a deacon, rejected the membership request of quixotic black minister Rev. Clennon King Jr. (no relation to the slain civil rights leader). Carter's campaign called Clennon King's attempts a stunt and "politically inspired," especially after President Gerald Ford's campaign sent a telegram to prominent black pastors, denouncing Carter's membership in a segregated church. But black ministers in Georgia, and even Coretta Scott King, publicly stood by Carter. Still, national headlines about this story gave anti-Carter liberals the chance to revel in the spectacle of the sanctified Holy Roller, who was challenging a half century of New Deal politics, getting his comeuppance.

On the campaign trail, Carter pointed out that Clennon King was "a Republican, not a Baptist, and not a resident of Plains." And he refused to resign from his church, saying he could no more do so than he could "resign from the human race."

"If it was a country club I would resign," Carter said, vowing instead to remain a church leader and fight to change the whites-only policy.

In the end, the incumbent, Gerald Ford, was an awkward candidate and an awkward man, haunted by the legacy of Richard Nixon and the pardon Ford granted him thirty-one days after Nixon resigned. On election day, Carter defeated Ford by a slim popular and electoral vote margin, by sweeping the South, including Texas and the "upper South" states of Missouri, Kentucky, Delaware, and Maryland. The Democratic ticket won Mondale's home state of Minnesota and the neighboring state of Wisconsin, along with the Rust Belt states of Ohio, Pennsylvania, and West Virginia, while holding traditionally Democratic strongholds like New York, Massachusetts, and the District of Columbia.

Carter improved on McGovern's paltry 31 percent share of white voters by 16 percentage points, and claimed 83 percent of the black vote—similar to McGovern. But unlike McGovern, he won a majority of voters ages 18 to 29, and tied among those ages 30 to 44.

Carter's victory was a schizophrenic amalgam of North and South, liberals and moderates, and religious voters (he lost white Protestants like himself, but handily won white Catholics) that would not be repeated for nearly a generation; it was a brief pause in what had become a growing Republican southern tide.

But Democratic Party leaders believed that Carter had won by running to the right, and they hoped to carry that received wisdom to the next election, presuming that Carter would hold up his end of the bargain by remaining scrupulously centrist, however much it enraged the old New Dealers. Instead, Carter's presidency proved to be a muddle, beset by international crises ranging from oil shortages to a hostage situation in Iran, and domestic malaise amid a moribund economy racked by inflation.

For African Americans, the failure of the Carter presidency produced a kind of despondency. Carter had placed black staff in prominent roles in his campaign, and he'd elevated civil rights figures like Andrew Young and Eleanor Holmes Norton, a veteran of SNCC and Mississippi Freedom Summer, to positions of power, and placed African Americans at the helm of the Department of Housing and Urban Development and even as secretary of the army (Clifford Alexander Jr.). But Carter often seemed at the mercy of events, rather than the master of them, as in the months between April and October 1980, when thousands of Cuban refugees began streaming into Miami as part of the Mariel Boatlift. Fidel Castro had permitted a mass exodus from the island amid growing economic deprivation, ultimately sending more than 125,000 migrants to the United States, including masses of unskilled laborers and hundreds of people purged from Cuba's prisons and insane asylums.

A month after the Cuban exodus began, Miami erupted in

riots when four police officers were acquitted by an all-white jury in the death of Arthur McDuffie. The African American insurance agent and former marine had been beaten to death in a frenzied traffic stop involving more than a dozen officers in the early morning hours a week before Christmas in 1979, his skull cracked open by the force of blows from a heavy-duty flashlight. Amid four days of mayhem that left eighteen people dead, 350 injured, and nearly twice that number arrested, along with more than $100 million in property damage, Democratic governor Bob Graham deployed thousands of national guardsmen to restore order in the smoldering black enclaves of Overtown and Liberty City. The Carter administration urged local leaders to take control, while the Justice Department prepared its own indictments. By the time Carter arrived in Miami to personally review the aftermath in June, promising $40 million in federal funds to rebuild the ruined neighborhoods, the sense that the administration had reacted too slowly, and done too little, too late, had set in. Just months before the election, the national image of Carter had calcified into one of weakness.

THE NOTION OF A BLACK PRESIDENT HAD TANTALIZED EVERYONE from Robert F. Kennedy to Martin Luther King Jr., who stated, the first time he was asked, that there had long been black men qualified for the nation's highest office. Surely the country that produced W. E. B. DuBois and Langston Hughes, Thurgood Marshall and Benjamin O. Davis, William Hastie and Charles Drew, Dr. King and his contemporaries had many black presidents in waiting. All that was needed was for the national imagination to see past the color of the candidate's skin.

As America reached the mid-1980s, black political leaders wondered if a singular figure existed, *then and there*, who could satisfy the yearning of a people and also survive the gauntlet of national politics. With the Gary Declaration a distant dream and

Shirley Chisholm's bid for the nomination having gone nowhere, the answer seemed to be a definitive no.

Ronald Reagan had captured the presidency in 1980, relegating Jimmy Carter to a single term in an election that saw the lowest voter turnout since 1948. Carter's 83 percent share of the black vote was a significant climb down for his party, offsetting even the 2 percent rise in black voter turnout resulting from a national push by civil rights organizations and labor unions, called "Operation Big Vote."

African Americans continued to laud the Carter administration's attention to job training programs, low-income housing, and urban revitalization, and his appointments of African Americans to prominent roles. But in the end, the laggard economy, a lingering energy crisis and the depressing, ongoing drama of the Iranian hostage crisis proved too much for the Democratic president.

Reagan was elected governor of California in 1966 on a platform that included opposing desegregation through open housing. As governor, he battled the Black Panthers over the open carrying of firearms and vocally opposed "socialist" Medicare, which, he'd warned in 1965, would destroy America. On the stump during the 1976 Republican presidential primary campaigns, Reagan often talked about how hard it must be for Americans to watch an able-bodied man in the grocery store using food stamps. In the South, the story morphed from "able-bodied man" to "strapping young buck."

Reagan kicked off his 1980 campaign in Philadelphia, Mississippi, where the bodies of Goodman, Schwerner, and Chaney had been unearthed a generation before. Reagan lamented the "humiliation of the South" via the Voting Rights Act and bemoaned the "Cadillac-driving welfare queen." He appeared onstage with former Mississippi governor John Bell Williams, an unrepentant segregationist, and his state campaign chair Trent

Lott, who like Reagan was once a Democrat, openly declared during the campaign that Democrat-turned-Dixiecrat-turned Republican Strom Thurmond would have prevented America from being "in the mess we are today" had he won the presidential election of 1948.

But Reagan promised a return to a robust economy and the restoration of American confidence and pride. And for all of Carter's attempts to dismiss him, Carter himself had failed to inspire the country, or his party. It was Reagan who managed to field a broad coalition that included a swath of white voters once loyal to the Democrats, plus 37 percent of Hispanics, and even 14 percent of African Americans. A Joint Center analysis noted that black Republican voter registration rose from just 2 percent in 1976 to 10 percent by 1979, and Carter received just 55 percent of the votes of black independents in 1980, two points lower than his share of the Hispanic vote.

Once elected, Reagan wasted no time putting his agenda to work.

Within his first two years in office, he had broken the national air traffic controllers union, slashed away at income tax rates, and eviscerated what was left of Johnson's Great Society programs. An assassination attempt in 1981 led the Democratic Congress to largely stand down, allowing much of Reagan's economic program to pass, and the country was soon mired in a deepening recession.

Reagan opposed U.S. sanctions against apartheid South Africa, a key plank for the Congressional Black Caucus. The administration argued that economic sanctions would hurt ordinary black South Africans and that Nelson Mandela's African National Congress was a terrorist organization. The new president was personally disarming and he was attracting his share of unexpected admirers (including soul legend James Brown), but liberal and African American Democrats were having difficulty abiding him.

In June 1982, Frank Watkins, a senior aide to Rev. Jesse Jackson, traveled to Indiana to meet with Mayor Richard Hatcher at his home in Gary. Watkins had written a detailed memo, directed at black political leaders, outlining why Jackson should run for president.

Watkins had been one of just two white attendees at the 1972 Gary conference, and he had Rev. Jackson's ear and trust. But Jackson had been cool to the idea of a presidential bid. Watkins hoped to enlist Hatcher's help, arguing that a Jackson presidential campaign could reignite the political consciousness of African Americans, who were foundering under the twin burdens of Reaganomics and a moribund national Democratic Party.

Hatcher knew Jackson well. They'd met in April 1966, as the young preacher launched Operation Breadbasket at the behest of the Southern Christian Leadership Conference (SCLC), in a chilly Capitol Theater on Chicago's South Side. Jackson had emerged from the embers of the civil rights movement with a national media profile and a growing following, through a combination of fortuitous timing and unabashed self-promotion.

Jackson had joined King's movement in Selma at age twenty-four after hearing the civil rights leader on the radio and was with King when he was assassinated in Memphis in 1968. Left behind at the Lorraine Motel, clad in a sweater on which he'd wiped his hand, stained with King's blood, Jackson was the first to address the media after the shooting, and he flew home to Chicago still dressed in those clothes. And while he elicited the constant skepticism of King's former associates, including Rev. Ralph Abernathy, Andrew Young, and King's widow, Coretta, Jackson did represent for many young African Americans an affirmation of black hope and self-love that was akin to what James Brown sang about in "I'm Black and I'm Proud."

Still as tall and as athletic as in his high school football days, Jackson had let his Afro grow long and his rhetoric had sharpened in the years after King's death. He used his years in the wilderness after King's assassination—having resigned from Breadbasket in 1971 in a disagreement with SCLC leaders over his fund-raising tactics and neglect in reporting Breadbasket's intake—to build his own organization: Operation PUSH, based in his adopted city of Chicago.

Jackson's weekly Saturday morning meetings at the Capitol Theater regularly drew a capacity crowd. The media—local and national, black and white—gravitated to the young, charismatic preacher in its hunt for a new "leader of black America."

Watkins believed Jackson was a natural candidate to vie to become the nation's first black president. Unlike Shirley Chisholm, he wouldn't dilute black enthusiasm with entreaties to women, and he was much better known on the national stage than Carl Stokes. Jackson's hybrid organization, Rainbow/PUSH (an amalgam of Operation PUSH and the Rainbow Coalition, named from a phrase Jackson borrowed from assassinated Chicago Black Panther leader Fred Hampton), knew how to register voters. Even if he didn't stand a chance against Reagan's reelection machine in 1984, Jackson would raise the national consciousness and make a future black president possible, Watkins argued.

Hatcher was persuaded and would sign on as Jackson's campaign chairman. But the greater leverage may have been exercised by Harold Washington, who had been a popular presence at the Saturday PUSH meetings and counted Jackson as an ally. Washington's November 1982 announcement that he was running for Chicago mayor came after he'd challenged his supporters to register a hundred thousand new voters. And they'd done it, with no small amount of help from Jackson's organization.

But leaders of the national Democratic Party seemed immune to the signs of growing black self-confidence in Chicago. As Jackson and Watkins awaited a flight at Washington's National Airport in January 1983, Jackson placed a call to

PUSH headquarters to check in and learned that former vice president Walter Mondale and Senator Ted Kennedy were on their way to Chicago to endorse Richard M. Daley, the son of the late Richard J. Daley, and Jane Byrne, the incumbent mayor, respectively, who were challenging Washington in the three-way February primary.

An angry Jackson prepared a telegram, signed by dozens of black political leaders inside and outside Illinois, imploring the national Democrats to remain neutral so as not to imperil Washington's historic bid. But Byrne had been an early endorser of Kennedy's primary challenge against President Carter in 1980, while Mondale insisted he'd been committed to Daley long before Washington announced back in November.

In Chicago, Mondale and Kennedy faced tense meetings with black leaders, during which they described their friendship and loyalty as the reasons for their endorsements of Byrne and Daley. "So we're not your friends?" Jackson snapped. Later he told aides, "If that's what liberal number one and liberal number two will do to us . . . if our 'closest friends' would run over Harold Washington in Chicago, we have to go in another direction."

Washington was elected mayor of Chicago in April 1983, driven by the wave of newly registered black voters and a Daley-Byrne split among white Chicagoans. Jackson quickly embarked on a national voter registration tour of his own, primarily targeting southern states, with their rich cache of unregistered African Americans. His nascent presidential bid had Hatcher's support, but not that of most other prominent black leaders, including Andrew Young and Coretta King, who publicly warned that Jackson wasn't viable.

Nevertheless, as he toured the country holding voter registration rallies, "Run Jesse Run!"—an exhortation originating from the pews of a small southern church—became a familiar refrain. In late October, Jackson taped an appearance on *60 Minutes* with reporter Mike Wallace and confirmed his intention to run.

When Jackson spoke at Morehouse College the day after the interview aired, he was introduced as a presidential candidate and received a thunderous reception. Four days later, in Washington, he officially announced he was running for president in 1984.

For a generation of young, liberal activists, Jesse Jackson's 1984 campaign was the most exciting thing happening in America. For the Democratic Party, Jackson's presidential bid presented a string of uncomfortable challenges. Robust enthusiasm among black voters was key to the party's national prospects and to leading candidate Mondale's hope of unseating Ronald Reagan, whose approval ratings had recently rebounded. But Jackson, who brought with him an agenda that had sent white voters first to Nixon, and then to Reagan, was preventing Mondale from having any chance of getting the black voters he needed to win in 1984. The party faced a dilemma because it could neither accommodate Jackson nor reject him.

Walter Mondale's deal brokering that set aside the Mississippi Freedom Democrats at the 1964 Democratic Convention, as well as his backing of Richard Daley over Harold Washington, continued to rankle Chicago's black political elite, putting Jackson's full and enthusiastic support of the ticket in question. Mondale, a longtime ally of the civil rights movement, was not without strong backers in the black political establishment, most of whom dismissed the Jackson campaign as an absurdity when the country was still wrangling over a holiday honoring Dr. King, which had been introduced and defeated by every Congress since a bill was introduced in 1968. Even after millions of petition signatures and mass rallies, including one that August that attracted two hundred thousand people to the National Mall for the twentieth anniversary of the March on Washington, and a song by Stevie Wonder, the bill was filibustered by Senator Jesse Helms in October 1983, the same month Jackson announced his presidential bid.

Members of the Congressional Black Caucus also had no interest in Jackson's symbolic runs for president when Reaganomics was cutting into the heart of their districts. Symbolism was a luxury too extravagant for their constituents to afford. As Detroit mayor Coleman Young put it at the time, the priority for the black political establishment was not electing one of their own to the White House, it was beating Ronald Reagan.

Still, black audiences flocked to Jackson's campaign as it barreled across the South, raising money through "love offerings" at church appearances to pay for that night's hotel rooms and the gas to get the campaign bus to the next stop. Jackson focused on two main issues: freedom for Nelson Mandela and black South Africans, as well as the rebuilding of infrastructure and eradication of poverty at home.

The Jackson campaign never thought they would beat Ronald Reagan, or even Walter Mondale, but they believed they were offering much more than a symbolic balm for the souls of black folk. The campaign surmised that if Jackson could build enough momentum, register enough voters, and claim enough delegates, he could be a force at the Democratic convention, winning important concessions in the platform. They even thought they could take away enough of Mondale's African American base to allow a more conservative candidate like Ohio senator John Glenn to emerge, forcing liberal Democrats to join with their camp to deny Glenn the nomination. (Glenn would wind up being a nonfactor in the primaries, while Colorado senator Gary Hart garnered major attention with his rebuke of Mondale's New Deal–era politics and his disdain for the politics of Jesse Jackson, whom he criticized for a multitude of sins, including what Hart and others viewed as Jackson's bias against the state of Israel.)

In January 1984, Jackson had breakfast with a black *Washington Post* reporter, Milton Coleman, who recalled Jackson saying,

"Let's talk black talk," before launching into a tirade about the fixation of liberal Jewish voters and donors in New York—a key part of the Democratic base—with Israel. "That's all Hymie wants to talk about, is Israel; every time you go to Hymietown, that's all they want to talk about," Jackson said, in what he must have thought was a "brother-to-brother" chat.

Coleman recounted the conversation to a colleague who was writing a piece about Jackson's fraught relationship with the Jewish community, dating back to his public embrace of Palestine Liberation Organization leader Yasser Arafat, and his persistent advocacy for an independent Palestinian state.

When Jackson's remark appeared in print, he first denied it—which was followed by a hearty defense from Nation of Islam leader Louis Farrakhan, who denounced Coleman and even seemed to threaten his life. But by February, Jackson admitted using the slur, issuing an emotional apology at a Manchester, New Hampshire, synagogue. But the damage was done.

Jackson's prospects fizzled, and he finished well behind Mondale and Hart in the Democratic primaries, winning just two states: Louisiana and his home state of South Carolina, plus the District of Columbia. Jackson had garnered more than 3 million votes and 18 percent of the popular tally, however, taking 466 delegates into the convention—just over a third of Hart's haul. Mondale easily won the nomination with nearly 2,200 delegates.

Jackson would have the chance to redeem himself at the convention in San Francisco, where he was slated to speak after New York governor Mario Cuomo, who articulated, at long last, a fulsome defense of his party's progressive legacy, which had been marginalized since the end of the Johnson era. "Do not forget that this entire nation has profited by these progressive principles," Cuomo told those assembled. "They helped lift up generations to the middle class and higher; that they gave us a chance to work, to go to college, to raise a family, to own a house, to be secure in our old age and, before that, to reach heights that our own parents would not have dared dream of."

On the evening before, Jackson and senior members of his campaign met in House Speaker Tip O'Neill's hotel suite, where Mondale's campaign manager, Bob Beckel, asked Jackson to join him on the balcony. Beckel pressed Jackson for a general idea of what he planned to say, emphasizing how important his words would be to Mondale, the party, and the country. Would Jackson do his utmost to encourage the full measure of African American support for the Democratic ticket, to which Mondale had added a woman, Geraldine Ferraro of New York? Or would he hold back?

"Beckel," Jackson said, "tomorrow night you're either gonna be a champ, a chimp, or a chump. But you're not going to know until tomorrow night."

After Cuomo finished, Jackson struck an inclusive tone. "Our flag is red, white, and blue, but our nation is a rainbow—red, yellow, brown, black, and white—and we're all precious in God's sight," he said. "America is not like a blanket—one piece of unbroken cloth, the same color, the same texture, the same size. America is more like a quilt: many patches, many pieces, many colors, many sizes, all woven and held together by a common thread."

Jackson touted the country's ending its "apartheid laws" and its achievements in voting rights. For the first time in a national convention address, he wove gays and lesbians into the "American quilt," alongside "the white, the Hispanic, the black, the Arab, the Jew, the woman, the native American, the small farmer, the businessperson, the environmentalist, the peace activist, the young, [and] the old."

By the time he wrapped up his speech, at nearly midnight, more than 33 million Americans had tuned in, and rousing applause and tears filled the convention hall. For African Americans and liberals who had longed to hear a message of redemption and national unity preached again from a Democratic platform, they were tears of joy. For many in the Democratic Party establishment, there were tears of relief.

In November, President Reagan was reelected, handing the Democrats a decisive defeat. But Jackson had proven that his candidacy was no novelty, and he prepared to run again in 1988.

Jackson had assembled a robust new team: Alexis Herman, who'd managed the convention floor for Jackson in 1984; Lavonia Perryman and Minyon Moore, of Operation PUSH in Detroit and Chicago; Jerry Austin, a veteran Democratic operative from the Bronx, as national campaign manager; Harold Ickes, whose father had been Franklin Roosevelt's secretary of the interior; and a talented union organizer from New York named Patrick Gaspard. Jackson moved his campaign headquarters from Washington, D.C., to Chicago and brought on Dr. Leon Finney, a longtime organizer and the head of the Woodlawn Organization, as his national finance chair.

Finney's grandfather, T. J. Huddleston, had built a family fortune on thousands of acres of land and twenty-seven funeral homes across Mississippi, while founding the Central Burial Association. His first cousin, Mike Espy, had in 1986 been elected the first black congressman from the state. Through Finney, Jackson gained access to the Hyde Park network of black business, civic, and labor leaders who had helped elect Harold Washington mayor in 1983. Finney had turned down Jackson's entreaties in 1984, but determined by 1988 that Jackson's campaign could do some good for black Americans.

The uninspiring Democratic field—Massachusetts governor Michael Dukakis, Senators Al Gore Jr. of Tennessee, Paul Simon of Illinois, Joe Biden of Delaware, and Gary Hart in a second bid from Colorado that was destined to end in sexual scandal; plus Missouri congressman Dick Gephardt and former Arizona governor Bruce Babbitt—was derided by some in the media, after the brief entrance of Colorado congresswoman Patricia Schroeder, as "Snow White and the seven dwarves." With no clear front-runner, and no marquee name on the ballot, Jackson's large campaign crowds and vibrant speeches were given notice.

The campaign was raising millions of dollars through the mail. Weeks into his job, Finney opened a closet at campaign headquarters in Chicago and discovered bags full of unopened envelopes. When the staff began to unseal them, they found money—lots of it—stuffed inside. The staff had ignored the mail in pursuit of more conventional fund-raising.

On Super Tuesday, a set of contests heavily concentrated in the South, Jackson won five primaries—as many as Gore and one fewer than Michael Dukakis. This was followed by a surprise March 26 victory for Jackson in Michigan, even without the endorsement of the African American mayor of Detroit, Coleman Young. This briefly earned Jackson the status of front-runner and the party's full attention.

Jackson broadened his message to appeal to a wider swath of liberal voices, earning an endorsement from *The Nation* magazine, which called his candidacy "a new civil rights movement with an added dimension of economic justice deriving in spirit from the last campaigns of Martin Luther King Jr. with the black working poor."

The forty-six-year-old's stump speech refrain, "It's our time!" didn't "just mean African American issues," one former campaign aide recalled. "He was the Left's standard-bearer in the race. If you were on that campaign, you'd fly to places like Medford, Oregon, and you'd think, 'There's not a single black person in this town. How am I gonna pull together a rally for Jesse?' And two days later there'd be twenty thousand white folks. White folks in overalls, Vietnam vets showing up and saying he was the only one speaking to their sense of not being part of the middle class American dream."

The excitement led *New York Times* columnist R. W. Apple in April to declare 1988 "the Year of Jackson—the year when, for the first time in American history, a black made a serious bid for the White House and was taken seriously by the electorate."

And this time, Jackson had the support of the black elite as well, including members of the Congressional Black Caucus; much of the civil rights movement's old guard, who some Jackson staffers suspected feared being left behind by their constituents; and the national black press.

"We used the same structure that we had for the civil rights movement to drive Jesse's campaign," Finney said. "Black business, black churches across the U.S. . . . . *Ebony* magazine, *Jet* magazine . . . Black radio carried our message. The black newspapers carried our message. And black folk were ready to believe in something. They were ready to dream. We had elected out of the city of Chicago the first black mayor. These black folk thought they could do anything. Even elect a black president."

In the end, Jackson won 6.6 million votes, double his total in 1984 and nearly 30 percent of the popular vote. He'd won nearly as many votes as Walter Mondale had in the 1984 primaries, and attracted twice as many white voters as he had four years earlier: more than 2 million according to a June 1988 analysis in the *New York Times*. Jackson, with more than 1,200 delegates, finished a strong second to Dukakis, whose base of immigrant Catholics and Jewish voters helped him secure the nomination with 9.7 million votes. But Dukakis performed dismally with black voters, who cast just 200,000 ballots for him, while Jackson's take consisted of two-thirds African Americans. Where in 1984 he had captured 77 percent of African American primary votes, Jackson now commanded 92 percent, a figure achieved by no one except LBJ.

By the time the Democratic National Convention convened in Atlanta on July 18, Jackson had won eleven contests: the

Alabama, Georgia, Louisiana, Mississippi, Puerto Rico, Virginia, and District of Columbia primaries, and the caucuses in Delaware, Michigan, South Carolina, and Vermont, and finished second in another thirty-three. He'd edged out Dukakis 35 percent to 31 percent in the Alaska caucuses and won the Texas local conventions (despite losing the Texas primary) and garnered 1,023 delegates to Gore's 374, and just 769 fewer than the nominee. When the final tally was called, after most candidates withdrew and threw their delegates to Dukakis, Jackson ended his campaign with 1,219 pledged delegates to Dukakis's 2,877, a final margin of victory for Dukakis of 70 versus 30 percent for Jackson, a larger percentage than any black candidate had ever received—or perhaps even hoped to receive—in a presidential nominating contest.

Hendrik Hertzberg, a veteran of the Carter administration, proclaimed that the results placed Jackson in the tripartite pantheon of black leaders with Martin Luther King Jr. and Booker T. Washington. And at a breakfast in Atlanta the day after the convention, onetime rival Andrew Young rose to speak, raised his glass to Jackson, and told him, "Jesse, you are now the moral leader of our country."

It wouldn't last.

CHAPTER 3

The Third Way

We have got to have a message that touches everybody, that makes
sense to everybody, that goes beyond the stale orthodoxies of left
and right, one that resonates with the real concerns of ordinary
Americans, with their hopes and their fears.

—Bill Clinton, address to the Democratic Leadership
   Council, May 1991

IT WASN'T LONG BEFORE THE DEMOCRATIC PARTY SHIFTED ITS
focus from accommodating Jesse Jackson and taking advantage
of how much he had grown the African American base to figur-
ing out ways they could marginalize him.

In 1984 and 1988, Jackson brought in more than 3 million
new voters. Heavily concentrated in the South, the gains helped
Democrats retake the U.S. Senate in 1986. His presidential campaigns cemented his role as the dominant civil rights leader of
his era and made him a political celebrity (he even hosted NBC's
Saturday Night Live in the closing weeks of the 1984 campaign).
He was black America's preeminent national figure. But in the

eyes of many leading Democrats, Jackson had wielded his triumphs like a sword, which hung over the party and Massachusetts governor Michael Dukakis, its 1988 nominee.

Before the July convention, Jackson openly and pointedly sought the vice presidency, and when Dukakis eventually chose Texas senator Lloyd Bentsen instead, Jackson's reaction seemed less than gracious, even to his friends. For some Jackson seemed to squander his triumph in the primary in a fit of pique, nursing his jilted status rather than pouring his energy into helping the hapless Massachusetts governor give life to his flagging campaign.

The 1988 election ended with a whimper, as Michael Dukakis threw away an early 17-point lead over Vice President George H. W. Bush. He was battered by his own stumbles as well as a relentless, race-tinged crusade by the Bush campaign that featured the grainy, menacing image of a black felon, Willie Horton, who had raped and assaulted a white couple while out of prison on furlough in Massachusetts, a program the governor inherited. But the Bush campaign, including campaign manager Lee Atwater and chief media strategist Roger Ailes, made good on its vow to make Horton a household name.

The tactic emerged from a series of focus groups with Reagan Democrats, through which the Bush campaign discovered that white voters responded to the kind of "tough on crime" messaging and racial scare-mongering that had been so effective in the Nixon era. The revived campaign model pricked at white America's deepest fears about street crime, as the crack cocaine epidemic continued to course through the arteries of major cities. Reagan's "welfare queen" was swapped out for the "Ubiquitous Black Thug." TV ads paid for by "independent expenditures" slid through the loopholes in post-Watergate laws, allowing millions of dollars to flood into elections without leaving a trace on the official campaign. Voter turnout reached a record low, and black voters, deflated and feeling that Jackson had been pushed aside, largely stayed home, too.

Democratic leaders saw a clear message: Even the most energetic campaign by a black liberal like Jackson couldn't reverse the track record of the past twenty-four years, which had been interrupted only once, in 1976, when Jimmy Carter ran to the right of Lyndon Johnson's legacy. Now, after the failure of Michael Dukakis, a liberal candidate from the Northeast, the core group of mainly southern and western senators and governors who focused on recapturing the White House saw little reason to court and solicit Jackson as an endorser in 1992, the way Mondale and Dukakis had felt they had to do. Instead party leaders had every incentive to view Jackson as a fulcrum, against whom the Democratic candidate could pivot toward working-class white voters.

By 1991, that lesson was top of mind for Bill Clinton, the governor of Arkansas, as he set his eye on the next presidential election.

Clinton and Jackson had become acquainted in 1982, when Clinton invited Jackson to attend the twenty-fifth anniversary commemoration of the integration of Central High School in Little Rock. The ceremony was followed by a small gathering at the Governor's Mansion with Jackson, Alexis Herman, Ernest G. Greene (five years Clinton's senior and a member of the Little Rock Nine, and a former assistant labor secretary in the Carter administration), and a handful of staff. As the evening stretched into the wee hours, participants began to peel away, leaving Jackson and Clinton to push on until nearly 4 A.M., discussing politics and "generally doing what both of them do: talk," as one aide put it. In the end, Hillary Clinton had to declare an end to the all-nighter. Jackson later recalled with a smile, "Hillary put me out of the governor's mansion."

Despite the cordiality of that night, Clinton and Jackson

were rivals. Clinton's 1988 convention moment had been a disaster; his overly long speech drew applause at the phrase "in conclusion." Clinton also found Jackson's unabashed liberalism starkly at odds with his and the "New Democrats'" formula for winning back white working-class voters in the South, the West, and the "culturally southern" voters in places like Ohio, western Pennsylvania, and Illinois.

Clinton led the centrist Democratic Leadership Council (DLC), which had a long game to launch a viable presidential candidate by 1996. But Clinton had no patience for the long game. He, like other charter members, including Al Gore and Missouri congressman Dick Gephardt, saw the DLC as a centrist vehicle they could ride to the White House.

The DLC had frequently invited Jackson to its annual conventions, but he always used the moment to criticize Democrats for talking about "opportunity, responsibility, and community" while essentially preaching Reaganomics, complete with conservative buzzwords like "equality of opportunity, not equality of outcomes."

When Clinton assumed the chairmanship of the DLC in 1990, the invitations to Jackson stopped.

The group's May 1991 convention in Cleveland was attended by a diverse group of political stars, including the city's young black mayor, Michael White; Congressmen Mike Espy of Mississippi and Bill Gray of Pennsylvania; the Democratic National Committee's first-ever black chairman, Ron Brown; and Virginia's newly elected first black governor, Douglas Wilder. The pointed message was that Jackson wasn't the only black leader who mattered. In addition, Clinton had his own relationships with black leaders, including Vernon Jordan, whom Clinton had known since 1973; Kansas City mayor Emanuel Cleaver, a Methodist minister bound for the House of Representatives; Carter-appointed Florida district judge Alcee Hastings; former

King aide Andrew Young; and John Lewis, the former SNCC leader elected to Congress in 1986.

The Cleveland summit would demonstrate that the party could take a new base into the next national election. Not only was Jackson conspicuously excluded, but so was George McGovern, a pointed rebuke that irritated liberal Democrats like Mario Cuomo, who saw no need to make the party "new."

Jackson organized a counter-rally on the Sunday night before the convention, but the protest was to no avail. Clinton was a bona fide hit in Cleveland, and his message for remaking the party so it could appeal to every region, class, and walk of life and could compete with Republicans for the American heartland was a balm to his stricken party. This New Democratic Party proclaimed its opposition to "quotas and special interests"—a barely concealed euphemism for African Americans and unions—and supported welfare reform and school choice.

In a June 1991 Associated Press interview, Clinton called out Cuomo and Jackson by name over their criticism of his and the New Democrats' vows to remake the party, and for Jackson's ridicule of the DLC as the "Democratic Leisure Class," saying, "I like Mario, but once again, he and Jesse are criticizing me without being specific about what they disagree with." He went on to say, "we're getting beat . . . and what's their explanation for why the middle class folks didn't vote for us in '88 when we had a clear shot? People aren't buyin' what we're sellin'."

The forces pushing Jackson to the margins weren't coming just from within the Democratic Party.

A new vein of civil unrest had opened in the Northeast, and it ran right through the heart of New York City—America's blue metropolis—filling the nightly news and the minds of white suburbanites with visions of the "urban nightmare" from which centrist Democrats were working so hard to disentangle the party.

The unrest touched off a new civil rights movement led by a onetime protégé of Jackson: Al Sharpton, who'd risen from boy preacher—at just nine years old he had already delivered sermons in Brooklyn churches and toured with Mahalia Jackson at the time of the March on Washington—to a road manager for soul legend James Brown to a growing national force in his own right.

Unlike Jackson and other traditional civil rights leaders, Sharpton had no roots in the South. He and his mother were forced to leave their middle-class home in Hollis, Queens, after becoming destitute in the wake of the family's abandonment by his father, who in 1963 ran off with Sharpton's eighteen-year-old half sister. The family moved to the rough projects of Brooklyn's Brownsville neighborhood.

In 1969, Jackson appointed Sharpton as youth director of Operation Breadbasket, and two years later, when Jackson split from the SCLC, King confidant Bayard Rustin gave Sharpton the cash to start his own organization, the National Action Network. By the early 1990s, Sharpton was carving a path separate from his onetime mentor, and more confrontational.

He became a staple in the New York City media after the shooting of four black men on a subway train by a white passenger, Bernard Goetz, three days before Christmas in 1984. Sharpton led mass marches denouncing the city's response to a wave of young black men chased down and killed by white mobs in New York's ethnically polarized neighborhoods: twenty-three-year-old Michael Griffith in Howard Beach, Queens, in 1986; sixteen-year-old Yusuf Hawkins in Bensonhurst, Brooklyn, in 1989; as well as the sensational trial and imprisonment of five black and Hispanic teenagers in the brutal rape of a white jogger in Central Park that same year; the men were found innocent decades later.

Heavy-set and frequently clad in a jogging suit in the style of the rap group Run-D.M.C., with long sideburns and pressed hair that hung down to his shoulders like his surrogate father,

James Brown, Sharpton cut a strikingly different figure from Jackson. He led marches through racially segregated neighborhoods, and battled city leaders with brash abandon. He would be dogged for years by a 1987 controversy over an alleged attack on a black teenage girl, Tawana Brawley, who accused six white men of raping her and covering her in excrement—an allegation later proven false—and survived a 1991 stabbing during a Bensonhurst march, to emerge as the most visible civil rights leader in an increasingly volatile city. Sharpton kept up a drumbeat of protests over racial profiling, police brutality, and the ongoing discrimination he called "not just a southern specialty."

The post–civil rights era had given way to the "no justice, no peace movement," in which activists took to the streets in 1960s-style marches but declined to adopt the neatly pressed Sunday garments or the pose of Gandhian nonviolence characterized by King's movement. In the Sharpton era, the threat of civil unrest churned beneath the surface of every protest, and civic (or corporate) leaders had little choice but to respond. Sharpton was the movement's primary organizational figure. Hip-hop artists like Public Enemy provided its soundtrack. And filmmaker Spike Lee provided the cinematic play-by-play for what felt, to some, like a racially apocalyptic America.

Angry protests, even riots, fueled by ethnic mistrust and decades of tension between communities of color and police, were erupting around the country: in Miami in 1989 following the police-involved shooting deaths of two unarmed black men; in Crown Heights, Brooklyn, in 1991 after a black child was struck and killed by a car in an Orthodox Jewish motorcade; and in Los Angeles in the spring of 1992 following the acquittal of four officers who brutally beat black motorist Rodney King—a mauling caught on videotape.

Even on college campuses, questions of race pervaded the discourse, from national debates over the merit of ethnic studies, to protests over the dearth of tenured black faculty. Questions roiled even staid Harvard University, where weeks of sit-ins brought a wave of black intellectual elites to the African American studies department, including Henry Louis Gates Jr., Kwame Anthony Appiah, William Julius Wilson, and Cornel West. At Harvard Law School, a young Columbia University graduate, Barack Obama, who had achieved a crackle of national notoriety as the first black president of the law review, attended a 1991 campus rally in support of Professor Derrick Bell, who had vowed not to return to the classroom until more diverse faculty were hired.

Jesse Jackson struggled to figure out where he, a civil rights leader from a different generation of activists—indeed, from what increasingly felt like a bygone era—fit in.

BILL CLINTON FORMALLY ANNOUNCED HIS CANDIDACY FOR PRES-ident in October 1991, just a few months after his triumph in Cleveland. He dove into the primaries the next year, confident that he could bring the "Reagan Democrats" home by neutral-izing the triumvirate of wedge issues—race, crime, and quotas—that had so advantaged the GOP.

The field of Democratic candidates was unimpressive, accord-ing to the Clinton team. Jackson was on the sidelines, saddled by lingering campaign debts, meaning that Clinton's only competitor for black votes in the primaries was Governor Douglas Wilder of Virginia, the first African American governor of any state since Reconstruction. He had the potential to do to Clinton with black voters what Jackson had done to Dukakis and Gore. In addition Wilder was a business-focused, bread-and-butter moderate, who could make a serious play for white voters. "He had a preexisting history, and was very well liked in the African American commu-nity," one senior member of the 1992 Clinton campaign said.

With African Americans making up 20 to 25 percent of the primary electorate, and 30 percent or better in states like South

Carolina, having a serious black challenger in the race would have been problematic for Clinton. But after declaring his candidacy for president in September 1991, Wilder withdrew before the start of the primaries, citing Virginia's fiscal woes and his need to focus on his job as governor.

"Once Wilder got out, Bill Clinton had an open field," the senior Clinton campaign staffer said.

Clinton recruited former members of Jackson's team, including Alexis Herman, Lavonia Perryman, and Minyon Moore. This prompted Jackson, referring to Moore's and Perryman's history with Operation PUSH, to crack, "we raise 'em up and you guys steal 'em."

With a clear path to the teeming black vote in the South, which was so important to the southern-packed schedule on Super Tuesday, Clinton worked to distinguish himself as the champion of the middle class, which involved sending a clear message to the white suburbs. For that Clinton would enlist Jackson's help, if not his consent.

In January 1992, with the Iowa caucuses looming, Clinton dramatically flew home to Arkansas to sign the death warrant for Ricky Ray Rector, a mentally damaged black man sentenced to die by an all-white jury in the 1981 shooting deaths of two men, including a police officer Rector had known for much of his life. The execution became a botched, torturous affair in which Rector seemed to believe that the executioners struggling to find a vein in his swollen arm were doctors who had come to help him. Afterward the prison chaplain resigned.

Jackson had publicly pleaded with Clinton to spare Rector's life, even urging top aides and supporters to send telegrams asking the governor to grant Rector an eleventh-hour reprieve. Instead Clinton made sure the execution went forward. The next day he went as planned to the Rainbow Coalition's presidential candidate forum in Washington, D.C.

As attendees streamed into the Omni Shoreham hotel for two days of panels featuring New York congressman Charlie Rangel, African American scholar Ron Walters, political scientist David Bositis, New York mayor David Dinkins, and others, Clinton strode into the room with full knowledge that the air was thick with the knowledge of Rector's death.

One by one, the Democratic candidates—California governor Jerry Brown, Iowa senator Tom Harkin, Nebraska senator Bob Kerrey, former Massachusetts senator Paul Tsongas, and former presidential candidate Eugene McCarthy—made their pitches for African American support. When Clinton's turn came, he fielded sharp questions, and calmly explained his views on the death penalty, coolly pointing out that he and Jesse Jackson disagreed on some things. But Clinton also emphasized where he agreed with Jackson: so-called motor voter laws to ease access to the polls, D.C. statehood, and the establishment of rural development banks like ones in his home state that could help lift black farmers out of poverty. But on the death penalty, he wasn't backing down.

"This was Bill Clinton, politically, at his absolute most brilliant," said one attendee. "It was like he was stabbing a knife right in the chest of the Republican Party. He was gonna go before Jesse Jackson's group and talk about why he executed Ricky Ray Rector. The next day, throughout the country, everybody was gonna know that Jesse Jackson and his friends were begging Bill Clinton not to execute Rector, and Bill Clinton just pulled the switch."

Clinton pulled this off with dexterity and charm, receiving warm applause as he left the stage. But he had sent a sharp message to white suburban voters that he was as tough on crime as any Republican, and he wasn't afraid to say so in front of America's most prominent civil rights leader. In one fluid motion, Clinton had inoculated himself against the deadliest weapon George H. W. Bush had wielded against Michael Dukakis in 1988.

As Bositis would later recall, after the conference, for all the attacks on Clinton's morality, his marriage, or his Vietnam service, "Republicans couldn't say a word about crime. Bill Clinton took crime as an issue away from them. And that time wasn't far removed from the crack epidemic. He took crime, and he took anti-black politics as a wedge issue away from the Republicans."

Clinton was sailing to the nomination, narrowly losing in New Hampshire but rebounding in the southern states, then Michigan and Illinois, and by late spring, across the Rust Belt and even in Jerry Brown's home state of California. But he still had more to deal with when it came to Jesse Jackson, who by late spring was pressing hard—and publicly—to be Clinton's running mate.

"Vice Prez Or Else!" blared a May 2 headline in the New York *Daily News,* which quoted Jackson warning the Democrats on behalf of black voters, in language reminiscent of his fiery stump speech in Gary in 1972, "We are ready for any opportunity to serve, but we are ready if we are ignored or rejected. . . . If I am rejected this time, I am prepared to react!"

The Clinton campaign reacted by ignoring Jackson.

Jackson's remarks were condemned for what many saw as a repeat of his 1988 attempts to bully the Dukakis campaign. "For all his brilliance, he hasn't figured out that it's not done that way—that to seek greatness is to fall short of it," wrote *Philadelphia Inquirer* columnist William Raspberry in May 1992. "Indeed it may be Jackson's tragic flaw that there is no overall cause that takes precedence over his personal prospects."

A month later, when Clinton was the presumptive nominee, he accepted Jackson's invitation to speak at another Rainbow Coalition conference in Washington, D.C., on June 13. Jackson had also invited twenty-eight-year-old Harlem rapper and activist Lisa Williamson, known as Sister Souljah. The onetime legislative intern in Washington was a veteran of the campus anti-apartheid movement at Rutgers University in the 1980s, and she now toured as a public speaker and poet, promoting a March rap album featuring cameos by Public Enemy leader Chuck D and N.W.A. ("Niggaz With Attitude") rapper Ice Cube. It had produced two controversial singles: "The Hate That Hate Produced" and "The Final Solution: Slavery's Back in Effect," which imagined a fictional vice president David Duke who reinstitutes slavery. Her music videos were banned from MTV but spun in heavy rotation on local music video shows in New York City.

One month before the conference, on May 13, the *Washington Post* had published an interview with Souljah in which she was asked if the violence during the Los Angeles riots, which raged from April 29 to May 4, after the Rodney King verdict, was wise.

"If black people kill black people every day, why not have a week and kill white people?" she replied. "In other words, white people, this government, and that mayor were well aware of the fact that black people were dying every day in Los Angeles under gang violence. So if you're a gang member and you would normally be killing somebody, why not kill a white person? Do you think that somebody thinks that white people are better, or above and beyond dying, when they would kill their own kind? . . . If my house burns down, your house burns down. An eye for an eye, a tooth for a tooth. That's what they believe. And I see why."

The uproar over the interview brought Jackson to New York, where he met with Williamson in hopes he could convince her to use her influence with young rap music fans differently. Beyond the invitation to the D.C. conference, Jackson hoped to get the young woman involved in future Rainbow Coalition activities in New York, and parenthetically, to gain a foothold for himself in the world of youth-centric direct action that Rev. Sharpton was making his signature. Williamson was added to a panel at the conference that included David Bositis, Harvard Law School professor Charles Ogletree, and Georgia state representative "Able" Mable Thomas, set for the day before Clinton's arrival. Jackson hoped that the older intellectuals would influence Williamson to soften her approach, ahead of her "coming-out party" the following day at the Washington event.

Bill Clinton had other ideas. He walked onto the podium at the Omni hotel in downtown Washington, before a hall packed with more than three hundred attendees and throngs of media. After a warm introduction from Jackson, Clinton delivered a rousing speech attacking President Bush's economic policies, drawing cheers from the almost entirely African American crowd. And then, in a moment that sliced across the warm crowd like a cold blade, Clinton delivered a broadside against both Sister Souljah and the man who had invited her, as Jackson sat grim-faced and captive onstage just behind him. Clinton's topical shift had the elegant feel of spontaneity, and the crispness of calculation. He said he "felt compelled to discuss racism with the audience," because "all Americans must speak out against it."

Addressing Souljah's remarks to the *Washington Post,* after pointedly noting her presence at the conference the day before, Clinton proposed that "if you took the words 'white' and 'black' and you reversed them, you might think David Duke was giving that speech." His words drew gasps from the audience.

Jackson was visibly shaken, later telling reporter Sam Fulwood III of the *Los Angeles Times*: "I do not know why he used this platform to address those issues. It was unnecessary. It was a diversion. . . . Perhaps he was aiming for an audience that was not here."

Fulwood and other journalists rushed to get comments from two black members of Congress who were there as Clinton's surrogates. He later wrote that when he and *New York Times* reporter Gwen Ifill compared notes, they found that California congresswoman Maxine Waters and John Lewis of Georgia had made virtually identical statements in support of Clinton. "Clinton had given them his talking points in advance, covering himself beautifully," Fulwood would later write.

Jackson's staff realized they'd been used. Some blamed Clinton's strategists, wry Texas transplant Paul Begala in particular; or the candidate's media team, George Stephanopoulos and Mandy Grunwald, who were waiting in the "spin room" to take questions from an eager press corps. Jackson's senior aides believed Clinton had acted without consulting his campaign manager, David Wilhelm, who was sympathetic to Jackson's liberal politics and dealt with the reverend day to day.

Privately, friends said, Wilhelm feared Clinton had taken too great a risk, of alienating Jackson, and black voters, for little reward. But as the pragmatists on the Jackson team saw it, this was Bill Clinton working the southern strategy from the Democratic playbook, and doing so brilliantly.

Or, as one leading civil rights leader stated more bluntly, by "pimp slapping Jesse Jackson in his own house."

Sister Souljah quickly called a press conference and blasted Clinton as a Vietnam draft dodger and philanderer who "could never quite get his own personal and social behavior together" and who "says he is not a racist but he tries to distance himself from Jesse Jackson—a candidate who has registered more voters, served the interest of poor blacks, poor whites, poor Latinos, unions, laborers, and farmers and by experience, intellect, and charisma, is far more qualified for the job." But the damage was done.

Three days later Jackson was still fuming when he appeared on CNN's *Crossfire* and said his demands for an apology had not been met.

"First of all, to imply, on a platform where the governor was my guest, that I condone violence . . ." Jackson trailed off. "I have reached out to Governor Clinton at his lowest moment, when he needed redemption, and a hand out, and a bridge. I ask him to be as sensitive to people in their low moments as he wants people to be to him in his low moments."

A group of New York pastors, led by Calvin Butts, denounced Clinton's use of a black organization to launch a play for the white suburbs. Butts, pastor of the storied Abyssinian Baptist Church in Harlem, made a point of inviting Williamson to speak at the church the next month.

In July, at a Rainbow Coalition retreat in Orlando, Florida, just before the Democratic National Convention was set to open in Souljah's hometown of New York City, Jackson huddled with top aides, and his assessment was succinct.

"Fuck Clinton," he told a senior aide. "I ain't campaigning for him."

Jackson's top strategists urged him not to risk all-out war with the Democratic nominee. If Clinton went down, Jackson didn't want to be seen holding the anvil—and anything less than full support during the campaign could jettison Jackson's ability to influence a Clinton administration.

"We have to elect the most liberal candidate who's electable and that happens to be Bill Clinton," the senior adviser told Jackson. "Which seems to be the position that progressives are always in." Indeed, Clinton was promising to restore targeted federal spending to rebuild infrastructure, boost resources for community policing, improve health care, and provide job training and business development if he won the White House, reasons enough for progressives to give the New Democrat a fair hearing.

Clinton had been laying down markers with young and black voters before Jackson's conference that mitigated any damage from his "Sister Souljah" moment. On June 3, Clinton had appeared on *The Arsenio Hall Show,* a nightly variety show hosted by the eponymous comedian. Clinton had gamely played the saxophone and chatted about Hall's pastor, and about being in South Central L.A. three years before the riots, meeting with community organizations and talking urban policy at a meeting at Congresswoman Waters's home. Just afterward he turned up on MTV, reinforcing his status as the candidate of the young, and of "tomorrow."

Even Clinton's membership in the segregated Country Club of Little Rock, which membership he had acknowledged on the dais at Rainbow Coalition in Washington to make the point that he, too, had made mistakes, but unlike Souljah, was owning up to them, couldn't derail his quest for the nomination or his solid support from black political leaders. The revelation drew protests from Sharpton, and the famous quip from California governor Jerry Brown that "even George Bush wouldn't dare play golf at an all-white golf club."

Clinton was going to be the Democratic nominee, and his new style of politics, which simultaneously pulled black voters in and pushed them away, was the party's path out of the political wilderness. Black voters, liberals, labor unions—and Jackson—had little choice but to get on board.

BILL CLINTON DEFEATED INCUMBENT PRESIDENT GEORGE H. W. Bush in November 1992 and carried with him to Washington the pent-up hopes and dreams of a party exhausted by decades of political despair.

Clinton and his running mate, Al Gore, whose father and Senate forebear had been one of just three Democrats from the South to refuse to sign the Southern Manifesto in 1956, had struck a generational blow, beating back the long shadow of Vietnam and the Democratic malaise that followed in Lyndon Johnson's wake.

And while he failed to win a bare majority of the popular vote, with third-party candidate Ross Perot taking 19 percent, Clinton held Bush to just 37.5 percent of the vote to his 43, securing an Electoral College landslide: 370 to 168. Victories in a handful of southern states—Georgia, Tennessee, Kentucky, West Virginia, Louisiana, and his native Arkansas—represented the best showing for a Democrat in the region since Jimmy Carter in 1976. Clinton carried the Rust Belt, with the exception of Indiana. He picked up the western states of Colorado, New Mexico, and Nevada, while sweeping the traditional Democratic strongholds in the Northeast and on the West Coast.

The election attracted the highest voter turnout since 1972, and the strongest showing among women, young voters, and African Americans since 1984. As a result, the incoming congressional class would be the largest since 1948, and the most diverse in American history, including the first Korean-American member (Republican Jay Kim of California) and the first Native American House member in sixty years (Democrat Ben Nighthorse Campbell of Colorado).

The number of Hispanics in Congress grew from ten to seventeen, bolstered by newly created seats that sent candidates like Luis Gutiérrez of Illinois to Washington. And the Congressional Black Caucus swelled from twenty-five members to thirty-eight, as post-census redistricting—and Jesse Jackson's voter registration campaigns in 1984 and 1988—created more than a dozen enclaves where black voters were registered in sufficient numbers to swing a Democratic primary.

Of the thirteen black candidates who entered those contests, all would enter the House of Representatives, including Cynthia McKinney in Georgia, Eddie Bernice Johnson in Texas, Carrie Meek, Alcee Hastings and Corinne Brown in Florida, Cleo Fields in Louisiana, Albert Wynn in Maryland, Bobby Scott in Virginia, and Mel Watt in North Carolina. Black candidates were elected for the first time since Reconstruction in North Carolina, Florida, Virginia, Alabama, and South Carolina, where a former high school teacher and human affairs commissioner named James Clyburn won a newly created seat.

The election brought six new women senators to the Capitol, including Carol Moseley Braun of Illinois, the first black woman ever elected to the United States Senate. Her campaign had been organized by the Hyde Park coalition that backed Harold Washington in 1983 and 1987 and Jesse Jackson in 1988. Her run was fueled by a core group of female attorneys in Chicago, who joined the outrage among national feminist, civil rights, and black legal organizations over President Bush's nomination of a black archconservative, Clarence Thomas, to fill the Supreme Court seat left vacant by the great Thurgood Marshall. Thomas had triumphed with the help of a stone wall of white male senators who dismissed the sexual harassment allegations leveled by a black woman, Anita Hill, who had worked with Thomas in the Department of Education's Office for Civil Rights. He also had the overwhelming support of African Americans, whose zeal to see Thomas confirmed reached 70 percent by mid-October 1991, higher even than that of Thomas's other core admirers: Republicans and men.

Moseley Braun joined fellow Democrats Dianne Feinstein and Barbara Boxer of California, Patty Murray of Washington State, and a reelected Barbara Mikulski of Maryland, plus one Republican, Nancy Kassebaum of Kansas, to form the largest female contingent ever in the upper chamber. The forty-seven women entering the House represented an increase of nineteen and consisted of thirty-five Democrats and twelve Republicans. The unprecedented election results led newspaper headline writers across the country to declare 1992 "the year of the woman."

Despite President Clinton's New Democrat pedigree, liberal activists hoped that backed by a Democratic-controlled Congress that better reflected the country's diversity, he would press for a bold, progressive agenda to turn the economy around and strike a blow for economic and civic fairness in the wake of the

Reagan-Bush era, with its emphasis on tax cuts and determination to undo the Great Society.

Clinton's political confidants had deep roots in the civil rights movement: fellow southerners like Vernon Jordan, Andrew Young, John Lewis, and even Jesse Jackson, who during the general election had worked hard for the campaign, traveling the country as a surrogate and even telling Clinton's campaign manager at one point, "Wilhelm, you want me to go to a Klan rally? You just tell me what the reason is and I'll go."

Clinton had acted quickly and built a diverse cabinet.

With Vernon Jordan leading the transition team, a first for an African American, Clinton chose Ron Brown, the DNC chairman, as secretary of commerce. He tapped his friend Mike Espy of Mississippi as secretary of agriculture, Alexis Herman to head the White House Office of Public Liaison, and a fellow Arkansan, Rodney Slater, as secretary of transportation.

"He ends up with prominent African Americans, credible African Americans that we knew, that we had worked with, that we were comfortable with," said Marc Morial, then a Louisiana state legislator, and whose father, Ernest "Dutch" Morial, had been mayor of New Orleans (a post Morial himself would attain in 1994). "We could pick up the phone. You had Henry Cisneros at HUD; you had Hazel O'Leary at the Department of Energy. Crucially, Clinton's director of personnel was an African American by the name of Bob Nash. So the guy vetting the team was himself a person of color."

Ron Brown was the best-known cabinet member on a national level, as a former deputy director of the National Urban League, a deputy manager of Ted Kennedy's presidential campaign in 1980, the head of Jesse Jackson's 1988 convention team, and the party's lead man in Washington as the DNC chair during the Bush years. He would be Clinton's key emissary to black business and political leaders around the country as they sought access to economic opportunities for their struggling communities.

Brown presented the incoming president with an ambitious agenda; he wanted to use the power of his office to inject real economic progress into the urban centers that had foundered in the decades since Lyndon Johnson's final act of civic stewardship: the signing of the Fair Housing Act in 1968. Decades of neglect, the crack epidemic, and generational despair continued to eat away at the heart of black America in big cities and small, rural towns. In the minds of black leaders, bringing these places back meant injecting federal dollars to rebuild businesses in communities that in some cases were torn apart by riots or abandoned by "white flight." Creating tax havens for investment—"enterprise zones"—and making loans available for small businesses could help bring commerce and jobs back to the urban centers where African Americans had, at various times, been steered and abandoned. It was an idea Jimmy Carter had championed, including in Miami after the 1980 riots, but Ronald Reagan had rolled such programs back, cutting urban investment to the bone. Brown and the president shared a belief with local black leaders that commerce was the lifeblood that could bring the urban core back from the dead. Black mayors and state representatives and business leaders were eager to get on the phone with Brown to pitch their vision for how to get the investments under way.

It was a promising start that was soon followed by a series of setbacks.

Within weeks of taking office, Clinton's campaign promise to gay and lesbian activists to end the military's ban on open service triggered a ferocious backlash from conservatives and from the military brass, and the administration quickly backed down, accepting a compromise excoriated publicly by gay rights groups, and privately by gay members of his own staff who viewed the rapid retreat to "Don't Ask, Don't Tell" as a cowardly and premature capitulation.

Next came the public outrage over a months-long armed standoff with a religious cult in Waco, Texas, that took the lives of nearly ninety people and ended with the Branch Davidian compound in flames. First Lady Hillary Clinton led an abortive effort to pass a national health-care bill; her secretive task force outraged even Democrats on Capitol Hill. The administration also faced a host of media scandals, including an alleged two-hundred-dollar haircut for the president that snarled traffic at Los Angeles International Airport and the firing of a handful of employees at the White House travel office. No story seemed too minor or too outrageous to captivate the Beltway press.

In April, the president nominated Lani Guinier to be assistant attorney general in charge of the Justice Department's storied Civil Rights Division. She was the biracial daughter of the first chairman of Harvard's Afro-American Studies Department, Ewart Guinier, a Jamaican-Panamanian immigrant who had been denied the opportunity to live in Harvard dormitories when he was a student there in 1929.

Guinier had known the Clintons since they were Yale Law School classmates; Bill and Hillary attended her wedding. The nomination was both an act of friendship and a demonstration of the president's commitment to restore the Civil Rights Division to the standard of aggressive pursuit of desegregation and voting access set during the Kennedy and Johnson eras and the Carter administration. Civil rights groups believed the division had waned in the intervening years.

But by June, Guinier had come under withering attack from the Right, including by conservative columnist George Will, who accused her of supporting both quotas (rather than affirmative action) and the creation of "race conscious" districts where only African Americans could be elected. Neither of those claims happened to be true. The attacks on Guinier as "Clinton's quota queen" on the editorial pages of the *Wall Street Journal* marked the inelegant reentry of the racial semiotics that had sidelined the Democratic Party since the waning days of Lyndon Johnson's presidency, the busing wars of the 1970s, and the welfare politics of the Reagan era.

The attacks built to such a fury that on June 3 Clinton called a news conference and withdrew Guinier's nomination, saying, improbably, that he hadn't read her academic tracts before naming her, and that having done so, he felt "they clearly lend themselves to interpretations that do not represent the views that I expressed on civil rights during my campaign and views that I hold very dearly, even though there is much in them with which I agree."

Black leaders in Washington and Guinier's longtime colleagues at the University of Pennsylvania were incensed, both with the decision and with Clinton's apparent cosigning of the Right's mangled take on her scholarship. To black members of Congress and to civil rights leaders, the dismissal of Guinier, who in her writing advocated doing away with the kind of "full slate" voting that Jimmy Carter had fought against as governor of Georgia, where black voters were forced to vote in an entire slate of often hostile white politicians in order to elect a single African American, felt like a betrayal, delivered by a president who professed to have a strong alliance with African Americans. More than nearly any other episode in Clinton's first term, the Guinier decision remained seared in the minds of even Clinton's strongest black supporters and of some of his friends and former aides. It was seen as a test of personal loyalty, and of fealty to the legacy of the civil rights era, that Clinton resoundingly failed.

"I could not believe that he mischaracterized her," Harvard professor Charles Ogletree, a future colleague of Guinier at Harvard Law School said, voicing alarm that Clinton would state "[that] after reading Lani's work that [he'd discovered] she was some sort of radical or 'race woman' in terms of law." That Clinton would accept that characterization of her, when her colleagues knew her to be a mainstream, even "middle of the road" scholar, struck some black Clinton supporters as a revival of his Sister Souljah strategy: an act of racial triangulation at the expense of a friend.

The decision outraged the Black Caucus, which collectively refused a White House invitation to discuss the canceled nomination. New York congressman Charlie Rangel, a member of the powerful Ways and Means Committee, began telling reporters that the caucus was considering partnering with Republicans to block Clinton's economic agenda in the House in retaliation. The decision put Clinton at particular odds with southern members like Jim Clyburn, who knew well what "full slate" voting had done to black voters for generations.

"[Clinton] not pursuing the nomination of Lani Guinier was one of the low points of his presidency," Ogletree said.

The wounds with the Black Caucus would heal, and there were significant successes, including the signing of a National Voter Registration Act in 1993, which eased the registration process for millions of Americans. A landmark budget bill was signed that had received no Republican support but would begin to close the yawning, Reagan-era budget deficits and ignite the lagging economy. But the Omnibus Crime Bill, which pledged to put a hundred thousand police officers on the streets and created a federal "three-strikes" provision that opened the door to lengthy prison terms for repeat offenders, ignited fresh criticism from civil rights leaders, including Sharpton, who accused the administration of failing to address racial profiling or the dramatic racial disparities in drug sentencing; of "federalizing capital punishment" by expanding the number of eligible crimes, and of unleashing what the National Action Network leader warned would be a new ground war between police and black and poor communities in cities like New York.

The crime bill came under attack from the Right, too, for its inclusion of "midnight basketball" to keep young men off urban streets, for its ban on the manufacture and sale of assault weapons, and for the inclusion of a Violence Against Women Act, which some conservative activists decried as "anti-men." Meanwhile, activists from groups like the NAACP, the Children's Defense Fund, and the American Civil Liberties Union worried that Clinton and the New Democrats were playing the Nixonian crime card for political gain.

When the crime bill passed with the support of two-thirds of the Democratic caucus, Senate Majority Leader George Mitchell declared that "on crime, the time is over when in fact or perception the Republican Party is seen as the party tough on crime. . . . [Now] it's the Democrats." Mitchell seemed to confirm suspicions that the party was turning on the most vulnerable in order to co-opt a powerful Republican theme. The bill split the Black Caucus. Key members, including Dellums, Waters, Rangel, John Conyers, and John Lewis, were among the sixty-four Democrats who voted no, while some of Clinton's staunchest allies, such as Bobby Rush, Alcee Hastings, Carrie Meek, Jim Clyburn, Kweisi Mfume, and Harold Ford Jr., voted in favor. For some members, the chance to advance a bill that might remove the scourge of guns and drugs from the streets of Chicago or Miami, and the promise of federal programs that might aid young, unemployed black men in Allendale County, South Carolina, or in Memphis, Tennessee, proved a more powerful argument than forestalling the Republican narrative of rampant, race-based criminality.

Crime would indeed begin to fall nationwide, driven downward by a strengthening economy, but the specter of the "Black Criminal Menace" would not be so easily dispelled. Nor would it remain any less politically potent for the opposition party.

During the summer of 1994, the nation was gripped by the June 13 murders of Nicole Brown Simpson and Ron Goldman on a quiet, tree-lined block in the Brentwood section of Los Angeles. The slow-speed chase, the sensational, twenty-four-hour cable news coverage, and the coming double-murder trial of football legend O. J. Simpson for the killings would tear open the age-old, unhealed wounds of race and sex—interracial marriage, interracial and domestic violence, and the policing of black men—that are the country's inescapable legacy. Simpson's innocence or guilt split Americans along racial lines, turning on questions of DNA, a "dream team" of legal stars, and a lead detective, Mark Fuhrman, who was said to have openly mused that he'd like to see the lot of blacks and Hispanics tossed onto a pile and burned.

The "O.J. jury"—nine black, one Hispanic, and two white—was selected for the "trial of the century" on November 3, five days before the midterms, which ended in a rout of the Democrats, causing them to lose the House for the first time since 1952.

Even the House leader succumbed to the tide of voter retribution, with Thomas Foley becoming the first Speaker to lose his seat since before the Civil War. With him went embattled House Ways and Means chairman Dan Rostenkowski of Illinois, and three prized chairmanships held by members of the Black Caucus, who, since the organization's founding, had never served in the minority. For the first time since the nineteenth century, Republicans swept House races across the once solidly Democratic South.

In the Senate, Republicans picked up both seats in Tennessee and added members in Arizona, Maine, Michigan, Ohio, Oklahoma, and Pennsylvania, where voters elevated evangelical congressman Rick Santorum to the upper chamber. On the day after the election, Alabama Democrat Richard Shelby switched parties, capping the Republicans' 53 to 47 majority.

The incoming class was the most conservative in a generation. The new House Speaker, Newt Gingrich, declared a "Republican Revolution." Just 45 percent of eligible voters had gone to the polls, and they were heavily seeded with conservative firebrand Pat Buchanan's pitchfork brigades, called to arms during the 1992 campaign to ride into Washington and drive liberalism out of town. Media headlines announced the revenge of the Angry White Male.

It wasn't that simple.

Midterm elections typically see lower turnout than a presidential race, but 1994 marked an inflection point in the political divergence between the old and the young, and between black and white voters, the latter of whom favored congressional Republicans by an unprecedented 12 points. Even in the 1980s, as Reagan Democrats leaned Republican in the presidential races, congressional Democrats had managed to split or even win majorities of senior citizens. Now, for the first time, those voters delivered a solid rebuke to the party of the New Deal, while exit polls showed white men favoring Republicans by a 60 to 40 margin. Among white men and women without a college degree, the decline for Democrats was stunning: 20 percent among the men and 10 percent among the women.

Just 37 percent of black voters went to the polls, along with only 20 percent of Hispanics. A *New York Times* article summarizing the election's aftermath pointed to signs that the black electorate had stayed away in revolt.

"Race was at the heart of this election," said Roger Wilkins, a professor of history at George Mason University in Fairfax, Virginia. "There is a fierce anti-black and anti-immigrant undertone to this switch to the Republican Party. The message was, 'Let us take this country back and make it a white country—a white male country—again.'"

The *Times* pointed to black voters declaring their frustration not just with Republicans, but with Democrats, who, while desiring black votes, rarely articulated a defense of black personhood in the face of conservative attacks. No longer was there a JFK willing to publicly challenge the country, or an LBJ to push his coregionalists on matters of civic fairness or even simple interracial civility. The Democrats had become the "tough on crime" party, the "hundred thousand cops" party, and the party that tossed Lani Guinier overboard.

It all left many wondering why they should come to such a party's defense in an off-year election.

"It was absolute disgust," said Robert Smith, a professor of political science at San Francisco State University. "Everyone from Ph.D.s to garbage workers were saying, 'This was white folks' business. They're going to make their decisions and make it among themselves.'"

CHAPTER 4

The "First Black President"

When Bill Clinton got elected, everybody started relaxing, and we started seeing an almost antithesis to activism. . . . Our political consciousness took a reverse. We went from Professor Griff to Lil Wayne.

—Rev. Al Sharpton, 2013

FOR THIRTY YEARS, THE STATE LEGISLATURES OF THE SOUTHEAST had resisted the generational tide that Lyndon Johnson grimly predicted as he signed the Voting Rights Act in 1964. Yet they had stayed nominally in Democratic hands, even while their constituents increasingly began to send Republican congressmen to Washington and to vote for Republican candidates for president.

Going into the 1994 midterms, nearly all of the black state legislators in the South were Democrats, and 99.5 percent of them were serving in the majority, and 91 percent remained in the majority afterward. Despite the Republicans' rollicking success in the election, only one-half of three southern legislatures flipped from Democratic to Republican control in 1994: the Florida Senate, and the North and South Carolina Houses of Representatives. This as Democrats went from twenty-one governorships to eleven, in defeats that stretched from Democratic strongholds like New York, where Mario Cuomo was defeated for a fourth term, to Alabama, the onetime fiefdom of George Wallace.

In a great bit of irony, the more white southerners voted Republican in federal elections, the more white southern Democratic politicians relied on black voters to stay in power in the states. And because they drew the maps, Democratic state legislators, including after the 1990 census, were able to gerrymander a small number of "black" congressional districts to satisfy the Voting Rights Act, surrounded by districts cleansed of black voters and increasingly Republican, but which didn't interfere with their own races. The remaining "mixed race" state legislative districts had just enough blacks to keep them Democratic, but not enough that a black candidate could win outright.

The "bleaching" of southern districts helped Republicans in Washington and kept Dixie Democrats in power at home. Republicans would need another sixteen years to complete Kevin Phillips's vision of a solid Republican South, but it would slowly happen as local Democrats were challenged by Republicans—or as many simply changed sides. In 1996 Republicans would take over the state legislature in Florida; in 1999 they would take Virginia; in 2000, South Carolina; in 2002, Texas; and finally, in 2010, North Carolina. But 1994 was a start.

In Washington, Republicans wasted no time putting their agenda forward. Newt Gingrich's "Contract with America" included "take back our streets" provisions to strip the social spending out of President Clinton's crime bill and redirect the funds toward building more prisons; it would also end welfare assistance to teenage mothers, put time limits on federal assistance, and add work requirements; caps would be placed on the number of children for whom an indigent woman could claim subsistence aid. There was a constitutional amendment requiring a balanced budget, a provision for congressional term limits, and of course, mandates for steep tax cuts: on business earnings, capital gains, and the incomes of the wealthiest Americans.

Gingrich vowed to pass it all and dared the president not to sign it.

By January, as Clinton delivered his State of the Union address, he was under attack by those in the Center-Right of his party who believed he had spent too much time on liberal obsessions like gays in the military and health-care reform. Of the latter effort, California Senator Diane Feinstein said the Clintons had been "listening to the 15 percent who don't have insurance, while Republicans listened to the 85 percent who do." She and the other New Democrats wanted the president to return to the moderate agenda he'd promised.

A chastened Clinton delivered. He adopted Vice President Al Gore's plan taking a stand against affirmative action; an effort to appease white working-class voters by proposing race-neutral solutions to poverty and infusing the party's rhetoric with the language of personal responsibility.

The president's January address went even further and denounced a "failed welfare system" that "rewards welfare over work . . . undermines family values . . . lets millions of parents get away without paying their child support . . . [and] keeps a minority but a significant minority of the people on welfare trapped on it for a very long time." And he boasted about having sent "the most sweeping welfare reform plan ever presented by an administration" to Congress and vowed to "make welfare what it was meant to be, a second chance, not a way of life," by offering federally subsidized child care and job training for a maximum of two years.

Clinton had co-opted the grace notes of the Republican message. And he never looked back.

Civil rights leaders were alarmed. Clinton wasn't just distancing himself from LBJ-style reform; he was plowing the late president's legacy underground. Jesse Jackson even threatened to enter the 1996 Democratic primary if Clinton didn't relent. The Clinton cabinet was split, too, with Gore at odds with Secretary of Labor Robert Reich, Alexis Herman, and Mike Espy over the shift toward more conservative social and economic policy.

But Bill Clinton knew the Republicans were rushing a welfare reform bill to the House floor, and he was determined to do an end run around Gingrich by proposing his own bill. His deputy chief of staff, Harold Ickes, began scheduling meetings for the president with constituent groups, and Clinton dispatched HUD secretary Henry Cisneros to Chicago to meet with a small group of mayors, hosted by Richard M. Daley, who'd been elected after Harold Washington's sudden death from a heart attack, not long after the latter was reelected to a second term. The mayors asked what would happen once scores of their citizens were kicked off public assistance with no jobs and no skills.

Cisneros's message was blunt: The president was going to sign welfare reform (though he would ultimately veto two Republican versions before reaching a compromise bill) but he would make sure the bill included job training, with the federal funding flowing to the cities.

Clinton's talent for wooing his opponents with careful compromise that left every side feeling like a winner would serve him well.

Around this time, the Clinton team also retreated from their vow to kill affirmative action, instead saying, "mend it, don't end it." And Clinton cheered up his disgruntled supporters by calling for a hike in the federal minimum wage. He was steering a careful middle path, touting "step by step" health-care reform and calling on the entertainment industry to police its moral practices (a priority of Gore's wife, Tipper), while also championing a national push to curb teen pregnancy. The package was served up as the "New Covenant."

Clinton's pivot toward a personal responsibility crusade came as organizers were preparing a Million Man March on Washington, D.C., on October 16, 1995. The massive gathering, conceived by Minister Louis Farrakhan and Ben Chavis, an ordained minister and former youth coordinator for Dr. King, attracted nearly half a million men to the National Mall to promote positive affirmations of black manhood, and to dramatize the ongoing need to address the crises in America's inner cities. It was as if even those elements considered the most radical in the African American community were triangulating along with Clinton. Both Jackson and Sharpton addressed the massive gathering, estimated at more than 830,000 people.

For the president's 1996 State of the Union address, delivered during his reelection campaign, he—not the Republicans—declared, "the era of big government is over." He followed that in August by signing a welfare reform bill called Temporary Assistance to Needy Families. The bill handed federal welfare funds to the states, added work requirements and a five-year lifetime benefit cap, barred illegal immigrants from working in licensed professions, and slashed overall social needs funding by $54 billion over a decade.

It could easily have been presented by the Nixon or Reagan administrations.

Civil rights leaders again objected, and two officials from the Department of Health and Human Services resigned in protest, including Peter Edelman, husband of Marian Wright Edelman, Hillary Clinton's longtime mentor at the Children's Defense Fund, for whom the First Lady worked in the early 1970s and on whose board she had served. Hillary Clinton viewed Marian Wright Edelman with a deference that made Edelman a near-matriarchal figure to the First Lady.

"His signature on this pernicious bill makes a mockery of his pledge not to hurt children," Edelman stated in a terse public statement. Privately, she had lobbied Hillary hard, pressing her to prevail upon the president to simply veto the Gingrich bill rather than present a welfare reform plan of his own, but it was to no avail. An aide to Hillary Clinton said the wedge driven between the two women over the bill was deep, and it hit Mrs. Clinton hard.

The president followed this in September by proposing the Defense of Marriage Act (DOMA), which defined marriage as being between a man and a woman. This further discouraged his supporters from the gay and lesbian community.

"I didn't think Bill Clinton was insincere in his message," said one former White House aide. "I just felt like he'd given up. The whole thing: 'the era of big government is over,' the welfare reform, DOMA, it just became a capitulation to the interests of the Right, and an unwillingness to fight. Because they'd lost on those two big issues—gays in the military and health care— they just kind of gave in and started fighting on small-bore issues instead, and triangulating, and trying to redefine him as a new kind of Democrat again."

And it worked—Clinton soundly defeated Senator Robert Dole in November 1996 and won a second term in the White House.

Clinton's victory was buoyed by a growing economy and accelerating job growth. The Democrats had put together an economic plan that was rocket fuel for the economy. As a result, the federal coffers were filling up, further boosted by George H. W. Bush's tax hike, which had doomed him with his own party. But now Clinton's approval ratings soared.

The president's policies were finally being materially felt in the cities, where Democratic power resided; in expanded federal hiring, with a 20 percent hike in the minimum wage; and in rural towns, where Head Start, a children's health insurance program, and expanded child tax credits began to lift the veil of economic calamity for millions of Americans, brown, black, and white.

Clinton's welfare reform concessions to liberal lawmakers, including the billions of dollars in job training and child care assistance, were flowing directly to big, urban municipalities, which were suddenly flush with federal housing vouchers that would help some two hundred thousand recipients move out of dilapidated public housing projects and into mixed-income rentals. There were earned income tax credits for the working poor, and tax credits for businesses to hire the underemployed who lived in designated "enterprise zones."

"In terms of income inequality, especially for black Americans, the Clinton years, especially his second term, were a golden age," said analyst David Bositis, with "major gains in terms of black household income, college attendance, unemployment. . . . On a whole variety of economic indicators it was really good times."

Indeed, by the end of the president's second term, the number of recipients of federal welfare programs would decline, from more than 14 million to fewer than 6 million, the lowest level since 1961. The number of Americans in poverty, which had grown by 7.4 million under Ronald Reagan and George H. W. Bush, would drop by 6.4 million. And the national unemployment rate, including the historically double-digit rates for black Americans, would fall to record lows, lifted by the creation of 22 million jobs, housing expansion, and an ominous but temporarily euphoric "dot-com" bubble.

Clinton even reached out to the man who had, at various times, been both ally and antagonist, naming Jesse Jackson, who by 1997 was hosting a weekly talk show on CNN, as a "roving ambassador" to promote democracy on the African continent. White House spokesman Joe Lockhart said Jackson, who had played a nongovernmental role in negotiating the release of American prisoners from Cuba, Iraq, and Syria, would undertake

unnamed "special projects" in Africa "to encourage greater respect for human rights and the improved functioning of democratic institutions throughout the continent, and build bridges to
further cooperation with Africa." It was an undefined role that
would allow Jackson to travel to African nations with the impri-
matur of the president. "It was kiss and make up," said one longtime Jackson aide of the president's gesture, "because they had
some really strained relationships during the 1992 campaign."

For black Democrats, Bill Clinton was a singular puzzle.
Clinton the *man* seemed quite clearly a friend. He had the affect
and the understanding, and the friendships, with Vernon Jordan
and with members of the "Arkansas Diaspora," like Danny K.
Davis, born in Parkdale, Arkansas, and by then a congressman
from Illinois; and John Stroger, the colorful first black president
of the Cook County, Illinois, board of commissioners. Clinton
had been friends for years with Congressman John Lewis, and
that gave him a kind of credibility rarely afforded to white politicians. He plied and charmed his friends and enemies alike with
invitations to dinner at the White House and junkets to golf.
Former aides described a joke between Clinton and Jackson that
if Jackson had been white and Clinton black, Clinton would have
been the preacher, and Jackson would have been president of the
United States.

"Bill Clinton could sit in a church pew and sing the songs
along with the choir," Jamal Simmons, an African American
former Clinton aide, said. " 'Lift Ev'ry Voice' would come on, at
a program at Howard University or somewhere, and he would
know the words to the second and third stanzas that black people
don't even know, like 'stony the road'—*who knows that part?* So
there was all that emotional stuff that mattered."

Clinton the *politician* was more complicated. He'd gotten
elected by proving to white suburbanites that he was unafraid to
speak hard truths to black leaders—"truths," it turns out, that

certain white voters believed *intuitively*, about the "black racism" of Sister Souljah and about the creeping danger of urban violence and riots. In 1996 he sailed to reelection by co-opting conservative themes on crime and welfare that revived the age-old caricature of black Americans as a kind of alien infection in the American host—one that had to be constantly isolated and treated with irradiating doses of austerity and "personal responsibility" to allow the body to live on in contagion-free neighborhoods, schools, and workplaces free from viral competition for jobs and advancement. Some, like Rev. Al Sharpton, privately worried that Clinton's cultural ease with the civil rights establishment caused the latter to give him too broad a pass on vital issues.

This may also have been because black Americans felt that with Clinton the policymaker they finally had a friend in the White House, which many had not felt for a very long time. "On a policy basis, people felt that he was looking out for them," Simmons said. "And they felt that way because he made sure to talk about it. And he didn't just talk about it at election time. He made sure to talk about it all the time."

"During the health-care fight," Simmons recalled, "Clinton gave a speech to the [Church of God in Christ, or COGIC] convocation in Memphis. The COGIC headquarters is located near a housing project. And it was the pulpit where Dr. King gave his last speech before he was killed. And [Clinton] gave this speech about 'Dr. King didn't die so that black kids could kill other black kids for their sneakers,' which some in the traditional civil rights community took offense at, like, '*what is he doing lecturing us about what we're doing?*' But in the room, and I think in a lot of church rooms, there were 'Amens' and shouts, that here was somebody telling the truth about what was going on in the community.

"When he left that church he got into his motorcade," Simmons said, "and we drove about two blocks away, through the project, where there were people lining the streets waving at him. I'm in the press van, and all of a sudden we hear on the radio, he's out of the car! Bill Clinton gets out of the limo and is shaking hands with people at a housing project in the rain. I remember the Secret Service agent losing his mind, and I turned to him and said don't worry about it, he's fine here."

"So on the one hand you had this 'New Democrats' theme from Bill Clinton," said Bertha Lewis, who worked on the 1992 Bill Clinton campaign and who would go on to lead the Association of Community Organizations for Reform Now, or ACORN, a political- and social-advocacy group for the poor that got its start as a welfare rights organization in Little Rock, Arkansas, in 1970. "But on the other hand, you had this younger couple in the White House in the nineties and black folks really did feel as though, if nothing else, these folks could actually see us. Bill Clinton would make appeals to black folks directly."

Clinton avoided the direct *legislative* confrontations on racial matters that his Democratic predecessors had faced during the height of the civil rights movement. He resisted entreaties from Sharpton and other civil rights leaders to proffer racial profiling legislation, and shunned a June 1997 effort by Congressman Tony P. Hall—a white, born-again Christian from Dayton, Ohio, whose devotion to the cause of alleviating world hunger led him to fast for three weeks in 1993 after his select committee on hunger was disbanded—to offer a congressional resolution in which the United States officially apologized for slavery.

Hall thought this could heal the nation's ongoing racial wounds, and he modeled it on Roosevelt's apology to Japanese Americans interred during World War II and Clinton's May 1997 presidential apology for the infamous Tuskegee experiments, which ensnared hundreds of black men between 1932 and 1972. But Hall's idea unleashed a torrent of angry phone calls and letters, and the measure attracted scant support from the Black Caucus, many of whose members called it a distraction. Even Jesse Jackson dismissed the idea as "race entertainment," likening it to a car wreck in which "you drive over somebody with a car, leave the body mangled, then you decide to come back later to apologize with no commitment to help them get on their feet."

While the idea did attract support from African Americans outside of Washington, Hall's resolution went nowhere. Clinton offered it no lifeline, while Speaker Gingrich dismissed it as "emotional symbolism" with no practical meaning. The president had in the preceding days empaneled an ambitious commission to study race in America, led by eminent black historian John Hope Franklin. Gingrich dismissed that, too, saying, "Any American, I hope, feels badly about slavery. I also feel badly about genocide in Rwanda. I also feel badly about a lot of things. . . . Finding new, backward-oriented symbolic moments so we can avoid real work doesn't strike me as a strategy that's going to solve the country's problems."

But Clinton could not avoid a collision with his political opponents on the matter of America's racial legacy.

The next March, siting on a 66 percent approval rating, Clinton left for an historic, twelve-day, six-country visit to Africa. The trip's focus was to create closer commercial ties with African countries. And it would be capped by a state dinner with South Africa's Nelson Mandela, who had gone from insurgent, to prisoner, to president. Clinton would also visit Gorée Island, where ships carrying frightened, captive human cargo once set sail for the Americas.

On his second stop, in Uganda, Clinton drew the ire of his conservative foes at home with a seemingly innocuous statement. "Going back to the time before we were even a nation, European-Americans received the fruits of the slave trade," Clinton said, as he and Hillary Clinton stood in a pastoral meadow, speaking to more than a thousand schoolchildren at a rural school. "We were wrong in that as well, although I must say, if you look at the remarkable delegation we have here from Congress, from our cabinet and administration, and from the citizens of America, you can see there are many distinguished African Americans who are in that delegation who are making America a better place today.

"It is as well not to dwell too much on the past," he said, "but I think it is worth pointing out that the United States has not always done the right thing by Africa."

Back home, conservatives were quick to react, with House whip Tom DeLay denouncing the president as "a flower child with gray hairs doing exactly what he did back in the 60s: . . . apologizing for the actions of the United States," and accusing Clinton of attacking his own country while on foreign soil. Writing on his own website, Pat Buchanan derided Clinton for "groveling" in Africa, while refusing to apologize "for his own sins" or to his sexual harassment accuser, Paula Jones.

It got worse in Rwanda, when Clinton expressed regret for U.S. inaction to stop the slaughter during that country's civil war; he essentially apologized for his own administration's reticence to intervene. Conservatives began dubbing this "Clinton's apology tour" and it didn't help when some on the left criticized the president for apologizing to Africans overseas, rather than to the descendants of the enslaved at home.

Rev. Jesse Jackson, who was traveling with the president, came to Clinton's defense by chastising the traveling press corps for failing to understand the emotional resonance of the trip for African Americans, before straying into a treatise about Martin Luther King's contributions to American democracy versus Thomas Jefferson's, which prompted a grim Susan Rice, then the assistant secretary of state for African affairs, to follow tersely with "As an African American, I would like to say that I think slavery is largely irrelevant to what we are about here."

By the fall the media had become fully engrossed in Clinton's affair with White House intern Monica Lewinsky, which capped a years-long frenzy of investigations and increasingly lurid allegations of sexual scandal, real estate chicanery, drug running, and even murder, which Clinton's foes hoped would drive him from office. Toni Morrison, the Nobel Prize–winning novelist, took to the pages of *The New Yorker* and gave voice to the whispers coursing through black America.

"Years ago," Morrison wrote, "in the middle of the Whitewater investigation, one heard the first murmurs: white skin notwithstanding, this is our first black President. Blacker than any actual black person who could ever be elected in our children's lifetime. After all, Clinton displays almost every trope of blackness: single-parent household, born poor, working-class, saxophone-playing, McDonald's-and-junk-food-loving boy from Arkansas."

Morrison argued that Clinton had been subject to unending hysteria from the Right, his privacy stripped away and his "un-policed sexuality . . . the focus of the persecution." He had been "metaphorically seized and body-searched" like any average black man within sight of a police car. The message, delivered even to the president of the United States, was as familiar to black America as the umbrage-laden argument that slavery no longer matters because its practitioners are dead. "No matter how smart you are," Morrison wrote, "how hard you work, how much coin you earn for us, we will put you in your place or put you out of the place you have somehow, albeit with our permission, achieved."

For all the complications of his relationship with black Americans, Bill Clinton seemed to represent the oft-imposed limits on their own collective voice, which, when used to name black suffering, in the present or the distant past, was quickly stifled by a conservative culture that demanded forgetfulness. Even the white president of the United States couldn't escape the commandment that unsanitized American history was never to be put on display. For many African Americans, Clinton's ready embrace of them, even in the thick of the fight over welfare reform, and his programmatic answers to their policy objections, which had palpably aided black households, were the "real" transgressions that triggered the relentless hunt through his sexual closet, in a bid to silence, destroy, and delegitimize a president who was doing good by black folk.

Clinton would survive impeachment and leave office at the height of his popularity, with the vast majority of Americans rejecting Republicans' attempt to do with the supreme act of congressional censure what they had failed to do in two elections: rid themselves of the Democratic president. But the impeachment saga would linger in the campaign of Clinton's vice president, as Al Gore sought to distance himself from the air of scandal as his party's nominee for president by running on his own merits. Despite separating himself from the still-popular Clinton, Gore's presidential bid did attract furtive support from black voters— with Gore earning a higher percentage of African American votes than even Clinton himself, and at 90 percent, a higher share than any Democrat except Lyndon Johnson—while George W. Bush's 9 percent matched Ronald Reagan's meager showing in 1984. For black voters, the sole issue was continuing the Clinton prosperity, and extending the policies that were bearing fruit in black communities.

Generations of historical experience had proven to African Americans that it really does matter who is in the White House, and how much they can influence him or her. It matters concretely in the lives of black Americans, who even at the turn of a new century continued to suffer disproportionate unemployment, poverty, and want, but who for a few short years in Bill Clinton's term had enjoyed, at long last, a deep breath of hope.

But the U.S. Supreme Court, and the state of Florida, had other ideas.

Gore won the popular vote by more than 500,000 ballots over Texas governor George W. Bush, but the five conservative judges on the Supreme Court, including David Souter and Clarence Thomas, both appointees of Bush's father, intervened to stop the recount in Florida, where Bush was clinging to a narrow 538-vote lead, giving him an Electoral College victory margin of a single vote.

The national media and Democratic circles were swarming with claims of voting irregularities and disenfranchisement in Florida. Emotions rocketed from rage to numb disbelief. Senior citizens—many of them Florida's Jewish retirees—were confused by the state's unwieldy "butterfly ballot" and wondered if they'd mistakenly voted for right-wing firebrand and World War II skeptic Pat Buchanan. Black voters complained of random traffic stops, of names disappearing from the rolls, and of outright police intimidation. The U.S. Commission on Civil Rights, the fruit of the 1957 Civil Rights Act, was vowing to investigate. It was discovered that Bush's younger brother, Jeb, the Florida governor, had initiated a purge of the state voter files, carried out by Katherine Harris, Florida's secretary of state (and a state co-chair of the Bush campaign), that had removed from the rolls thousands of eligible voters whose names merely bore a similarity to those of convicted felons.

Florida was one of a handful of states—all of them in the South—that permanently stripped the voting rights of those convicted of felony crimes unless the governor individually restored them. The law was a vestige of the Black Codes enacted at the end of Reconstruction, when Union troops withdrew from the southern states on the condition that those states permit their black male citizens to vote.

Southern legislatures and governors responded with an array of laws to get around the Fifteenth Amendment and push the freedmen back into their place. The new southern constitutions created various exemptions from the voting mandate: for felons and vagrants and those deemed morally or mentally unfit, and for those unable to pay a fee or recite an arcane stanza of state law. And they invented a host of new felonies (even loitering could result in a prison camp stay!) that state police applied with abandon, sweeping up black men like kindling and filling southern jails with those who would forever be separated from the vote.

When the Florida Constitution was reaffirmed in 1968, with felon disenfranchisement intact, the state, like most in the region, had been embroiled in years of sit-ins, marches, arrests, "wade-ins" to desegregate Florida beaches, and even spasms of rioting, which brought Dr. King to St. Augustine in 1964 to enjoin young activists that "violence is not the answer."

Jeb Bush had frequently clashed with black state legislators, including Kendrick Meek, whose mother, Carrie P. Meek, was elected to Congress with the "Clinton Class of 1992"—the first black member of Congress from Florida since Reconstruction. When the governor decreed the end of affirmative action in the state, the younger Meek backed massive student protests and even staged a sit-in at Bush's Tallahassee office with a fellow state legislator, Representative Tony Hill.

In the lead-up to the 2000 election, Meek and a group of legislators and civil rights leaders had mounted a massive voter registration drive modeled on Jesse Jackson's 1984 and 1988 campaigns. Driven by lingering anger over Clinton's impeachment, black voters responded to entreaties to "arrive with five" family members or friends at the polls, and to sardonic warnings from Jackson, to "stay out of the Bushes."

After the U.S. Supreme Court rebuffed Gore's challenge of the Florida vote, he gave in. His concession on December 13 called for national unity and quoted his father in saying, "No matter how hard the loss, defeat might serve as well as victory to shape the soul and let the glory out."

For many Democrats, there was no glory in concession. The election had borne out their deepest suspicions that those who long opposed the full enfranchisement of Americans living on the margins and who fought to impeach Bill Clinton—a president who succeeded in investing in the nation's urban core, fought the worst and deepest Republican cuts to the federal programs that gave the economically disadvantaged a fighting chance, and dared to speak out loud about America's historic faults—would certainly reverse it all if they assumed the power of the White House. Back would come the deep cuts to the social safety net and the steep upper-income tax cuts of the Reagan era. And gone would be the chance to entrench and extend the Johnsonian policies that gave life to inner-city and rural economies. Considering how much was on the line, Democrats had trouble understanding why their party and its leaders had no fight left in them.

On January 6, 2001, in the joint session of Congress, a group of House members, drawn mostly from the Congressional Black Caucus, decided it was time they insisted on being heard. One by one, the thirteen members rose on the House floor and walked to the podium to voice their objections. Vice President Gore stood on the dais, wielding the gavel in his final act as Senate president, presiding over the joint session that would make George W. Bush the president of the United States.

The protest began with an objection from Palm Beach, Florida, congressman Peter Deutsch, whose own district had seen scores of seniors confused by the poorly constructed ballot. Deutsch objected to the lack of a quorum as the senators filed into the chamber. He was gaveled down.

Gore began to certify the states and their electors one by one, tallying which electors had voted for him and which had voted for Bush. When Florida's time came, Congressman Chaka Fattah of Pennsylvania, who had been tasked with reading the

state tally, began by saying, "This is the one we've all been waiting for."

"Is there objection?" Gore asked, after the totals, eked out
by recounts that dragged on into mid-December before the Supreme Court put a stop to them, were read.

"Mr. President, I object to the certificate from Florida," said
Alcee Hastings, a former county judge appointed to the federal
bench by President Jimmy Carter, and who represented a deep
blue district spanning Palm Beach and Broward counties.

Hastings, like his colleagues, knew that according to the
rules, members were required to submit their challenges in writing, cosigned by a member of the Senate.

"Is the gentleman's objection in writing and signed by a member
of the House of Representatives and by a senator?" asked Gore.

"Mr. President, and I take great pride in calling you that,"
Hastings said, pointedly referring to Gore's honorific in his final
day, "I must object because of the overwhelming evidence of official misconduct, deliberate fraud, and an attempt to suppress
voter turnout."

The chamber reverberated with disapproval, and Gore gaveled Hastings down. He reminded Hastings that no debate was
allowed.

"Thank you, Mr. President," said Hastings.

It was if the two southern men were simply exchanging pleas-
antries, rather than engaging in a tug-of-war over history and, in
the hearts of many dispirited Democrats, the very meaning of the
right to vote. Many in the caucus were unclear precisely what the
rather opaque Gore believed, beyond his passion for issues relating
to the environment. He had, after all, been the architect of some of
Bill Clinton's most onerous and conservative ideas. But Gore was
viewed as a good man. And he was losing as a good man.

"To answer your question, Mr. President, the objection is in writing; signed by a number of members of the House of Representatives, but not by a member of the Senate."

Hastings was again gaveled down. Twelve more would follow.

"Mr. President, it is in writing and signed by several House colleagues on behalf, and myself, of the 27,000 voters of Duval County in which 16,000 of them are African Americans that was disenfranchised in this last election," said Corinne Brown of Jacksonville.

"Is the objection signed by a member of the Senate?"

"Not signed by a member of the Senate," Brown responded. "The Senate is missing."

"Mr. President, it is in writing and signed by myself and several of my constituents from Florida," said Carrie Meek. "A senator is needed, but missing."

To scattered boos in the chamber, Barbara Lee of California rose to speak "on behalf of many of the diverse constituents in our country . . . and all American voters who recognize that the Supreme Court, not the people of the United States, decided this election."

Patsy Mink, of Hawaii, who in 1990 had become the first Asian American woman elected to Congress, regretted that she possessed "no authority over the United States Senate," and that "no senator has signed."

"Is your objection signed by a senator?"

Maxine Waters of California was a firebrand, a vehement ally of Jesse Jackson who became first a friend, and then a staunch supporter of the Clintons. Waters had seen firsthand the devastation of the Rodney King riots in South Central Los Angeles, and the rebuilding made possible by the Clinton federal outlays. According to associates, Waters delivered the blunt message to Democratic senators during the impeachment saga that a vote to convict Bill Clinton meant "you're dead to black people." Now she was watching the Clinton-Gore era end with a whimper.

"The objection is in writing," Waters shot back at the chair. "And I don't care that it is not signed by a senator."

"The chair would advise that the rules do care," Gore replied with a weary smile, as the Republicans in the chamber erupted in applause.

And so it went. Eddie Bernice Johnson of Texas cited the "hundreds of thousands of telegrams and e-mails and telephone calls" her office had received, and was gaveled down. Elijah Cummings of Maryland stated his objections, and was gaveled down, as was Sheila Jackson Lee of Texas, Cynthia McKinney of Georgia, Eva M. Clayton of North Carolina, and Bob Filner of California, who had no written objection and was not a member of the Black Caucus, but rose to speak "in solidarity" with his colleagues.

"It's a sad day in America, Mr. President, when we can't find a senator to sign the objections," Representative Jesse Jackson Jr. said as he was ordered to suspend.

The protest lasted eighteen minutes.

As Vice President Gore prepared to resume certifying the states, the objectors walked out.

They had learned, in stark fashion, what their party was willing to fight to the end for, and what it was not.

The 2000 election had not been a total loss. Democrats had grown their Senate ranks from forty-six seats to fifty, tying the Senate. In New York, the seat of the legendary Daniel Patrick Moynihan had gone quite decisively to former First Lady Hillary Clinton.

Replacing Moynihan, a key architect of the "War on Poverty," was an important undertaking. His 1965 report, "The Negro Family: The Case for National Action," commonly called "The Moynihan Report," had helped to define the country's, and his party's, approach to the nagging issues of poverty and urban decay. Moynihan, the erudite Horatio Alger figure who in the lore of Washington rose from Hell's Kitchen to Harvard, and whose own father's abandonment of the family led to childhood encounters with want, had done more than almost any single political figure to popularize the belief that the primary cause of black suffering was the proliferation of unwed mothers and fatherless children.

Moynihan's detractors saw him as a victim-blaming enabler of those who substituted racial stereotypes and moral shaming for a frank examination of the country's racial hierarchism, and the matrix of governmental policies, federal, state, and local, that had systematically kept black families in poverty. To his supporters, he was a good man willing to tell the truth, even at the expense of political correctness. For millions, he had helped erect the intricate web of social services, social workers, and federal aid programs that for decades defined what it meant to be poor in America.

He had been a key ally of both Democrats and Republicans on the subject of welfare reform, supporting efforts by Ronald Reagan in 1984, and Bill Clinton in 1994, to cull the aid rolls and hold absent fathers to account, earning him both praise and scorn from those in the thick of the battle for social uplift.

When Moynihan announced his plans to retire two years before the 2000 election, several names had popped up, including those of Andrew Cuomo, son of the former three-term governor, and Robert Kennedy Jr., son of the late senator and nephew of Camelot. But senior pols in New York State and Democrats in Washington, D.C., had someone else in mind: Hillary Clinton.

The First Lady had weathered the public humiliation of her husband's infidelity, and she was emerging as a genuine political star, whose poise under the media glare had cast her in the unexpected role of national heroine. A Gallup survey at the close of 1998 found her favorability rating peaking at 67 percent. When Moynihan announced his retirement, her phone started ringing.

The First Lady spent considerable time ingratiating herself with Senator Moynihan—and attempting to do so with his considerably more skeptical wife—even traveling to the couple's five-hundred-acre farm in Pindars Corners, a rural hamlet outside Albany, in the summer of 1999, to launch her "listening tour" of the Empire State, trailed by a roving pack of media.

The campaign quickly became a national sensation, as the First Lady launched her historic run, rebranded simply as "Hillary"— with enough of the Clinton brand to gain from the booming economy, but just the right amount of distance to make her intriguing in her own right. The campaign assembled a team of experienced locals, including Rangel's former campaign manager, Bill de Blasio, who worked to get around the caricature of a celebrity carpetbagger who couldn't decide whether she was a Cubs or a Yankee fan that was almost inevitable in the brutal New York City tabloids.

Hillary faced Rudy Giuliani, the hard-charging New York City mayor, who was deeply unpopular among black New Yorkers, but whom many white residents credited with turning the city around.

African Americans made up nearly 16 percent of the state's massive population, with more than 2 million of the state's 3 million black citizens living in New York City, where a third of the statewide vote resided. And while upstate voters tended to lean conservative, the Clinton campaign had every incentive to maximize turnout among black, Hispanic, and white liberal voters in New York City, where they made up more than a quarter of the vote. But Hillary also had to keep her eye on the "law and order suburbs"—a quarter of the state's electorate—and on the rural swaths upstate where agricultural prices counted more than anxiety about overzealous cops.

It was a balancing act that saw the candidate ping-ponging across the state, talking "dairy price supports" in Utica and policing in the Bronx. With a thriving economy and plunging crime rates across the city (and nationwide) shifting public attention away from "owning the night" and taking back the streets from real and imagined bogeymen, Mrs. Clinton had considerable space to give ear to black New Yorkers' laments without alienating Osceola County.

Soon, however, Hillary's campaign was seized by a trio of police-related incidents. First was the trial of four police officers in the February 4, 1999, killing of Amadou Diallo, a West African street vendor gunned down by plainclothes officers from Giuliani's Street Crimes Unit. During a hunt for a serial rapist, the officers fired forty-one shots at a bewildered Diallo, nineteen of which struck the twenty-three-year-old as he fumbled for his keys in the vestibule of his Bronx apartment. Second were the trials, starting in December 1999, of police officers who beat and assaulted a Haitian American man, Abner Louima. He was sodomized with a broom handle inside a holding cell following his arrest outside a Brooklyn nightclub. There was also the March 16 fatal shooting of an unarmed man, Patrick Dorismond, by an undercover narcotics officer. Witnesses said Dorismond was killed after insisting he had no drugs to sell, and got into a shoving match with the man he didn't realize was a policeman. The public outrage was compounded when, in the immediate aftermath of the Dorismond killing, Giuliani released the dead man's sealed juvenile arrest record to the media, as he defended the officer's actions. It was just two weeks after the officers in the Diallo shooting were acquitted by a jury in upstate New York.

In response to all three of these incidents, Rev. Al Sharpton was leading daily marches to City Hall and to police precincts in Brooklyn and the Bronx, resulting in hundreds of arrests. It wasn't long before they were joined by the Service Employees International Union's massive New York local, 1199, New York City led by Patrick Gaspard, a former organizer in Jesse Jackson's 1988 campaign and the successful effort to elect former mayor David Dinkins, and a mentee of Bill Clinton's former deputy chief of staff Harold Ickes.

Gaspard and Sharpton were longtime allies, and de Blasio was Gaspard's closest friend. Giuliani's campaign seized on the connections to try to tie the Clinton Senate campaign to "Reverend Al," whom Giuliani campaign manager Bruce Teitelbaum derisively called "Hillary Clinton's key advisor." Sharpton's name remained a potent deterrent to white voters in the suburbs and upstate, where polls found Giuliani struggling to overtake the First Lady, while she was beating the Republican candidate in New York City by a margin of 3 to 1.

The Clintons had had a long and complicated relationship with Sharpton, who had been a persistent critic of the president's urban policies, including welfare reform and the 1994 crime bill, which helped stock New York's police force with fresh personnel. Sharpton had been among the New Yorkers who denounced Clinton's treatment of Sister Souljah in 1992, and he was privately disdainful of what he viewed as the capitulation of black elites, and even of some of his mentors in the civil rights movement like Jesse Jackson, to a Clinton presidential agenda characterized by "Sister Souljah moments" of triangulation.

The Clinton campaign had been careful not to embrace Sharpton, but they didn't want to alienate him, either. Hillary had accepted a January invitation to Sharpton's annual Martin Luther King Day celebration, in which she described Diallo's killing as a "murder," drawing the ire of New York police unions. But Hillary had since been careful to avoid a direct confrontation with police or, by extension, their supporters.

Sharpton, who in 1996 had himself entered the mayoral primary, spoiling for the chance to take on Giuliani, was now teaming up with Charlie Rangel to demand federal oversight of the New York City Police Department. The two accompanied Diallo's family and Dinkins to a March 2 meeting with Clinton deputy attorney general Eric Holder, to press for a federal civil rights indictment of the acquitted officers.

Next came a meeting with Hillary Clinton—an awkward confab to which her campaign invited Sharpton's nemesis, former mayor Ed Koch. The Giuliani team fired off a letter that seized on the Holder meeting, the Justice Department review of the Diallo shooting, and President Clinton's first remarks on the case. At a March 3 fund-raiser Clinton had stated that while he was loathe to second-guess the jury, "I know most people in America of all races believe that if it had been a young white man in an all-white neighborhood, it probably wouldn't have happened."

The Giuliani letter was quickly circulated to the New York media. It pronounced: "Even President Clinton, following in the footsteps of Al Gore, Bill Bradley and Hillary Rodham Clinton, has now started to read aloud from the Al Sharpton playbook, parroting Sharpton's description of the Diallo case as being based primarily on race."

Hillary's campaign spokesman, Howard Wolfson, replied with a terse non sequitur: "The mayor knows that Hillary Clinton is a New Democrat who supports a balanced budget, targeted tax cuts, and welfare reform. All the mayor can do is keep tearing New Yorkers apart."

Despite the reticence of her spokesman, and with even Giuliani's traditional supporters in the New York tabloids accusing him of "vilifying the corpse" of Dorismond, Hillary dove in, telling nearly a thousand parishioners at Harlem's Bethel AME Church in late March that the mayor "has led the rush to judgment" against the dead man, adding, "that is not real leadership."

By April, polls showed voters overwhelmingly sour on Mayor Giuliani's handling of the police incidents, with many even believing his actions had contributed to a rise in police brutality. And Hillary had solidified the support and the enthusiasm of black New Yorkers, who were already poised to go to the polls in large numbers to support Al Gore for president, but who now had a down-ticket race to drive up their numbers in a nonswing state. Giuliani seemed well on his way to a humiliating defeat, delivered mainly at the hands of his own city.

One month later, Giuliani threw in the towel, shocking the local and national media in a May 19 news conference that included the announcements that he was suffering from prostate cancer and that he was leaving his wife, TV newswoman Donna Hanover, to be with his "very good friend," socialite Judith Nathan. It was a bizarre segue with shades of Nelson and Happy Rockefeller's unhappy jaunt through the New York gossip pages in 1964.

Giuliani's rambling exit, in which he mused that he hoped to one day discover how he had managed to erect a "barrier" between himself and minority New Yorkers, had in the view of many New York political watchers been an act of preemptive self-rescue. Giuliani's successor in the Senate race, a prickly young Suffolk County congressman named Rick Lazio, would fare no better.

FOR ALL HER STARDOM, AND HER HISTORY-MAKING SENATE RUN, Hillary Clinton was not destined to remain the only, or even the brightest, Senate star.

In 2004, Barack Obama, freshly elected to the United States Senate from Illinois, arrived in Washington with his young family to the clack of flashbulbs and a crush of media interviews—the *Today* show, *Entertainment Tonight*, and CBS News. Interviewers marveled at the senator-elect as he held his six-year-old daughter, Malia, on his lap and Michelle bundled three-year-old Sasha. Invitations and offers of transition help poured in, but the senator and his staff accepted very few. Obama did respond to the kind notes and offers of help with settling in from Hillary Clinton.

The two had their ideological differences. For one, they had been on opposite sides of the Iraq War, which was still raging as Obama came to Washington. Senator Clinton had voted to authorize President Bush's actions in Iraq; Obama, eight days before, while still an Illinois state senator, had taken the stage at an antiwar rally in Chicago's Federal Plaza along with Rev. Jesse Jackson and a group of local clergy and civic leaders to protest such an invasion and to express deep skepticism with Bush's case for war. But the two senators shared a lot in common, including their Illinois ties and, not least, their political stardom. Hillary Clinton was perhaps the one member of the body who fully understood what it meant to have more than sixty news organizations descend on Washington to mark the occasion of one senator's swearing-in.

With John Kerry's listless 2004 campaign behind them, and Democrats dispirited over George W. Bush's reelection—as well as the loss of their Senate majority leader, Tom Daschle, whose seat Republicans had claimed as a singular prize—Hillary and her team put their arms around Obama, whose victory was a rare flash of good news.

Obama had been on the Clintons' radar since he breezed through the Illinois primary. "Part of what both Clintons like to do is to help support up-and-coming political talent," one former staffer to Senator Clinton said. "It was, 'you're a megawatt star, I was a megawatt star,' so how do you navigate?"

Obama's national political rise had begun considerably less auspiciously. He parlayed a stint organizing low-income tenants on Chicago's far South Side in the mid-1980s into the platform for a respectable career in the Illinois Senate a decade later; his brief stardom as Harvard's first black law review editor had produced the opportunity to write a well-received autobiography in between. But he'd stumbled, too, deciding in 2000 to challenge Bobby Rush, the Black Panther turned congressman, for the seat in Chicago's First Congressional District, held by some of the city's most storied black politicians: Oscar De Priest in the 1930s; William Dawson from the early 1940s until 1970; Ralph Metcalfe, a former Olympic sprinter who'd finished second to Jesse Owens in the 1936 Olympics in Berlin; Harold Washington, who convinced black Chicagoans they could conquer the world; and now Rush, who had traveled the long trajectory from brash young militant, posing for photos with a pistol in his hand, to a cosponsor of the Brady Bill and the assault weapons ban, arguing that the weapons of war being glamorized in hip-hop songs were killing young black men on the streets of the South Side.

It was a bold and risky proposition. Chicago was a city of traditions, a black cultural Land of Oz whose historic pedigree included *Ebony* and *Jet* magazines, Katherine Dunham and Gwendolyn Brooks, Richard Wright, Gordon Parks, and Nat King Cole. It was the place where George Ellis Johnson Sr., born two years before Dr. Martin Luther King Jr., came with his parents as a small child from Richton, Mississippi, and grew up to found Johnson Products, which by the 1960s was the leading black hair care company in the country, the facilitator of the sky-high Afro, and the advertising sponsor that brought *Soul Train* into America's living rooms. Chicago, and its hybrid black and Jewish Hyde Park elite, took its politics as seriously as its culture (and its food); its political elites took their loyalties more seriously than all three.

In the state senate, Obama operated with the quiet backing of Emil Jones, the powerful senate majority leader, who'd been an Obama mentor since his organizing days, and who worked behind the scenes to help Obama outmaneuver Alice Palmer, the popular state senator who vacated her seat to run for Congress in a three-way primary against Jones and Jesse Jackson Jr. Palmer had promised to support Obama for her state senate post, but when her congressional prospects fizzled and she tried to regain her seat instead, Jones's staff quietly helped Obama's team draft the petition challenges that ended her bid. Jones, the affable but tough barrel of a man, who shared a chain-smoking habit with his young protégé,

Obama, blithely shrugged off the machinations in conversations with colleagues as a simple case of Palmer not properly informing the Senate leader of her plans ahead of time.

If Obama often deferred to Jones, he rarely did to the state's black establishment, eschewing their clubbish politics and, with Jones's encouragement, wooing "downstate" white fellow senators instead, joining late-night card games with Republican members who wielded powerful swing votes. Some of Obama's black colleagues took an open dislike to the young man from Harvard and Hawaii, whom they derided as an arrogant, overeducated outsider who had "taken" Palmer's seat. At one point Jones had to separate Obama and another black lawmaker, Rickey Hendon, on the Illinois state senate floor.

There was nothing new about black ambition challenging black power, and Obama was hardly the first upstart politician to take on the African American establishment. Charlie Rangel, after all, won his seat by challenging the legendary Adam Clayton Powell in a Democratic primary in 1970. And John Lewis took on his friend and former SNCC associate Julian Bond in a blistering 1986 campaign for the Georgia congressional seat that then–state senator Bond had helped to draw under the Voting Rights Act, and for which Bond had openly voiced his intention to run. But the Chicago old guard had as little patience for Obama as he had for the glacial pace of legislative politics. They viewed him as a neophyte who hadn't earned the right to enter the pantheon of the black Chicago elite.

So while Obama's congressional bid attracted the support of a small network of young black and white Chicago entrepreneurs and a high-profile endorsement from the *Chicago Tribune,* Bobby Rush had Jesse Jackson; Illinois's senior senator, Dick Durbin; and the former president of the United States, Bill Clinton, in his corner, along with a hundred South Side ministers ready to organize the community.

Obama's message of cross-ethnic outreach, which had been a standard feature of his public discourse, fell flat on the campaign trail. "We have more in common with the Latino community, the white community, than we have differences," he would say in sidelong references to Congressman Rush. "[And] it may give us a psychic satisfaction to curse out people outside our community and blame them for our plight, but the truth is, if you want to be able to get things accomplished politically, you've got to work with them."

Rush, along with the third candidate in the race, Donne Trotter, a dapper, silver-haired pol with a family history dating back to turn-of-the-twentieth-century Chicago and a particular distaste for his Senate colleague, dismissed Obama as a man who "went to Harvard and became an educated fool," flaunting an "eastern degree" and dismissing the power of protest politics.

It wasn't a complete picture. Obama was familiar with protest movements, having joined the anti-apartheid cause as a student at Occidental College and supporting the student movement to diversify the faculty at Harvard Law School. But the point wasn't missed by black Chicagoans, as Rush barnstormed the churches on the South Side, flaunting his deep ties to a community where he and the Panthers had literally bled in the cause of justice.

Obama lost, and lost badly, ceding the primary by an overwhelming 59 to 29 spread, after which Rush went on to claim nearly 88 percent of the general election vote in the overwhelmingly Democratic district. Obama's political friends, including Leon Finney, whose Woodlawn Organization was represented by Obama's law firm; Timuel Black, who, like Finney, taught with Obama at the University of Chicago; and Judge Abner Mikva, a former Clinton administration lawyer who had tried to recruit a young Obama out of law school, were completely unsurprised. Most of them had stuck with Bobby Rush, too.

"There was no gnashing of teeth and rending of garments over it," said Finney. "He ran, he lost. As I thought he would."

Four years later, and after intense lobbying of his wife, Michelle, Obama decided to try one last tilt at Washington, and this time he was aiming even higher: for the U.S. Senate seat being vacated by Republican Peter Fitzgerald, the man who had removed Carol Moseley Braun from her historic perch in 1998.

Moseley Braun's original victory had proven that a black candidate could win statewide in Illinois, despite an electorate where just 1 in 10 voters was African American. And 2004, like 1992, was a presidential election year, when the larger voter base meant more black, Latino, and young voters in the mix. And this time, Obama had the Hyde Park machine behind him.

Obama had maintained the fund-raising contacts he'd culled from Illinois Project Vote, which he'd been hired to run after law school ahead of the 1992 campaign (the job he took instead of working for Judge Mikva). And he had in his favor Jones's tireless lobbying for support from state unions, donors, and political leaders, and sheer, unmitigated luck, as one after another, first his primary opponents, and then his general election foe, Jack Ryan, fell away to personal and sexual scandal, leaving only an out-of-state black conservative iconoclast and sometime cable television gadfly named Alan Keyes standing in his way.

Suddenly Obama was a political star, one who by the summer of 2004 was well on his way to becoming only the third African American ever elected to the U.S. Senate, and the fifth, counting Reconstruction, to serve there. Obama's senior campaign team secured the coveted keynote for him at the 2004 Democratic National Convention, where his message of racial and regional ecumenism played much differently than it had when he was taking on an African American icon in Chicago.

The soon-to-be senator's call to ignore the "cynics" and the "dividers" and press on toward national healing, his praise of

America's social advancement, and his pronouncement that "there's not a liberal America and a conservative America; there's the United States of America," that "there's not a black America and white America and Latino America and Asian America; there's the United States of America," brought the convention in Boston to its feet, and some in the convention hall to tears.

When it was over, no less a doyenne of the Chicago elite than Oprah Winfrey declared Barack Obama to be "the One," and serious politicians, including the senior senator from Illinois, began whispering that despite his lack of time on the national stage, his dearth of national political experience, and his name (which was unhelpfully evocative of "Osama bin Laden" and compounded by the middle name Hussein), could one day be the country's first black president. Even formerly skeptical black Chicagoans embraced the possibilities.

"He was like the brother from another planet," said Harold Lee Rush, a longtime Chicago radio personality, and Congressman Rush's cousin. "Nobody knew where he came from, but we claimed him because he claimed us."

But Obama was not, in the strictest sense, correct about America's invisibly united status. John Kerry's running mate, North Carolina senator John Edwards, had made "two Americas" the theme of his primary campaign when he was vying for the nomination. Edwards spoke of the stark divide between the affluent who enjoy excellent schools and the poor communities whose school buildings are crumbling and barely contain decent resources; between the powerful "haves" who enjoy top-notch health care, and whose interests are argued by a phalanx of lobbyists, and the humble "have-nots" just struggling to get by. It was a message reminiscent of Mario Cuomo's "shining city on a hill" address at the Democratic convention a generation earlier in 1984, in which Cuomo put the lie to the Reaganite vision of a glorious flawless America.

Indeed, the country that was so rapt by Obama's inclusive message was home to many divides, of class and gender, and along racial lines, with black, Latino, and Native Americans frequently on the wrong side of the statistical tracks, laboring under higher unemployment and poverty rates, living in under-resourced communities and grasping more tenuously than their white counterparts for a piece of the American dream. Racial division seethed beneath the surface of American life, even if the fires were no longer burning in the streets.

In Illinois, Obama was running for election in a state with vast reaches of "culturally southern" towns—"sundown towns," where blacks who found themselves in town after dark could almost certainly expect an encounter with police. Sure, down-state voters might consent to sending an African American to Washington. The trouble might come if the Obamas tried to move in next door. Indeed, Senator Moseley Braun had been only the second black American sent by statewide voters in any state to the Senate, and the first, Edward Brooke, had left Congress in 1979.

Even Chicago, with its vibrant black cultural heritage, re-mained nearly as segregated in its neighborhoods and public schools in 2004 as it was in 1966, when Dr. King moved into slum housing to dramatize the plight of the city's poor. Long after the demise of official "redlining," the bulk of the city's black residents remained virtually walled off by the Eisenhower expressway, on the city's south and west sides. Even affluent and liberal Hyde Park had in the recent past seen battles to resist de-segregation and busing that were as ferocious as the antibusing frenzy that roiled cities like Boston in the 1970s.

And yet Obama had, by virtue of luck, or rhetorical skill, or simply his upbringing in three worlds—the peculiarly mid-western, pragmatic idealism of his mother's family, the exotic multiculturalism of Hawaii and Indonesia, and the brown skin that he inherited from his Kenyan father and that he lived in every day—been able to traverse that paradox with no trace of malice or affect. And just as Moseley Braun had triumphed in a campaign that often spoke more to gender and national politics than to race, Obama's campaign traversed the racial plain largely by setting it aside.

"You know when you're in a setting where you're the only black person in a room, and there are tensions there on your part, and their part?" said one longtime Chicago pol who campaigned with Obama in all-white communities during his U.S. Senate campaign. "With Barack that tension doesn't exist. You know how there's something you may say, or the way you act, that causes that tension to exist that you're completely unaware of it? With him it dissipates. It may be because his mother was white, and his white grandparents raised him."

Obama often said on the stump, "People are really hurting across Illinois. It's a jobless recovery. Laid-off industrial workers are now competing with their children for seven-dollar-per-hour jobs at Wal-Mart. Fifty-year-old white workers are facing nearly the same future as young African American men from the South Side, fifty percent of whom are out of work and out of school. . . . If I'm elected you get a three-for: you get a Democrat, greater diversity, and someone with backbone who will fight the Bush agenda."

And in even the sundown towns of Illinois, the message, devoid of explicit racial content, got through.

"So I'm sitting across the table from this little old white lady," the longtime Chicago pol continued. "And she says, 'I'm eighty-four years old, and I certainly hope I live long enough, 'cause this young man's gonna be president one day, and I want to be around to vote for him.'"

Whether in downstate Illinois or at the Democratic National Convention, Barack Obama was speaking to the America that—as Tony P. Hall discovered with his slavery resolution in 1997 (and again when he reintroduced it in 2000), and which Howard Dean discovered during the primary, when he wandered into the racial and political thicket of "Confederate flags" and "pickup trucks" as shorthand for the white southerners he hoped to win back to the Democratic fold—wants very little to do with the past, other than to point to the glory of its progression and then move on to more productive things. An America that above all, desires from its politicians, white and especially black and brown, a certain benign forgetfulness on the subject of race, which allows the broad strokes of history to be retained, but only as poetic allegory.

A certain ethnic agnosticism, an attractive nuclear (traditional) family, and displays of genteel public (Protestant) piety have long been key to successfully "crossing over" and transgressing the confines of racially or ethnically provincial politics. Thus John Kennedy needed to comfort the nation as to his Catholicism; Republican Ed Brooke became the first nonappointed black senator in 1966 by declaring, to the *Washington Post:* "I want to be elected on my own ability. Only then do you have progress . . . people should not use race as a basis for labeling me," only to be defeated after two terms by a Democratic congressman, Paul Tsongas, who declared it "the other side of racism" for Democrats to hesitate in defeating a "symbol" (Brooke had also gone through a bitter and public divorce, and made a second-term glide from the quintessence of moderation to vocal support for busing to desegregate schools). Eschewing explicit racial appeals was how Doug Wilder triumphed as a candidate of economic and not racial reform. And it was why Barack Obama, with his ecumenical racial vision, was well positioned to become the president of the United States.

Obama was not, strictly speaking, addressing the America where black and brown politicians often preside in unmixed communities of color, where the question of "remedies" is very much on the table, and where the purpose of remembering history is to correct it. In communities where ongoing strife is heavily seeded by the lingering sins of the past, forgetfulness is viewed as anything but benign. Almost from the start, many of the political and ideological leaders of *that* America eyed Obama with suspicion.

Associates said support for his Senate bid from home-state congressmen like Bobby Rush and Danny Davis was tepid at best, as was that of Rev. Jackson, who had hoped to see his son and namesake vault from the House to the Senate—a possibility that "Junior" believed (and told Obama as much) his father's own missteps had helped to foreclose in November 1999, when Jackson swept into Decatur, Illinois, a downstate, blue-collar town once known as "Striketown, U.S.A.," following the suspensions of a group of black students after a fight at a football game. Jackson launched protests, waving the banner of Selma and facing down the governor himself, only to find out, via videotape, that the young men had been brawling after all. Obama, who enjoyed a respectful, if nominal relationship with Jackson and a friendship with his son, was a much more careful man, and far less eager to turn up the wattage on racial outrage. Turning it down was the way to get more done.

On the day of his keynote speech in Boston in 2004, Obama was reintroduced to Rev. Sharpton before a meeting of black convention delegates. The introduction was made by their mutual friend Charles Ogletree, who had taught both Barack and Michelle at Harvard Law and whose own orientation was that of an activist, having represented clients ranging from the victims of the 1921 race riots that led to the burning of "Black Wall Street" in Tulsa, Oklahoma, to Anita Hill, to rapper Tupac Shakur.

Obama and Sharpton had met before, at Rainbow/PUSH and other events, but they didn't know each other well, and Ogletree thought they should.

The state senator stuck out his hand, then launched into an explication of his planned keynote, his multiracial vision, and what he hoped to accomplish in the United States Senate, noting that he'd lived in New York City for a time, during some of Sharpton's toughest fights. Sharpton, seven years older than Obama and a man who lived very much in the America of remedies, but who also knew well the limits of flight for a black leader who made them his calling, stopped him midsentence, with a knowing smile.

"You do what you've got to do tonight," Sharpton said. "I understand, you're speaking to the whole party and the whole country, and you've got to get elected statewide in Illinois. Don't worry about it, because I'm gonna take care of the brothers and sisters tomorrow night."

The two men would develop a quiet understanding and, with time, an increasing bond, based on Sharpton's belief that there were many lanes along the road to African American advancement; politicians were meant to trod in one, and civil rights leaders in another. "No politician ever marched against himself," Sharpton would often say. He believed it was his duty to speak to black needs as a civil rights leader, and to challenge power to relinquish the resources that advancement required, while Obama, as a symbol of the black excellence the country was capable of producing, could use his growing platform to cajole the nation to embrace its better angels and do what is right. It was an arrangement that suited both men just fine.

CHAPTER 5

Kanye

[To become president], Obama is gonna have to be the least angry black man in America.

—Unknown

"I hate the way they portray us, in the media. . . . If you see a black family, it says they're looting . . . You see a white family, it says they're looking for food."

Kanye West had gone off script, and his nerves were visibly jangling as he stood beside a grim-faced Mike Myers on an NBC soundstage.

It was September 2, 2005, nine months into George W. Bush's second term, and the network was airing a live telethon for the victims of Hurricane Katrina, which had violently struck coastal Louisiana and Mississippi a week before, killing more than 1,800 people, many of their bodies floating down rivers of mud. Meanwhile, tens of thousands were stranded on rooftops or in their homes, or crowded inside the filthy Superdome in New Orleans. The devastating storm had flattened a populated area spanning a breathtaking ninety thousand square miles.

West was voicing the outrage felt by many African Americans about the language the media was applying to images of people fleeing the water and desperately grasping for whatever food was left in grocery stores. If they were white, the media called them "flood victims." If they were black, they were "looters."

The NBC control room was on alert for any profanity from the rap star and fingers hovered over the switch to trigger the two-second delay. But no one realized that West had veered so wildly off script. Or perhaps they believed he would find his way back.

He didn't.

"And you know, it's been five days, because most of the people are black," the rapper continued, wandering further and further from the scripted words meant to compel donations. He grew increasingly emotional and was struggling to put his thoughts together in a straight line.

"With the setup, the way America is set up to help the poor, the black people . . . the less well-off, as slow as possible," Kanye continued, allowing that the Red Cross, for whom the telethon had been organized, was "doing *everything they can.* We already realize, a lot of the people that could help are at war right now, fighting another way, and . . . *they've given them permission to go down, and shoot us.*"

Myers shifted back and forth, unsure where to go from there. He scratched the side of his nose and tried to return to the script.

When it was Kanye's turn again, he didn't stammer.

"George Bush . . . doesn't care . . . about black people."

Myers turned and looked directly at West, as if he wanted to say something. Instead, the camera cut away. (Myers later told *GQ* magazine he was proud to have been "the guy next to the guy who spoke a truth," and in 2010 West was goaded into an awkward retraction on the *Today* show, as host Matt Lauer pressed him to apologize to the former president.)

Conservatives immediately erupted online. The rapper's comments were cut from the telethon's West Coast broadcast, and after NBC and the Red Cross were bombarded with angry phone calls, they issued statements distancing themselves from West's words. Six days after the telecast, West was drowned out by boos from forty thousand fans during a season kickoff concert for the National Football League at Gillette Stadium, outside Boston.

George W. Bush, in his memoir, would later describe Kanye's rebuke as the worst moment of his presidency. Worse than the terrorist attack on September 11, 2001. Worse than any day during two land wars. Worse than the day Hurricane Katrina tore New Orleans apart. Worse, because the normally brash and temperamental young rapper, who two weeks before had made the cover of *Time* magazine as the phenom of rap mogul Jay-Z's record label, had in unsteady fashion affixed the Bush administration's failures to racism.

Nothing infuriated white Americans more, and those on the right were particularly determined to turn this accusation back on the accuser and by doing so, to defang it. As black conservative writer John McWhorter put it: "We associate a person charging racism with powerlessness. . . . But West's charge came from a position of, actually, rather awesome power. To call someone a racist today is only a notch or two less potent than calling them a pedophile. Racism may still be 'out there,' but it is socially incorrect. It is whispered, hedged, released unintentionally amidst frustration. It is an embarrassment, disavowed even by racists."

Whatever cultural power West and his words might have had (apparently even over the president of the United States), he had inelegantly but powerfully summarized the anxieties of many black Americans about the power they *lacked*, even to save their own lives. Louisiana's population was one-third black—a percentage outmatched only by Mississippi and the District of

Columbia—and a third of the black and Hispanic population lived below the poverty line; the poorest residents living in the basin of a topographical soup bowl, stuck in a low-lying landmass often beset by flooding, encircled by high but faltering levies meant to keep Lake Pontchartrain and the Mississippi River at bay. A succession of Democratic leaders had been complicit in the neglect of the low-lying wards, including Louisiana's governor, Kathleen Blanco, and New Orleans's African American mayor, Ray Nagin, whose evacuation plans proved woefully inadequate as the waters rose, and who had been reduced to profanity-laced tirades when the federal government was slow to respond with emergency help, making Nagin appear as the very picture of the impotency of black power.

For so long African Americans had seen the federal government as their sometimes reluctant savior of last resort, on the right to vote, the right to march, and the right to go to school. Blacks had never been able to rely on state authority, which for so long had been trained against them. But now the federal authorities had failed them, too.

For Barack Obama, Katrina was a particular test. As the Senate's lone black member, and with mainly black families left chanting for help inside the Superdome, or fleeing Louisiana for Texas or Florida, labeled "refugees" inside their own country, the press was putting immense pressure on him to react. He was traveling overseas when the storm hit, but quickly telephoned Bill Clinton upon his return, signing on to his efforts with George H. W. Bush to raise funds for Katrina relief and, with Senator Hillary Clinton and Barbara Bush, to tour the Houston Astrodome, where thousands of displaced New Orleanians had been moved to temporary shelter.

But as the senator was boarding his flight to Houston on September 5, three days after Kanye West's tirade, the media was less interested in what Barack Obama planned to do there than what he would say. After all, he had come to national prominence as an eloquent spokesman for racial and political reconciliation. And Katrina was quickly becoming a tale of poverty and race. Would Barack Obama be the conciliator, or would he join Kanye and the growing body of black opinion that agreed with him?

Obama and Hillary Clinton each called for an independent commission to investigate the federal response. But when long-time Chicago reporter Lynn Sweet asked the senator to respond to West's broadside against President Bush, he demurred. No, the failed federal response was not due to New Orleans being "disproportionately black," Obama said. No, the local and state officials were not primarily at fault. And no, the Katrina tragedy was not a failure of "personal responsibility" by the victims.

Obama told Sweet that Katrina showed "how little inner-city African Americans have to fall back on," in a world where largely affluent federal officials blithely assumed they could simply "hop in their SUVs, and top off with a $100 tank of gas and [get some] Poland Spring water," as they sped out of harm's way. Sure, "inner city blacks" were underresourced, both in New Orleans and in underserved communities around the country. "But that has been true for decades," Obama said.

And to West's rebuke of the president, he added: "What I think is that we as a society, and this administration in particular have not been willing to make sacrifices or shape an agenda to help low-income people."

It wasn't a dodge. Obama had long balanced a number of competing inner visions. He was equally the product of his grand-parents' traditionalist midwestern probity and his mother's internationalist humanism. But he was also influenced by the liberation theology of his mentors in Chicago, including his pastor, Jeremiah Wright of Chicago's Trinity United Church of Christ, and Roman Catholic firebrand Michael Pfleger, who ran an activist ministry that had aided a young Barack Obama during his days as a community organizer. The two men preached social justice in the blended context of race and poverty, and Obama believed deeply both in the racial ecumenism of most Americans and that the country was often guilty of profligacy toward its poor.

After Sweet's interview with Obama on the tarmac, she wrote that she found him to be conspicuously "measured" in warning against the "false dichotomy" that stated that either personal responsibility or collective societal failure alone was to blame for New Orleanians' agony.

Even when Barbara Bush further damaged her son's image by saying that among the displaced she'd met in Houston, nearly "all want to stay in Texas," having been "so overwhelmed by the hospitality"—and went on to say the people sleeping inside the arena were "underprivileged anyway, so this is working very well for them"—Obama refused to be drawn in. On the day after the visit, his office released a statement: "There's been much attention in the press about the fact that those who were left behind in New Orleans were disproportionately poor and African American. I've said publicly that I do not subscribe to the notion that the painfully slow response of FEMA and the Department of Homeland Security was racially-based. The ineptitude was colorblind."

Katrina sank Bush's approval ratings among African Americans, only 15 percent of whom rated the federal government's response as "good" or "very good" by the time Gallup released its September 14 poll, while just under half of white Americans thought the response was fine. And while 60 percent of African Americans said they believed the federal government responded so slowly because many of those in distress were black and 63 percent said the failure was because they were poor, just 12 and 21 percent of whites, respectively, said the same. More blacks blamed President Bush than Mayor Nagin for the post-Katrina debacle, while whites said the reverse. In every sense, it was clear that even the aftermath of the natural disaster was being viewed from two very different worlds, one white, one black.

Bush's approval ratings with white Americans, already stuck in the 40s due to disapproval of the Iraq War, stayed there, though when asked "the question," 7 in 10 white Americans believed that President Bush did indeed "care about black people," while 7 in 10 black Americans agreed with Kanye West.

DEMOCRATS AWOKE THE MORNING AFTER THE 2006 MIDTERM elections basking in the glow of a victory not seen since 1992. They would again control both houses of Congress, making California congresswoman Nancy Pelosi the first female Speaker of the House. Harry Reid was elevated to Senate majority leader, with Democrats' fifty-one-seat majority sealed by the consent of two independents. Eighty-seven women now served in Congress, the vast majority of them Democrats, and twenty-three were women of color. The Democratic Party even grabbed a majority of governorships.

In many of the races, victory had come on the strength of black and Hispanic votes, as the white electorate split down the middle, 51 percent for Republicans, 47 percent for Democrats. A postelection analysis found that the uptick in black turnout alone was enough to deliver Democratic Senate seats in Missouri, Ohio, Pennsylvania, and Virginia, where Republican George Allen's defeat was fueled by controversy over an apparent racial slur. Surging black turnout in Pennsylvania, Michigan, and Tennessee helped reelect Democratic governors and helped Deval Patrick become the first black governor of Massachusetts.

Nationally, Democrats triumphed despite losing white men by nearly 10 points, by edging out Republicans among white women and overwhelming them among nonwhite voters, including Hispanics, who just two years earlier had given more than 4 in 10 of their votes to President Bush.

Republican National Committee chairman Ken Mehlman

had carried out a reparative campaign to begin to woo African American voters, including a public apology the previous summer for the GOP's "southern strategy"; he had risked the ridicule and opprobrium of his party's base by saying, during an address before the NAACP, that "some Republicans gave up on winning the African American vote, looking the other way or trying to benefit politically from racial polarization." He added, "I am here today as the Republican chairman to tell you we were wrong." Nevertheless, black voters were now seemingly out of reach for Mehlman's party. At the time Mehlman spoke, the NAACP was in the midst of an IRS investigation of its tax status, launched in 2004 after its chairman, Julian Bond, made comments critical of President Bush.

Now, a year after Mehlman's attempt at rapprochement, the three prominent black Republicans seeking statewide office in swing states went down to defeat: Ken Blackwell for a U.S. Senate seat in Ohio, Lynn Swann for governor of Pennsylvania, and Michael Steele for a Senate seat in Maryland. Blackwell, the archconservative former Ohio secretary of state whose machinations many Democrats blamed for John Kerry's narrow defeat in 2004, received just 20 percent of the black vote in his Senate bid—less than half the haul white Republican George Voinovich had received when he was reelected governor in 1994. Swann, a onetime NFL star, received just 13 percent of the black vote. Steele, the affable Maryland lieutenant governor who ran a campaign supported by some prominent African Americans, including Mike Tyson and Radio One founder Cathy Hughes, and whose campaign ads rarely mentioned his party, received the highest black vote total of the three, at just 25 percent.

Black voters continued to nurse their lingering anger over Katrina—to which they added frustration with the war in Iraq and the ongoing complaints of harassment and intimidation of black and brown voters at the polls. Since 2004, more than forty thousand voting-related complaints had been logged by a national election hotline. The complaints in 2004 ranged from the presence of plainclothes sheriffs along polling routes in Florida, to men carrying official-looking clipboards and driving sedans with law enforcement–style insignia on them challenging voters in Philadelphia, to the discovery that groups with official-sounding names had distributed flyers in Lake County, Ohio, warning that anyone who had registered to vote through the NAACP was ineligible, and flyers in Milwaukee from a fictitious group called the Milwaukee Black Voters League warning that anyone who had cast a ballot in an election that year could not vote in November. In 2006, flyers listing the wrong election day were distributed in multiple states, and there were reports of clipboard-toting "poll watchers" who asked for identification in predominantly black precincts. Sometimes the intimidation was unsubtle. Election protection organizations in 2006 fielded complaints of harassing robocalls targeting Democratic voters in New York, Florida, Virginia, and New Mexico. Tennessee Republican candidate Bob Corker was forced to demand that radio ads that featured jungle drums in the background when black U.S. Senate candidate Harold Ford Jr.'s name was mentioned be pulled off the air. The Tennessee Senate race was also beset by intimations of interracial sex in a TV ad that featured a white woman who appeared to be naked, cooing into the camera for Ford to "call me." Ford narrowly lost his bid to become the state's first black senator. And brochures distributed in several states in 2006 warned that going to polling places could prompt FBI background checks or even arrests for unpaid tickets, unpaid child support, or for vague and mythic "voter fraud."

The level of mistrust among voters of color was profound. An October 2006 Pew poll found that only 3 in 10 African Americans believed their vote would count in November, a view only 8 percent of whites shared.

Obama spent fall 2006 on the road, drawing large crowds as

he rallied Missouri Democrats for Claire McCaskill's Senate bid, Florida voters for gubernatorial hopeful Jim Davis, and Bay State throngs for Deval Patrick's historic bid. He was the party's star attraction, more sought after even than former president Clinton. Obama had a new, bestselling book, *The Audacity of Hope,* and the rapt attention of the national media. He was viewed as a singularly unifying figure, who enthralled the largely white audiences of party activists who yelled "we love you!" as the young senator spoke to the country's most idyllic possibilities. Obama frequently overshadowed the candidates he'd come to stump for.

Anytime it needed to drum up the enthusiasm of the party's liberal wing—the labor organizers and old New Dealers, and left-of-center stalwarts—the Democrats sent in Barack Obama. But when it was time to rally African Americans, the party sent Bill Clinton to town. Obama was still largely unknown among African Americans, while the former president was the singular draw.

On the day after the 2006 midterm elections, Obama held his first formal meetings with a small group of advisers to explore the possibility of running for president. He'd been hearing talk about his running while he traveled the country. And the next presidential election would be an open contest, with no incumbent in place, and a deeply unpopular Republican exiting the White House.

Hillary Clinton had been exploring a run, too, and polls showed her with a commanding lead over any other political figure, Democrat and Republican. Her team knew she could raise the money and put together the organization, and her husband, the former president, stood proudly offstage as she delivered the keynote speech at the DLC convention in December. Still, some of her staff wondered if they could really be sure the candidate field was closed, since repeated calls to recruit key potential staffers like David Axelrod and Patrick Gaspard, whose union's endorsement would be key to any campaign and whose closest friend had run

Hillary's 2000 Senate campaign, were going unanswered. Some top aides suspected they knew why. But most in Hillary's inner circle didn't know that Axelrod already had a candidate, and that, according to close associates, Gaspard had decided not to work for Clinton the day she voted in favor of war with Iraq.

On January 16, 2007, the top aides' suspicions were confirmed when Obama announced that he was forming a presidential exploratory committee. In a video on his website, Obama railed against the "smallness" and bitter partisanship of the politics he'd encountered on Capitol Hill. He lit into the Iraq War—Hillary's Achilles' heel—and set his official announcement date for the following month.

Many in the Clinton camp were stunned, including the former president and the senator herself. Hillary's intentions had long been known. She was the party's natural heir, and Bill Clinton was its centripetal force. The former first couple were aware of the glow around Obama, and they had even heard the siren calls for him to enter the race, but, according to a former aide, "Hillary, and Bill Clinton particularly, were thinking, 'There's no way he's gonna run.'"

Four days after Obama's announcement, the Clinton team released a video in which she declared, "I'm in it to win it!" She announced the start of a "listening tour" with her supporters, reminiscent of the launch of her Senate bid at Pat Moynihan's New York farm. She vowed to "renew the promise of America" after eight years of George W. Bush. She would seek "the right end" to the war in Iraq, which had cost Bush's party so dearly in the midterm elections of 2006. It would cost Mrs. Clinton much more.

ON THE EVE OF THE 2000 DEMOCRATIC NATIONAL CONVENtion in Los Angeles, former BET anchor Tavis Smiley, a onetime aide to Los Angeles mayor Tom Bradley, launched the State of the Black Union, modeled on the 1972 National Black Political Convention. The event would be televised each year on C-SPAN and brought together prominent black scholars, journalists, authors, political leaders, and civil rights activists from around the country to discuss black America's communal health in the areas of politics, economics, and social welfare.

This year, 2007, it was set for February 10, and invitations to the event at Hampton University in Virginia had been sent to all the major Democratic presidential hopefuls. Hillary Clinton's campaign quickly confirmed her attendance. Though she had a commanding lead in the polls, including a 2-to-1 advantage over Obama with African Americans, the campaign was taking no chances.

The Obama campaign declined. February 10 had been fixed as the date for his official presidential announcement in Springfield, Illinois, and they were expecting a capacity crowd.

Smiley's team pressed and kept pressing. They had assembled a who's who of the black intellectual and civic elite: Revs. Jesse Jackson and Al Sharpton, Cornel West, former Virginia governor Douglas Wilder, Radio One founder Cathy Hughes, Marian Wright Edelman, actor Tim Reid, radio host Tom Joyner, and even Chuck D, founder and leader of the legendary rap group Public Enemy. More than eleven thousand people had registered for the daylong Q&A session, and the organizers believed that Obama, whose star had risen largely in the D.C. political media, ought to tell African Americans who he was, and why they should support him over Senator Clinton for the White House.

After days of back-and-forth, Obama picked up the phone and called Smiley, offering to come to Hampton after his announcement. Smiley declined. Obama next suggested sending Michelle, who knew his political platform better than anyone, and whose legal and intellectual pedigree was as impressive as his own. Michelle had been a standout at Princeton University and

Harvard Law School. Her family had ties to Chicago's storied political machines: Her father was a Democratic precinct captain, and her former boss, Valerie Jarrett, worked in Richard M. Daley's City Hall. She'd even grown up in the orbit of Rev. Jackson, whose daughter Santita was a friend and high school classmate. The Obamas sometimes socialized with Jesse Jr. and his wife, even attending each other's weddings. And though Junior viewed Obama as both a rival and an ally, the younger Jackson had been an early and enthusiastic supporter of Obama's Senate campaign. Michelle Obama would not only ably represent her husband, the candidate; she'd be coming home.

Again, Smiley rejected this offer, and when Obama suggested that he send a detailed letter laying out his reasons for running for president, the negotiation was at an end.

Smiley was no incidental figure. He had risen in stature as a social commentator, from BET to a weekly platform on Tom Joyner's top-rated morning radio show. He'd produced bestselling books based on the State of the Black Union series, which proposed a national agenda for black America, and a plan of action to arrest the political, economic, and social ills of black communities. Smiley and Obama had a passing friendship, as two members of a rising black intellectual elite. But Obama had risen on tracks defined by racial reconciliation, whereas Smiley had done so through a talent for confrontation.

Now Smiley would direct that talent toward a sharp debate over Obama's claim to national leadership and his place in black America.

Four days before the conference was to start, on February 6, the *Virginian-Pilot* ran an interview with Smiley in which he was asked if he thought America was ready for a black president. He responded: "The question is, is Barack Obama the right person? Obama has not had the quintessential black experience in America—*raised in Hawaii, spent time in Indonesia, biracial family* . . . Barack Obama is no Shirley Chisholm. When Shirley Chisholm ran in '72, when Jesse ran in '84 and '88, they had long-standing relationships with the black community."

Smiley's challenge to Obama's "black experience" was rich with irony. Chisholm had positioned herself as precisely the kind of hybrid candidate Obama was attempting to be—declaring that she wanted to empower not just blacks but also "women, young, Spanish-speaking peoples" and "all of those forces in America that have never had any real input into who's going to be the chief executive of this land." Like Obama, Chisholm had neither the consent nor the support of the black political and intellectual elite, who dismissed her campaign because, in their view, she put the aspirations of women ahead of the cause of racial justice.

Obama, like Chisholm, the immigrants' daughter, had an upbringing framed by an international context but lived in brown skin in America. And the defining feature of the "black experience"—whether in Hawaii or Chicago's South Side—was simply being black and experiencing the social consequences.

And so, Obama and his team saw no need to genuflect before the black elite at Smiley's conference or anywhere else.

Instead, despite the five-degree temperatures in Springfield, the Obamas and their young daughters were greeted at 10 A.M. by an enthusiastic, and overwhelmingly white, crowd of sixteen thousand. After an introduction by Illinois's senior senator, Dick Durbin, who had encouraged him to mount a presidential bid, Obama bounded onto the stage to a U2 anthem: "City of Blinding Lights."

"I know it's a little chilly, but I'm fired up!" he told the crowd, borrowing a riff from an old NAACP call-and-response chant, which he would use often on the campaign trail: "Fired up, ready to go!"

The night before, Obama had reluctantly sidelined his pastor, Rev. Jeremiah Wright, who was to give the invocation, but who instead prayed privately with the family and Durbin before the announcement. The decision followed the publication of a *Rolling Stone* article that called Obama's association with Wright "as openly radical a background as any significant American political figure has ever emerged from, as much as Malcolm X, as Martin Luther King Jr.," citing one of Wright's sermons, in which the preacher declared that "racism is how this country was founded and how this country is still run," saying of Americans, "we believe in white supremacy and black inferiority and believe it more than we believe in God."

The article cited the men's long relationship: Obama's consecration of his Christian faith at Wright's church, and Wright's role not just as the man who married the Obamas and baptized their children, but as a "sounding board" for the candidate to ensure he kept a level head. The *Rolling Stone* piece followed a January 21 profile of the 8,500-member Trinity United Church of Christ in Chicago that was arranged by the Obama campaign, to combat the insinuations rippling through conservative media that he was a Muslim, an insinuation that in one fell swoop exploited anti-Muslim prejudice, while reminding the more closed-minded among white voters of Obama's black, foreign father and his cross-cultural, blended family. Despite the candidate and his team's best efforts, suspicion about Obama's identity was going to be a feature of the campaign.

While this was going on in Springfield, Cornel West was on-stage in Hampton satirically laying the blame for Obama's absence on his white senior staff. "Look, Obama is a very decent, brilliant, charismatic brother, there's no doubt about that," West said, as Smiley looked on. "The problem is he's got folk *who are talking to him, who warrant our distrust.*"

West speculated that Obama "going to Springfield the same day Brother Tavis has set this up for a whole year" was by design, and that Obama being in Springfield "is not fundamentally about *us,* it's about *somebody else*! He's got large numbers of white brothers and sisters . . . who have fears and anxieties, and he's got to speak to them in such a way that he holds us at arm's length—enough to say he loves us but doesn't get too close to scare them away."

The audience jeered Obama, as West, his voice rising from just above a whisper to just below a shout, asked rhetorically of the absent Obama: "*I want to know how deep is your love for the people, what kind of courage have you manifested in the stances that you have and what are you willing to sacrifice for.* . . . . I don't care what color you are. You see you can't just take black people for granted because you're black. We want to know what your record is. Where's your courage, what are you willing to sacrifice!"

The boos for Obama rained down as Smiley read "Brother Baracks'" regrets and announced that the candidate would appear in a *60 Minutes* broadcast that night.

A *Los Angeles Times* article that same day questioned whether Obama would be a "black president" and featured skeptical reviews of his candidacy by black political activists, including a former Obama nemesis from Chicago, Northeastern Illinois University professor Conrad Worrill, who was quoted as saying: "When white folks begin to put their arms around a black person, there's always suspicion." Worrill added a comment reminiscent of Bobby Rush's indictment of Obama when Rush and Obama were electoral rivals: "The question is: Will this generation of new, college-trained beneficiaries of the black political power movement in America fight for black political interests?" It was an almost exquisite irony. Barack Obama was catching hell for not being "black enough" while at the same time his political enemies were preparing to savage him as exotically, radically black.

That Sunday evening, Obama rebutted these critiques with trademark understatement in his *60 Minutes* interview, as he addressed the growing fascination with his racial identity.

"If you look African American in this society, you're treated as an African American," he said flatly. "It's interesting, though, that now I feel very comfortable and confident in terms of who I am and where I stake my ground."

But Obama had other patches of ground to take. He needed to conquer the territory occupied by the black political establishment in Washington, which didn't know him and which saw itself as the political gatekeeper for black America, and he needed to take and hold the political battlefield littered with black America's doubts and prove to black voters that he, with or without the blessing of their traditional leaders, could fulfill their wildest political dreams.

A week before Springfield, Emil Jones, Obama's political mentor, traveled to the Democratic National Committee's winter caucus in Washington, D.C. All of the major candidates were there, pressing the flesh at the Washington Hilton, at a time when Bill and Hillary Clinton were burning up the phone lines looking to lock down Hillary's African American political support base. Hillary already had endorsements in hand from a third of the Congressional Black Caucus, many of whose members had long personal ties to the Clintons and believed Mrs. Clinton's victory to be a foregone conclusion. Few of them knew Obama well.

At the caucus meeting, Jones listened patiently as DNC staffers talked about the party's bounty of candidates and said they all intended to stay neutral.

"I'm a member of the DNC, and I'm not neutral," Jones blurted to the room when it was his turn to speak.

He then launched into his pitch, taking particular note of the front row, where Donna Brazile, Minyon Moore, and other Democratic political veterans sat quietly. Many in the room owed long and valuable careers to the Clintons. Some had already committed to Hillary's campaign—Moore as its director of African American outreach. Others were on the verge of doing so.

Undaunted, Jones spoke on behalf of Obama, whom he thought of as a son and who he believed had a real chance of becoming the first black president of the United States.

"Each of us at one time has gone around to all these schools and talked to all these black youngsters and encouraged them to stay in school, and told them you can be anything you want to be," Jones thundered to the room. "And now is the time." Jones argued that Obama had the characteristics to lead the country. "He's young, he's articulate, he knows the issues," he said. "We as a caucus should be behind Barack Obama."

And then Jones leveled the unkindest cut of all.

"We don't owe anybody anything," he said. "What Clinton did for the blacks he did because he was *supposed* to do it. He got our votes, so we were entitled to everything we got. He didn't do us any favors. We don't owe anybody anything."

His words had the sting of accusation. And many in the room felt duly accused. As Jones finished, Moore stood and walked out of the room.

Some in attendance resented what they viewed as Jones's attempt to lecture and manipulate the caucus on the basis of race. Others simply felt they could not afford the psychic luxury of another exciting but ultimately doomed black candidate for president when they believed a second Clinton presidency would mean tangible benefits for their communities. They were incredulous that with the White House finally in reach, the party's most faithful base was being asked to gamble on the almost unthinkable possibility that just forty years after Dr. King was laid in the ground, a black man from Hawaii with the middle name Hussein could become president of the United States.

The men and women who had fought hostile forces to have a place in the Democratic Party and had painstakingly built black political machines, from Atlanta to Chicago to Detroit—men like Alabama Democratic Conference chairman Joe Reed, who tirelessly rounded up black votes for the Humphrey ticket in 1968 and was now Hillary's point man in the South—were less interested in symbolism than in the practical impact of having an ally, meaning a Democrat, in the White House for the next four years.

"You don't have all these gymnasiums and things named for Joe Reed because he was interested in symbolic stuff," political scientist David Bositis said. "He was interested in jobs and roads and highways."

The same political machines had rejected Jesse Jackson's long-shot candidacies in 1984 and 1988, when he would have faced a popular, sitting president and his anointed successor. But 2008 would not be 1988. George W. Bush had no heir apparent, and even if he had, Bush's embrace would have doomed that person. The country was restless, in the throes of an unpopular war and hungry for a change of leadership. A winnable election was at hand, and no Democrat—black or white—wanted to throw it away.

When South Carolina state senator Robert Ford endorsed Hillary, he said of Obama, "It's a slim possibility for him to get the nomination, but then everybody else is doomed. Every Democrat running on that ticket next year would lose—because he's black and he's top of the ticket. We'd lose the House and the Senate and the governors and everything."

"I'm a gambling man," Ford added. "I love Obama. But I'm not going to kill myself."

Ford said it was "humanly impossible" for Obama to win the share of white votes needed to win most states, adding: "Black Americans in the South don't believe this country is ready to vote for a black president."

These doubts rang true in millions of African American

homes, barbershops, and beauty shops, and on black radio. Obama's candidacy ignited sharp debates and divided black households, with parents siding with Clinton and children with the Illinois senator. One spouse might favor Barack and the other rally to Hillary. Many black women saw as much of themselves in Hillary as they did in Obama.

Some wondered whether Obama's audacity was a bridge that simply stretched too far, and whether he was casting his lot too high in attempting to go from the Illinois Senate almost straight to the White House, as a relatively unknown black man. Others feared that if Obama soared too high, an extremist would try to assassinate him, the same way the country had been robbed of JFK, RFK, and Dr. King. Indeed, early on, Senate Democratic leader Harry Reid urged Obama to request Secret Service protection, which he and his family received when most presidential candidates were still unbound by onerous security.

Still others saw in Obama's candidacy a ruse designed to rob black people blind. Cathy Hughes, a pioneer in her own right as the lone black woman to launch a national radio network, derided Obama in near-apocalyptic terms in public and in private conversations, implying that his true aim might be to trick African Americans into sabotaging their own interests. On CNN, weeks after the State of the Black Union, Hughes called the young candidate "a dazzling deception," pointedly noting that Norman Lear was among Obama's "big supporters" and adding, "He feels like a Hollywood movie: The movie *Wag the Dog*."

Others believed in Obama's potential but simply thought it was Hillary's turn. "I want Barack Obama to be president . . . in 2016," Andrew Young would tell an Atlanta forum in December 2007. "You cannot be president alone. To put a brother in there by himself is to set him up for crucifixion. His time will come and the world will be ready for a visionary leadership." (That month, Obama would land the endorsement to beat them all: Oprah Winfrey, whose blockbuster announcement before a massive crowd in Iowa was answered by a video endorsement of Hillary Clinton by legendary poet Maya Angelou. Many of Winfrey's white female fans accused her of abandoning the historic race by a viable woman, while many who admired Angelou were dismayed by her siding against a viable black candidate.)

And some questioned, as Cornel West, Conrad Worrill, and Tavis Smiley had done, whether Obama, with his eclectic background and racially ecumenical themes, had black America's interests in mind at all.

Obama had a ready answer when he spoke to an enthusiastic, mixed-race crowd of three thousand in Columbia, South Carolina, a week after his announcement in Springfield. He was riffing on state senator Ford's comments.

"Can't have a black man at the top of the ticket," he'd drawled in a preacher's cadence, as the crowd booed. "When folks were saying, '*We're going to march for our freedom*,' they said, '*You can't do that*.' When somebody said, '*You can't sit at the lunch counter. . . . You can't do that*,' we did. And when somebody said, '*Women belong in the kitchen not in the boardroom. You can't do that*,' yes we can." The crowd thundered back, "Yes we can!"

And to those who questioned whether he was "black enough," Obama answered on March 7, from Brown Chapel AME, the historic church in Selma, Alabama, that launched the march across the Edmund Pettus Bridge, as the major Democratic campaigns converged for the annual commemoration of the 1965 voting rights demonstration that turned into "Bloody Sunday."

Addressing a gathering that included pastor C. T. Vivian, whom Dr. King had praised as the greatest preacher he'd ever heard; Rev. Joseph Lowery, the aging SCLC leader and an early Obama enthusiast; and John Lewis, the organizer of the commemorative events and the most sought-after endorser from the Congressional Black Caucus, Obama spoke in his characteristically inclusive fashion, saying: "We're in the presence today of giants whose shoulders we stand on, people who battled, not just on behalf of African Americans but on behalf of all of America."

Obama was seeking to bring together his all-encompassing vision of an America without borders of identity with the deepest aspirations of African Americans, who needed to see themselves in him.

"There was something stirring across the country because of what happened in Selma, Alabama, because some folks are willing to march across a bridge," he continued in the chapel, alluding to the Kennedy administration airlift to Africa that brought his father and other young, ambitious intellectuals to the United States in the early 1960s, and his Kansan mother, whose ancestors owned slaves. "So they got together and Barack Obama Jr. was born," he said. "So don't tell me I don't have a claim on Selma, Alabama. Don't tell me I'm not coming home to Selma, Alabama. I'm here because somebody marched!" The speech would be swiftly criticized for jumbling the timeline of his own birth in 1961, four years before the march he was implying inspired his parents' confidence to pursue an interracial union. But Obama's task in Selma was not to write a public biography of his family; it was to connect himself to the larger body of African American history, and to inspire skeptical black voters to believe. And he sought to interweave the commemoration of the past with a call to responsibility aimed at black households, complete with admonishments to turn off the TV and help children with their homework, and to get "cousin Pookie" off the couch, out of his "bedroom slippers," and to the polls, as the correct way to honor the generation that bled on the Pettus Bridge and across the American South. It was a juxtaposition that would serve Obama well on the stump and in the broad main of American politics, but in time it would invite sharp criticism from African American thought leaders.

In June, Tavis Smiley would have his opportunity to quiz Obama on matters of race, as the eight Democratic candidates met at Howard University for their third debate, hosted by Smiley and broadcast on PBS. The debate—held in the wake of a 5–4 Supreme Court decision banning the use of race by school districts in assigning children to public schools to achieve diversity—was ground the media presumed Obama, as the lone black candidate, would take easily. Instead, it was Hillary Clinton who drew the most vigorous applause, for stating "there would be an outraged outcry in this country" if HIV/AIDS afflicted white women at the rates that black women were being infected, and when she declared that "You can look at this stage and see an African American, a Latino [New Mexico governor Bill Richardson], a woman contesting for the presidency of the United States. But there is so much left to be done, and for anyone to assert that race is not a problem in America is to deny the reality in front of our very eyes." Backstage afterward, Charles Ogletree, Obama's former Harvard professor, and Senator John Edwards ribbed Obama for getting beaten by a white woman at an historically black college.

Of all the ironies of the Obama rise, none attracted more commentary than his growing friendship with Reverend Sharpton, the bogeyman of racial politics in New York, who had gone on to become a radio talk show host, a senior statesman of the civil rights movement, and someone Democratic candidates for president sought for endorsement.

Sharpton and Obama solidified their growing friendship in the winter of 2007, when Rev. Jesse Jackson was becoming increasingly disgruntled with Obama's campaign, which he saw as insufficiently attentive to his legacy, particularly as he watched them court celebrities like Oprah, while rarely asking him to barnstorm on the campaign trail.

Jackson mounted multiple attacks on Obama in the fall,

accusing the candidate of "acting like he's white," during remarks at historically black Benedict College in Columbia, South Carolina, according to the *State* newspaper. Jackson was chiding the Illinois senator for avoiding strong statements on the Jena Six, a group of black teens charged with felony offenses in Louisiana after a fight that injured a white student from Jena High School, where African American students had discovered a noose hanging from a tree on the "white side" of the yard after a group of black students dared to sit down beneath the tree to get some shade.

The arrests and what many deemed excessive charges against the teens over a high school fight drew tens of thousands of protesters to the small Louisiana town in the fall, including Jackson. As he traveled across South Carolina on a voter registration tour in September, he told the paper, "If I were a candidate, I'd be all over Jena," calling the young men's arrests and pending trials "a defining moment, just like Selma was a defining moment." Jackson later reiterated his support for Obama and said he didn't recall the "acting white" remark, to which the Obama campaign had responded that the candidate's statements on Jena were made in consultation with his national cochair: Jesse Jackson Jr.

Jackson took another, more veiled swipe at Obama in October, telling the *Los Angeles Times* editorial board that the "thing of the hour is . . . who can have the most anti-Iraq policy," as if Obama's war opposition, launched at a Chicago rally at which Jackson was the star, was little more than a fad. Jackson added, "Well, the absence of the Iraq war, which is important, is not the presence of reinventing America."

"I've said I would vote for Barack because he's my neighbor," Jackson told the *State*. "I have very strong feelings for Hillary because we've worked together 30 years. I'm not really campaigning for anybody."

The next month, Charlie King, the National Action Network's executive director and a longtime Democratic Party activist, called Sharpton in his Harlem office to relay an invitation from Bill Clinton, who was flying to his and Hillary's home in Chappaqua, New York, and wanted to talk.

Sharpton traveled up to the Clintons' home in Westchester County and the two met for about an hour, during which the former president pressed Sharpton to come out publicly for Hillary. His reasons ranged from their New York connection to what she could accomplish as president for the African American community.

On the drive back to New York City, Sharpton pondered his prospects, between the probability of Hillary and the possibility of Obama, who was soon calling, too, with an invitation to dinner at Sylvia's soul food restaurant in Harlem.

The dinner on November 29 attracted national media attention, as the "post-racial" candidate dined on fried chicken and corn bread with the civil rights activist, who, having become a vegetarian, had only coffee.

At Sylvia's, the two talked about Obama's civil rights agenda, including his vow to reinvigorate the Justice Department's Civil Rights Division and Voting Section as president, his support for federal action to combat racial profiling by police, and even his reverence for the late Thurgood Marshall, one of Sharpton's heroes.

Afterward, Obama headed for a fund-raiser at Harlem's legendary Apollo Theater, where he told the capacity crowd: "I'm in this race because I'm tired of reading about Jena, tired of reading about nooses. I'm tired of hearing about a Justice Department that doesn't understand justice!" It was a riff that could have come from Sharpton himself.

On the same night, Hillary Clinton spoke at Harlem's Abyssinian Baptist Church at the invitation of Congressman Rangel. The two events couldn't have been more different: one staid and driven by Rangel's political machine, and the other rowdy and full of impatient energy. At the Apollo event, Cornel West, who had been converted from an Obama critic to a campaign surrogate through the lobbying and cajoling of mutual friends, including Charles Ogletree and Michael Eric Dyson, who had arranged personal meetings between the professor and the candidate, congratulated the crowd for being "on the right side of history." Comedian Chris Rock pointedly added, "You'd be really embarrassed if he won, and you wasn't with him." Rock joked in a pained voice: "'I had that white lady. What was I thinking? What was I thinking!?'"

Sharpton didn't attend either event. Instead, he spent the evening at the Havana Club, the private cigar club that had become his nightly haunt. Sitting inside the club's comfortably appointed rooms, Sharpton decided he would choose Obama. His staff thought he'd lost his mind.

Days after the twin events, Sharpton called Senator Obama, telling him that his support would be genuine, but not entirely public. He wouldn't go so far out on a limb that Obama would have to saw the branch off to save his support with white voters.

Obama appreciated Sharpton's support, and would have been happy simply knowing that Sharpton didn't intend to hurt him with black voters. Sharpton wasn't even certain Obama had a chance, friends said, but he was mindful of the black establishment's dismissal of Shirley Chisholm, and of his own 2004 presidential bid. "I'm not going to do to you what some of the older guys have done to us," he told Obama.

The next month, just days before the Iowa caucuses, the Obama campaign learned that Sharpton had been asked to give the keynote address at a forum planned by one of the Hawkeye State's few black interest groups. The campaign's senior leadership was worried because Sharpton's message would surely be strongly rooted in racial justice, which contrasted sharply with Obama's message of racial unity. Obama told his staff he would call Sharpton.

During the call, the senator explained his dilemma. As deeply as he believed in racial justice, it wasn't his campaign's focus. Sharpton said he'd think about how to handle it, but just over an hour later, he called back to say he was turning down the invitation.

"There's no way I'm not going to do Al Sharpton," the civil rights leader said. "So the best thing to do is I just won't go."

The men's relationship grew from there, giving the candidate an invaluable validator among African Americans. But an even more powerful validation was coming to the Illinois senator, and from a most unexpected state.

CHAPTER 6

Hope and Change

We've been asked to pause for a reality check. We've been warned against offering the people of this nation false hope. But in the unlikely story that is America, there has never been anything false about hope.

—Senator Barack Obama, primary concession speech in
  Nashua, New Hampshire, January 8, 2008

OBAMA'S VICTORY IN IOWA SENT SHOCK WAVES THROUGH THE black electorate. If Obama could win lily-white Iowa, they wondered, could he fulfill King's dream and win it all?

The Clintons, meanwhile, for the first time faced the possibility that the Obama moment had broken the spell of Hillary's inevitability. Obama was claiming the fertile political territory of "hope" and "change," to which Hillary responded, "We can't have false hopes. We've got to have a person who can walk into that Oval Office on day one and start doing the hard work that it takes to deliver change."

The Obama campaign had its own response. "False hopes?

Did John F. Kennedy look at the moon and say, 'Ah, thought so, too far. Reality check. Can't do it'? . . . Dr. King standing on the steps of the Lincoln Memorial, looking out over that magnificent crowd, the reflecting pool, the Washington Monument [saying] 'sorry guys, false hope. The dream will die. It can't be done!' . . . We don't need leaders to tell us what we can't do. We need leaders to tell us what we can do, and inspire us to do."

Obama's frequent invocations of Kennedy touched a nerve in Clinton World. Bill Clinton had idolized John F. Kennedy since he was a teenager and had long cultivated a relationship with Senator Ted Kennedy, whom he was courting to support Hillary's campaign. The former president believed that the Clintons and Kennedys belonged side by side on the long road of history. But the Kennedy mantle was no easy load to bear. And in New Hampshire, the Clintons discovered how ill-fitting the robes of history can be.

Hillary was asked if she cared to react to Obama's remarks, including his references to Dr. King.

"I would," Senator Clinton said, "and I would point to the fact that Dr. King's dream began to be realized when President Lyndon Johnson passed the Civil Rights Act of 1964; when he was able to get through Congress something that President Kennedy was hopeful to do, [that] the president before had not even tried. But it took a president to get it done. That dream became a reality. The power of that dream became real in people's lives because we had a president who said, 'We are going to do it,' and actually got it done."

Hillary's words were not untrue. King and the other civil rights leaders had used the power of protest, and the power of negotiation, to cajole the nation into truly seeing itself for the first time and to move politics along. They'd pressed Eisenhower and Kennedy but ultimately it was Johnson who would spur passage of the most comprehensive civil rights legislation in the country's history.

But Hillary's words seemed to undercut the importance of John Lewis and Stokely Carmichael and Julian Bond and millions of African Americans who had demanded "freedom now," the manful demands of Malcolm X and Muhammad Ali, and the womanly cries of Fannie Lou Hamer, Angela Davis, Diane Nash, and Shirley Chisholm. King's legacy had a visceral resonance with African Americans that was not to be taken lightly, even by a political friend with the surname Clinton.

As the controversy rocketed around the blogosphere and the mainstream press, Hillary was being assailed for impolitic treatment of Dr. King's legacy, for appearing to liken herself to Johnson the "doer," and Obama to King the "dreamer," and diminishing both black men in the process.

The Clinton campaign made attempts at damage control, dispatching Hillary's African American surrogates to defend her. Sympathetic blogs and liberal media watchdogs pointed out that early posts and stories truncated her quote in a manner that distorted its meaning.

None of it helped. Bill and Hillary Clinton suddenly found themselves in an unfamiliar place: at odds with a large body of black Americans, and sharply so.

At a town hall discussion in Hanover, New Hampshire, in support of Hillary's campaign, a student said to Bill Clinton that "one of the things that Senator Obama talks a lot about is 'judgment.'"

Clinton, leaning with one elbow on the podium, festooned with a blue and white Hillary banner, launched into an aggressive broadside against Obama's claims of "superior judgment" and his claim to have been against the Iraq invasion from the beginning. A visibly agitated Clinton set down his notes and began to walk toward the questioner, pointing his finger and delivering a stern lecture on "judgment" and his estimation of his wife's chief rival for the nomination.

"[S]ince you raised the judgment issue, let's go over this again," Clinton began, his voice just above hoarse, but rising. "That is the central argument for his campaign." He mocked Obama's entrance into the race, boiling it down to " 'it doesn't matter that I started running for president less than a year after I got to the Senate, from the Illinois state senate; I am a great speaker and a charismatic figure, and I am the only one who had the judgment to oppose this war from the beginning, *always, always, always. . . .*' "

After Clinton went point by point through the lead-up to the war, he challenged Obama's fundamental claim that he was always against attacking Iraq.

"It's wrong that Obama . . . never got asked one time, *not once,* 'well, how could you say that, when you said in 2004 you didn't know how you would have voted on the resolution?" Clinton said. "You said in 2004 there was no difference between you and George Bush on the war, and you took that speech you're now running on off your website in 2004, and there's no difference in your voting record and Hillary's ever since?"

Clinton ended his tirade with a flourish of exasperation, drawing a patter of applause from the room, where most attendees seemed astonished by what they'd witnessed. "Give me a break. This whole thing is the biggest fairy tale I've ever seen," the former president said.

If the former president was growing brittle, Hillary's stress and exhaustion seemed to finally give way, too, as she sat down in a Portsmouth coffee shop with a group of sixteen "undecided" women voters. The weary candidate was sipping coffee and wearing a ready smile. But when the final question came, it was surprisingly personal: As a woman, given how tough it can be "just to get out of the house, how do you do it? How do you stay so upbeat, and so wonderful?" Hillary clasped the microphone and leaned forward on the table, seeming at once relieved and released. "It's not easy," she said. "And I couldn't do it if I just didn't passionately believe it was the right thing to do."

And then she grew emotional, placing her hand under her chin. And her voice began to crack. "You know I have so many opportunities from this country. . . . I just don't want us to fall backwards."

She continued over the gentle applause: "This is very personal for me, it's not just political. It's not just public. I see what's happening and we have to reverse it. And some people think elections are a game, and it's like, who's up and who's down. It's about our country. It's about our kids' futures. And it's really about all of us together."

This moment would be parsed and mocked by pundits and by opponents. *New York Times* columnist Maureen Dowd wryly asked whether Hillary could "cry her way back to the White House," while others likened her emotion to the glint in Edmund Muskie's eyes on a cold Manchester day in February 1972 (Muskie's emotionalism during a speech against the city's hard-right *Union Leader* cost him any momentum he had against his Democratic presidential primary rival, George McGovern). But it was clear to those who knew Hillary Clinton, who knew her as the girl who had been moved by Dr. King, as the young woman who admired Edward Brooke, and who had both labored for and disappointed Marian Wright Edelman in her transition from child advocate to First Lady, that even though she had never had the connection to African Americans her husband did, she felt she'd lost something important in New Hampshire.

When the votes were cast, Hillary delivered her own shock to the pundit class by winning the New Hampshire primary. But that night, Obama answered with a speech that in defeat moved a nation and created an iconography that proved unstoppable, even for the Clintons. It called on a refrain he had used on the campaign trail many times before.

"[W]e have faced down impossible odds," Obama said, calling for a "new majority" that would stretch across political parties to take the nation in a fundamentally different direction.

> When we've been told we're not ready or that we shouldn't try or that we can't, generations of Americans have responded with a simple creed that sums up the spirit of a people: Yes, we can. It was a creed written into the founding documents that declared the destiny of a nation: Yes, we can. It was whispered by slaves and abolitionists as they blazed a trail towards freedom through the darkest of nights: Yes, we can. It was sung by immigrants as they struck out from distant shores and pioneers who pushed westward against an unforgiving wilderness: Yes, we can. It was the call of workers who organized, women who reached for the ballot, a president who chose the moon as our new frontier, and a king who took us to the mountaintop and pointed the way to the promised land: Yes, we can.

Hillary Clinton had won New Hampshire, but she and her husband had done real damage to themselves. On the day of the primary, in an interview on CNN, Donna Brazile, a bona fide Clinton insider and friend, called the former president's words and tone "depressing" for African Americans to hear.

New York Times columnist Bob Herbert slammed the Clintons for "chastising the press for the way it was covering the Obama campaign," and the former president for his remark about "fairy tales." He derided the spectacle of "Mrs. Clinton telling the country we don't need 'false hopes,' and taking cheap shots at, of all people, the Reverend Dr. Martin Luther King Jr."

Wrote Herbert: "We've already seen Clinton surrogates trying to implant the false idea that Mr. Obama might be a Muslim, and perhaps a drug dealer to boot." Hillary had indeed been forced to rebuke campaign surrogates, including chief strategist Mark Penn, for suggestive comments about Obama's admissions of experimenting with drugs as a young man. Inside the Obama team there was a strong belief that much of the whisper campaign against Obama's religious faith originated inside the Clinton camp, and from Penn in particular.

But next up was the South Carolina primary, and when Congressman Jim Clyburn of that state publicly declared his disapproval of the Clintons' tone and the invocation of King to deride the Obama campaign, the Clinton campaign knew that zero hour had been reached.

Clyburn, a tough, gravelly-voiced man with roots in the Gullah low country, had come through the crucible of the civil rights struggle and was now the third-ranking member of the House leadership. He was among the leading politicians, black or white, in a state where 4 in 10 Democratic primary voters were African American. He had not declared for Clinton or Obama, and his support would be critical for winning the Democratic nomination.

Clyburn and Bill Clinton had a long relationship, dating back to Clinton's first term as Arkansas governor, but the congressman had been agitated by what had happened in New Hampshire. Clyburn had been telling associates that he had his political view and his personal view of who should get the Democratic nomination in 2008. He believed, as did many of his colleagues, that Hillary would ultimately prevail, but personally he was for Obama.

He and the Illinois senator had formed a relationship during Obama's brief time in Washington. Few members of the Congressional Black Caucus had gotten to know Obama, who, like most senators, had only infrequent contact with members of the House. Obama attended Black Caucus meetings sporadically, but when he did, he often sat beside Clyburn, and the two would talk about politics or current events, and the strange alchemy of Washington. Clyburn was among a handful of Washington hands Obama sought advice from as he made the decision to run for president. Thus Clyburn was one of the few members in either chamber not to be taken by surprise when he announced.

Clyburn had been traveling overseas during the New Hampshire primary, but when the *New York Times* reporter Carl Hulse reached him and read him both Clintons' comments over the phone, Clyburn was stunned.

"We have to be very, very careful about how we speak about that era in American politics," he said. "It is one thing to run a campaign and be respectful of everyone's motives and actions, and it is something else to denigrate those. That bothered me a great deal."

As to President Clinton's pronouncements about Obama's Iraq stance being a "fairy tale," Clyburn focused not on the war but on the senator's candidacy itself: "To call that dream a fairy tale, which Bill Clinton seemed to be doing, could very well be insulting to some of us."

The *Times* article indicated that Clyburn's displeasure might shake him out of his neutral stance ahead of the January 26 South Carolina primary, the very thing the Clinton team feared. The campaign quickly scheduled call-ins for the former president on Friday, January 11, to the *Tom Joyner Morning Show,* the number-one morning show in black U.S. households, and to Rev. Al Sharpton's syndicated afternoon program, *Keeping It Real.* Bill Clinton told Joyner the campaign was now "in a genuine fight, and no one should be able to accuse someone like Hillary of being a racist." He explained to Joyner, and later to Sharpton, that "fairy tale" referred to the Obama campaign's presentation of the senator's opposition to the war as unswerving, not to his campaign. "There's nothing fairy tale about his campaign," Clinton told Sharpton. "It's real, strong, and he might win."

A frustrated Clinton told Sharpton he would respect any black voter who chose Barack Obama over Hillary. But he laid into the Obama campaign for "sowing divisiveness when Obama had vowed to run a different kind of race."

The Obama team knew a victory in South Carolina would put the campaign in the thick of the delegate race, and as Obama told his senior staff, a defeat could be the end of the game. And key to South Carolina was separating the Clintons from black voters.

The day of the Clinton radio call-ins, Obama's South Carolina spokeswoman Candice Tolliver told Ben Smith of *Politico* that Hillary Clinton would have to decide if she owed anyone an apology. A memo went out to reporters under Tolliver's name that described a series of events that began the previous December, when Hillary's New Hampshire campaign cochair, Bill Shaheen, spontaneously raised the issue of Obama's prior drug use; it extended to campaign strategist Mark Penn's repeated use of the word *cocaine* on television in reference to Obama, to Hillary's remarks on Dr. King versus Lyndon Johnson, and to Clinton surrogate Andrew Cuomo, the New York attorney general, who said after New Hampshire that the race can't be bought or won through TV, that "you can't shuck and jive." Cuomo's spokesman insisted later that the comment did not refer to the Illinois senator.

The memo quickly leaked, causing furious Clinton supporters to charge the Obama team with race-baiting. The Clinton camp deployed their top African American surrogates to respond. Ohio congresswoman Stephanie Tubbs Jones dismissed the idea of a pattern of racial comments out of Clinton World as "ridiculous," saying, "all of the world knows the commitment

of President Clinton and Senator Clinton to civil rights issues—
and not only the commitment in terms of words but in terms
of deeds." Texas congresswoman Sheila Jackson Lee said "any
school child" knows that King's words "moved people to action."

Some Clinton advisers said they should simply end the discussion, but the campaign was in no mood to back down. During
a January 13 appearance on *Meet the Press,* Hillary fielded Tim
Russert's first question, which went directly to the ongoing controversy: "First, with respect to Dr. King, you know, Tim, I was
fourteen years old when I heard Dr. King speak in person. He
is one of the people that I admire most in the world, and the
point that I was responding to from Senator Obama himself in a
number of speeches he was making is his comparison of himself
to President Kennedy and Dr. King. And there is no doubt that
the inspiration offered by all three of them is essential. It is critical to who we are as a nation, what we believe in, the dreams and
aspirations that we all have.

"But I also said that, you know, Dr. King didn't just give
speeches," she continued. "He marched, he organized, he pro-
tested, he was gassed, he was beaten, he was jailed. He understood
that he had to move the political process and bring in those who
were in political power, and he campaigned for political leaders,
including Lyndon Johnson, because he wanted somebody in the
White House who would act on what he had devoted his life to
achieving."

Clinton accused the Obama campaign of deliberately distorting her and the former president's remarks, referring to news of
the leaked South Carolina memo and insisting that she wanted
neither race nor gender brought into the campaign.

The Clintons were losing and "they were really pissed-off," a
former campaign aide said. "Not because they were losing to an
African American man, but to a man who had been in the Senate
all of two years. They couldn't understand it. It had nothing

to do with him being an African American man for crying out loud. I just think the loss in Iowa just really freaked everybody out. . . . That this guy, who was very politically talented, but really, what has he done?"

The attempts at damage control weren't working, not least due to the ongoing missteps of surrogates, including BET founder Bob Johnson, who on January 13 told a South Carolina crowd that "as an African American, I am frankly insulted that the Obama campaign would imply that we are so stupid that we would think Hillary and Bill Clinton, who have been deeply and emotionally involved in black issues since Barack Obama was doing something in the neighborhood—and I won't say what he was doing, but he said it in the book—when they have been involved," adding, "That kind of campaign behavior does not resonate with me, for a guy who says, 'I want to be a reasonable, likable, Sidney Poitier *Guess Who's Coming to Dinner?* And I'm thinking, I'm thinking to myself, this ain't a movie, Sidney. This is real life."

The bank shot at Obama's youthful drug use landed like a bottle rocket, and Johnson quickly demurred, saying afterward that his comments were meant to refer to Obama's time as a community organizer and nothing more. Johnson called any suggestion to the contrary "irresponsible and incorrect."

At an event in New York on January 14, Senator Clinton received a mix of polite applause and scattered boos when she called on the more than two thousand people there to fulfill King's unfinished legacy, and drew her strongest applause by praising Barack Obama.

"We may differ on minor matters, but when it comes to what is really important, we are family," she said. "Both Senator Obama and I know that we are where we are today because of leaders like Dr. King and generations of men and women like all of you."

Both campaigns were sensing that the war over Dr. King's legacy was getting out of control. "How race got into this thing is because Obama said 'race,'" Congressman Charlie Rangel told a local news outlet. "But there is nothing that Hillary Clinton has said that baffles me. I would challenge anybody to belittle the contribution that Dr. King has made to the world, to our country, to civil rights, and the Voting Rights Act, but for [Obama] to suggest that Dr. King could have signed that act is absolutely stupid. It's absolutely dumb to infer that Dr. King, alone, passed the legislation and signed it into law." The segment had been taped four days earlier, but the timing couldn't have been worse, coming one day before King's birthday and a week before the national holiday.

The next day, the Clinton campaign released a statement from Hillary Clinton that said: "Our party and our nation is bigger than this. Our party has been on the front line of every civil rights movement, women's rights movement, workers' rights movement, and other movements for justice in America. We differ on a lot of things. And it is critical to have the right kind of discussion on where we stand. But when it comes to civil rights and our commitment to diversity, when it comes to our heroes— President John F. Kennedy and Dr. King—Senator Obama and I are on the same side."

Obama was in Nevada, but he called a news conference that evening to say, "I don't want the campaign at this stage to degenerate into so much tit-for-tat, back-and-forth, that we lose sight of why all of us are doing this. We've got too much at stake at this time in our history to be engaging in this kind of silliness. . . . If I hear my own supporters engaging in talk that I think is ungenerous or misleading or in some way is unfair, I will speak out forcefully against it. I hope the other campaigns take the same approach."

Obama called the Clintons "good people" who have

"historically and consistently been on the right side of civil rights issues." He added, "I think they care about the African American community and that they care about all Americans and they want to see equal rights and justice in this country."

Clyburn weighed in as well, telling PBS host Charlie Rose that he would do his "level best to help get beyond the unfortunate circumstances that we find ourselves in." Within days, Rangel went on MSNBC to voice his regrets for throwing a grenade onto the field when the candidate he supported was seeking to walk away, and Bob Johnson announced he'd sent a letter of apology to Obama for comments he called a hasty attempt at humor.

But it didn't end there. The Clintons were infuriated when Obama implied that Ronald Reagan had fundamentally changed America with his ideas, in a way that Clinton had not; more so when Dick Harpootlian, the colorful former prosecutor and one-time chairman of the South Carolina Democratic Party, went on CNN to accuse Bill Clinton of launching race- and gender-tinged attacks designed to discourage and suppress black votes, and of inventing charges of voter suppression by Obama campaign operatives in Nevada. Harpootlian called Bill Clinton's tactics "reminiscent of Lee Atwater."

Bill Clinton shot back at a CNN reporter, Jessica Yellin, as he exited a campaign event in Charleston three days before the South Carolina primary: "There are still two people around who marched with Martin Luther King and risked their lives: John Lewis and Rev. Andrew Young. They both said that Hillary was right and the people who attacked her were wrong, and that she did not play the race card, but they did. So I don't have to defend myself from Dick Harpootlian. I will just refer you to John Lewis and Andrew Young. And let him go get in an argument with them about it."

With the polls slated to close in South Carolina in fewer than twenty minutes, at 7 P.M. in the Saturday election, the former president struggled to contain his irritation as he stood alongside Florida congressman Kendrick Meek, Stephanie Tubbs Jones, and other campaign supporters in a parking lot in Columbia, taking questions from a claque of reporters who had chosen that spot to wait for the returns to come in. Hillary Clinton had already headed to Tennessee, leaving her husband to shepherd the final leg of the primary.

Asked if he was proud of what he'd done in South Carolina on his wife's behalf, Clinton said his role had mainly been to go around the state answering voters' questions. He then offered that it was "immensely impressive to me to see in the audiences whether they were predominantly African American, predominantly white, or totally integrated, there has not been a great deal of difference in the questions people ask."

It was an answer to a question that hadn't been asked.

When ABC's David Wright asked, "What does it say about Barack Obama that it takes two of you to beat him?" Clinton laughed.

"That's just bait, too," he said. "Jesse Jackson won South Carolina twice, in '84 and '88. And he ran a good campaign, and Senator Obama's run a good campaign here. He's run a good campaign everywhere . . . he's a good candidate, with a good organization."

Clinton's remarks instantly became the headline for every news outlet, seemingly everywhere. The former president was accused of playing the race card on the popular liberal blog Daily Kos, he was derided as the "big mouth of the South" by the conservative *New York Post,* and pundits made a meal of him on cable TV, accusing him of indiscipline and classlessness, of botching his wife's presidential campaign, and worse, of conflating the candidacies of Jesse Jackson and Barack Obama solely because both men are black.

The Obama team couldn't believe Clinton had stepped so forthrightly into the breach. One top campaign aide said, "Our reaction to the former president was, please keep talking."

"South Carolina was deeply troubling," said another. "Everyone understood his passion for his wife, and we always assumed he'd be out there litigating a case for her. And we assumed that if he attacked Obama, he would go after the experience question, which was the natural place to go. We never expected the tone; the ways that he was clearly, utterly dismissive, in the way that frankly we've seen too many white people can be about black people with potential, for a long time in our history." The attacks, the aide said, "really put an ugly shade on the president, and I just think it was unbecoming of him and desperate, and it was hard for us to not see it through the prism of race. Especially given that he was doing it in South Carolina."

The Clinton team quickly dispatched its top African American surrogates, including Representatives Tubbs Jones and Meek, to contain the fallout, with Meek insisting the former president had been asked a question about historic contests involving African American candidates. Pro-Hillary bloggers seized on the claim, accusing the media of attempting to manufacture a scandal. But the transcripts, released by ABC, didn't bear it out.

Obama was declared the winner of the South Carolina primary almost immediately after the polls closed, with MSNBC calling the race just after 7 P.M. and the *New York Times* following suit twenty minutes later. And he'd won in commanding fashion, taking 55 percent of the vote in the three-way race, to Senator Clinton's 27 percent and just under 18 percent for South Carolina native son John Edwards, who represented the neighboring state. Obama had taken 78 percent of the black vote and a quarter of the ballots cast by whites. His victory, which was much more substantial than the polls or the pundits had anticipated, and the storm of denunciation over Clinton's remarks in Columbia, seemed to touch a raw nerve for the man once dubbed the "first black president."

By nightfall, Clinton, who friends said had a longtime habit of calling at all hours, was burning up the phones, reaching out to old friends from the black political community, including members of the Congressional Black Caucus, with heated questions: Didn't they know him? Wasn't it clear that what was being said about him wasn't true? It was a plaintive call for support, and for resolve in his defense. He railed not just against Obama but against Clyburn, too, accusing him of taking sides against Hillary.

"It was probably the only argument I've had with Bill Clinton," one longtime Clinton friend said. "I said to him, 'You're reading this wrong. Clyburn is not trying to do anything to hurt you.'" But Clinton was not in any mood to hear his friend's assurances that Clyburn had merely assumed that Hillary would win in the end, and "didn't want the president to do or say anything that alienated black voters so that they weren't still highly energized to come out and vote for Hillary" when the primary contests were over.

But friends and veteran staffers of the former president said he took the negative reaction to his statements during the campaign, dating back to New Hampshire right through to that parking lot in South Carolina, as a personal affront, and that he was equal parts shocked and enraged at the criticisms, given what he saw as his long-standing commitment to engaging and aiding the African American community, using the power he'd managed to accumulate as a governor, and as president.

Clinton was still angry when he finally reached Clyburn, at close to 2 A.M. on Wednesday, January 27. The former president wasn't walking anything back. He vowed to fight anyone who meant to question his racial bona fides. It was part warning, part entreaty. Eventually, he also reached Jesse Jackson, who was traveling in India for a commemoration of Mahatma Gandhi. This time he had Congressman Meek on the call as he launched into a vigorous self-defense. Hadn't Jackson won South Carolina twice? *That was a fact, right?* And how could anyone construe his remarks to be racist? He blamed the Obama campaign for fanning the flames. Jackson agreed that Clinton's statement sounded factual, and he would soon say as much to the *New York Times*.

Rev. Sharpton appeared on ABC's *The View* later that day and told the hosts that the country was hearing "race charges" and "race-tinged rhetoric" rather than solutions to real issues. He said of the former president, "I think it's time for him to just be quiet. I think it's time for him to stop. As one of the most outspoken people in America, there's a time to shut up, and I think that time has come."

It was a great irony that a man who had so shrewdly and flamboyantly used the art of racial rebuke to propel himself into the White House, and his wife, who had traversed the ideological aisle to make common cause with the Kingian ideal that inspired her as a young girl, were now the ones being rebuked. The freighted history of race inside the Democratic Party and in American politics was not what this campaign was supposed to be about. But it was tearing away at Hillary's campaign.

In 1992, Clinton had scolded Sister Souljah as a way of letting white voters know he would speak up for the interests they believed the party had set aside. Barack Obama was now having a "Sister Souljah moment" at the Clintons' expense. And black Americans were standing up to the "first black president" and exposing the title's inherent lie, since no nonblack person, however close his ties to African Americans, and whatever tropes of blackness he was believed to display, could ever bestow the achievement of "first black president" on black America. In rebuking Bill Clinton, black America was coming to an unspoken understanding: "We *don't* owe the Clintons anything. We can have a real 'first black president' of our own."

ON THE MORNING AFTER THE SOUTH CAROLINA PRIMARY, THE *New York Times* ran an op-ed by Caroline Kennedy, daughter of John F. Kennedy, titled "A President Like My Father," in which she endorsed Barack Obama for president. News of the endorsement broke just after the polls closed on Saturday night, adding a further blow to the already fraught Clinton campaign. In the spring of 2007, Kennedy and her children had quietly slipped into the audience at the back of the ballroom at the Sheraton hotel in New York to hear the Democratic presidential candidates address the National Action Network's annual convention. Her children had heard all the excitement over Barack Obama and wanted to hear him for themselves. After the speech, she telephoned her uncle, Senator Ted Kennedy, to tell him Obama was worth paying attention to.

Bill Clinton had wanted nothing more for Hillary than an endorsement from Senator Kennedy. He had courted and plied the aging Massachusetts senator, but the Clintons' behavior in the preceding month had deeply disturbed Kennedy, who found the former president's statements to be dangerously racially divisive. The day after Caroline's op-ed ran in the *Times,* Senator Kennedy formally endorsed Obama as well.

A month later, John Lewis would also endorse Obama.

In Georgia, anger at the congressman's early endorsement of Hillary over Obama in October 2007 hit a fever pitch after South Carolina, and it grew even stronger after Obama won a commanding victory in Georgia on February 5, 2008. The Illinois senator bested Clinton 66 to 31 percent and won 90 percent of the black vote. In an exclamatory flourish, Obama beat Clinton by a margin of 3 to 1 in Lewis's district.

Soon afterward, Markel Hutchins, a thirty-one-year-old Atlanta attorney, announced that he would challenge Lewis in the next Democratic primary, slated for June. Hutchins accused the civil rights icon of being out of touch, having rejected the candidacy of the potential first black president. It was Lewis's first primary challenge in sixteen years.

Hutchins stood little chance against the sitting congressman and civil rights legend. But it was a shot across the bow to Lewis and other black politicians, raising the specter that Jesse Jackson Jr. had warned of in the early months of the campaign. Jackson had phoned fellow Black Caucus members as Obama's national cochair to warn them of the consequences of falling "on the wrong side of history," including public ridicule on black radio, particularly Tom Joyner's popular morning program, and of primary challenges. The warnings aggravated some senior members of the Obama campaign, and the candidate himself, who felt they went too far, but they stuck in the minds of black Congress members.

"The African American community had become so fiercely 'Obama' after South Carolina," said one black Hillary Clinton supporter, "that many of the [Black Caucus members] felt that even if they didn't know Senator Obama, they were gonna have to switch, because the black community was saying we're not tolerating anybody who does not support Obama."

Lewis had begun to waver, telling reporters he was considering switching his support. "In recent days, there is a sense of movement and a sense of spirit," Lewis told the *New York Times* on February 15. "Something is happening in America, and people are prepared and ready to make that great leap." He said he planned to cast his vote for Obama at the August convention.

Lewis made it official on February 27, explaining in a written statement that he wanted to be on the side of the people of his district, and that, "after taking some time for serious reflection on this issue, I have decided that when I cast my vote as a super-delegate at the Democratic convention, it is my duty . . . to express the will of the people."

Lewis was soon joined in shifting his endorsement by other Black Caucus members from Georgia, Virginia, Ohio, and New Jersey. On February 28, Lewis told a local Georgia TV reporter that his decision to abandon the campaign of his friend Mrs. Clinton was among the hardest things he'd ever done. He compared it to the march over the Edmund Pettus Bridge in 1965. "It was easier to walk across that bridge and face those state troopers and be beaten and left bloody," Lewis said. "This has been hard. This has been difficult. But there comes a time when you have to make a decision."

The Clinton campaign quickly issued a statement calling Lewis "a true American hero," adding, "we have the utmost respect for him and understand the great pressure he faced. And Senator Clinton enjoys incredibly strong support from superdelegates around the country from all regions and races."

Michael Eric Dyson later said, "There is no question that John Lewis was made to bow in front of the manifest power, will, desires, and agenda of the masses of black people. There was no more clear case of the black masses leading its leaders."

"To me, there's a historical consideration in this," Congressman John Conyers, who had served his Michigan district since 1965, told *The New Republic* on the day of Lewis's formal announcement. "How in the world could I explain to people I fought for civil rights and equality, then we come to the point where an African American of unquestioned capability has a chance to become president and I said, 'No, I have dear old friends I've always supported, who I've always liked.' What do you tell your kids?"

In March, Representative Sheila Jackson Lee, a Hillary supporter, was booed in her Texas district at a meeting of Baptist ministers, prompting Dyson, an Obama surrogate, to admonish the audience that the congresswoman had the right to make her own choice.

As the March 4 Ohio primary approached, Stephanie Tubbs Jones began to see prominent pastors and local politicians in her district who'd worked with her for years shifting their support from Hillary Clinton as they felt the rolling tide of black support for Obama's candidacy.

"The majority of the people of color in her district were very supportive of Obama," said Tubbs Jones's longtime friend Marcia Fudge, a former Cleveland-area mayor who succeeded the late congresswoman in the House. "Even those who had before said to Stephanie, 'If Hillary's your candidate I'm gonna be with you,' as the time got closer they were calling her and saying, 'I know I said I was gonna be with you, but I can't do it. I'm gonna endorse Obama.' And that was happening on a fairly consistent basis as the primary got closer."

TUBBS JONES REACTED BY DOUBLING DOWN ON HER SUPPORT FOR Hillary and by ramping up her public scorn for Obama. She became the campaign's fiercest attacker on cable news shows, questioning everything from Obama's experience to his record on the Iraq War. When Will Burns, a promising young former political staffer running for alderman in Chicago, and whose family had been members at Tubbs Jones's church since he was a child, addressed the congregation from the pulpit and praised Obama, Tubbs Jones refused to speak to him after service. But she also reaped a whirlwind of criticism, which friends termed abuse.

"She was called 'handkerchief head,' 'sellout' . . . you name it," said Fudge. "She always held her head up, she never let it get to her, but you could tell that it was wearing on her. At one point we were at a meeting and someone said to her, 'I hope you die.'"

"She was treated like she was treasonous," said Emanuel Cleaver, who in 1991 became the first African American mayor of Kansas City, Missouri, and who won election to Congress in 2004, eventually becoming the chairman of the Congressional Black Caucus. "But the more she was attacked, the more committed she became. She had had a relationship with the Clintons since she was a prosecutor. And she said, you guys can do what you want to do, but I'm not going to abandon somebody I've had a relationship with for over twenty years. And she didn't drop back."

"One of my campaign themes was 'vote your future, not your fears,'" Cleaver added. "And then to have black people so openly saying, if you don't vote for the black person, you are a handkerchief head . . . it was a tough time, [and] I think African Americans are going to look back on that and say, maybe we were a little thoughtless in what we were doing."

Obama wanted no part of it and grew increasingly irritated by surrogates who fanned the flames, including Jesse Jackson Jr., who found himself increasingly on the outside of the Obama inner circle. Soon, however, Junior would have another task, one that would grow more difficult over time: managing his father.

IT HAD BEEN JUST OVER A YEAR SINCE THE FIRST ARTICLES ABOUT Rev. Jeremiah Wright appeared in the *Chicago Tribune* and *Rolling Stone*. During that time, a steady stream of e-mails had poured into the in-boxes of reporters and voters alike: Obama's Chicago church "has a non-negotiable commitment to Africa. . . . *Notice too, what color you will need to be if you should want to join Obama's church . . . B-L-A-C-K!!! . . .* Doesn't look like his choice of religion has improved much over his (former?) Muslim upbringing. *Are you aware that Obama's middle name is Mohammed?* Strip away his nice looks, the big smile and smooth talk and what do you get? *Certainly a racist, as plainly defined by the stated position of his church! And possibly a covert worshiper of the Muslim faith, even today.* This guy desires to rule over America while his loyalty is totally vested in a Black Africa!"

As the campaign had picked up steam, so did the volume and outlandishness of the charges: Obama was not just a Muslim radical, he was actually *Kenyan born* and not a U.S. citizen at all. He was the product of a forty-seven-year conspiracy between his teenage mother and officials in Africa and Hawaii to place a Manchurian candidate in the seat of American power! And Michelle Obama hated white people and wrote as much in her Princeton thesis!

Moreover, white people weren't even *allowed* inside Trinity Church, which was little more than a "black separatist cult" allied with Nation of Islam leader Minister Louis Farrakhan! Some of the questions about Obama's faith had their origins in the Clinton campaign, and strategist Mark Penn's desire to dirty up the candidate who the Clinton team believed was getting a free ride from the media. Others swirled in the ideological basin of right-wing blogs, e-mail lists, and talk radio. Obama was forced into repeated assurances that he was a Christian and to distance himself from his provocative pastor.

The Wright revelations—snipped from selected sermons, bandied about on cable talk shows, and sometimes fueled by Wright himself—represented a growing danger to the campaign. After this, Obama instructed his staff to pull copies of every sermon Wright ever preached and review them, to insulate the campaign from further revelations. David Axelrod agreed, but the assignment fell by the wayside—an oversight Obama and his team would regret.

In March, after the *Wall Street Journal* ran an article that questioned whether speeches and sermons by Obama and Wright violated the church's tax-exempt status, ABC News' chief investigative reporter, Brian Ross, fielded a request from the executive producer of *Good Morning America* to do their own piece on the church and the Obama-Wright relationship. Ross asked his staff to purchase DVD copies of every Wright sermon they could find on the church's website.

What they discovered would upend the campaign.

In a sermon delivered five years earlier, on April 13, 2003, Wright engaged in a lengthy exposition that was profoundly political. "This government," Wright said, referring to the United States at its creation,

> lied about their belief that all men were created equal. The truth is they believed that all white men were created equal. The truth is they did not even believe that white *women* were created equal, in creation, nor civilization. The government had to pass an amendment to the Constitution to get white women the vote. Then the government had to pass an equal rights amendment to get equal protection under the law for women. The government still thinks a woman has no rights over her own body, and between Uncle Clarence [Thomas], who sexually harassed Anita Hill, and a closeted Klan court, that is a throwback to the nineteenth century, handpicked by Daddy Bush, Ronald Reagan, Gerald Ford, between Clarence and that stacked court, they are about to un-do *Roe vs. Wade*, just like they are about to un-do affirmative action. The government lied in its founding documents and the government is still lying today. Governments lie.

The sermon was expansive, reprising "the government lied" riff to include the Tuskegee experiments, the HIV virus, and the failure to find weapons of mass destruction in Iraq.

"Prior to the Civil Rights and equal accommodation laws of the government in this country," Wright thundered, "there was black segregation by the country, legal discrimination by the government, prohibited blacks from voting by the government [sic], you had to eat and sit in separate places by the government, you had to sit in different places from white folks because the government said so, and you had to be buried in a separate cemetery. It was apartheid, American style, from the cradle to the grave, all because the government backed it up."

"But guess what?" Wright intoned. "Governments change. Under Bill Clinton, we got a messed-up welfare to work bill, but under Clinton blacks had an intelligent friend in the Oval Office. Oh, but governments change. The election was stolen. We went from an intelligent friend to a dumb Dixiecrat. A rich Republican who has never held a job in his life; is against affirmative action, against education . . . against health care, against benefits for his own military, and gives tax breaks to the wealthiest contributors to his campaign. Governments change. Sometimes for the good, and sometimes for the bad."

Wright walked his listeners through a litany of American horrors: the theft of Native American land and the consigning of the remaining tribal nations to scattered reservations; the internment of the Japanese; and the enslavement of Africans:

> When it came to treating the citizens of African descent fairly, America failed. She put them in chains. The government put them in slave quarters. Put them on auction blocks. Put them in cotton fields. Put them in inferior schools. Put them in substandard housing. Put them in scientific experiments. Put them in the lower-paying jobs. Put them outside the equal protection of the law. Kept them out of their racist bastions of higher education, and locked them into positions of hopelessness and helplessness. The government gives them the drugs, builds bigger prisons, passes a three-strike law, and then wants us to sing "God Bless America." Naw, naw, naw. Not God Bless America. *God Damn America!* That's in the Bible. For killing innocent people. God Damn

America for treating us citizens as less than human. God Damn America as long as she tries to act like she is God, and she is Supreme.

For the first time, Obama's opponents had something to work with, something that could render the candidate's essential narrative of racial equanimity as an insidious lie. Conservative media kept up a steady drumbeat against the pastor, the church, and the Obamas, rife with insinuations that behind the Ivy League educations and the portrait of midwestern probity and nuclear family bliss lay a pair of stealth black radicals, waiting to ensnare white America in a bloody, political revenge fantasy.

(Months later, in July, this image would be lampooned on the cover of *The New Yorker,* which depicted a "fist bumping" duo clad in Muslim garb [Barack] and an Angela Davis–style Afro, combat fatigues, and machine gun [Michelle], with an American flag burning in the Oval Office fireplace and a picture of Osama bin Laden on the wall. The cover would produce torrents of outrage from liberals and African Americans, who saw no humor in the parody.)

With snippets of Wright's sermons in heavy rotation on YouTube and in Republican TV ads, Obama called a meeting with his senior staff. The politics called for Obama to say he was no longer associated with the church. But according to one former adviser, "It took a while to get there. And I think it says something about his loyalty and his respect for not just this man and this church in particular, but the institution of churches in general. It's like, 'I'm not gonna go there unless I have to.'"

Obama told a reporter from the *New York Times* that neither he nor Michelle was at the church on the day the sermon was delivered. The campaign issued a statement in which the senator condemned Wright's language. More news outlets called, in rapid succession. The Wright remarks had touched off a full-blown media frenzy.

Obama knew there was no way around the uproar. "If people have full information and decide on the basis of that information that I'm not qualified to be the president of the United States, then that's their decision," he told his team.

The candidate and his team decided to try for the long ball. They'd put the truth out there and let the chips fall where they may. Obama was a student of history, and he remembered that John F. Kennedy had faced a country deeply skeptical of his Catholicism, but rather than ignoring the public's angst, JFK had taken it head-on. The campaign announced that Obama would give a speech on race the next month, during a planned trip to Philadelphia to campaign for the Pennsylvania primary.

In Chicago, Wright's longtime friends and colleagues accused the media of distorting Wright's sermons and making a caricature out of a man who'd spent his life in the service of the poor, the locked out, and his country. Wright was a marine and navy veteran who as a young medic had monitored the intravenous drip as doctors at Bethesda Naval Hospital operated on President Lyndon Johnson's gall bladder, a memory revived in an interview with Wright in late April by Bill Moyers, a fellow member of the United Church of Christ denomination who at the time of the surgery was Johnson's press secretary. Wright had even received a personal letter of commendation from the president, dated December 19, 1966.

Trinity was unique inside the body of the United Church of Christ—a liberal, socially active, and mainly white denomination whose adherents have included John and John Quincy Adams, Julian Bond, Moyers, and Howard Dean. Wright, a gifted orator and son of a Baptist preacher, had joined the denomination after being unable to find a Baptist church home. He became the senior pastor of the church on Chicago's South Side in 1972.

Wright injected a fiery, Afrocentric vision into Trinity. Frequently dressed in a flowing dashiki, he preached "liberation theology," fixing on Jesus as a liberator of the poor and oppressed. Wright's flamboyance in weaving the fight for racial justice into the gospel left the church, and its most famous member, wide open to attack.

"They gave only a very selected part of that sermon," said Timuel Black, a Chicago historian and longtime civil rights activist who'd helped to organize the Chicago contingent of the March on Washington in 1963. "Wright started that sermon talking about the continuous injustices" inflicted by the government of the United States. "Louis Armstrong said in the 1950s that if the president of the United States couldn't help those children in Little Rock, then to hell with the United States," said Black. "I know that because I knew him. [He used] almost the same words as Wright. They only took the ending to try and demonize Obama."

Others pointed out that Rev. Martin Luther King Jr. denounced the Vietnam War in 1967 by calling the United States "the greatest purveyor of violence in the world today," and on the day he died, King was preparing a sermon he intended to deliver at Ebenezer Baptist Church in Atlanta, titled "Why America May Go to Hell."

But those arguments came to nothing.

On March 15, Tavis Smiley was speaking at a banquet in Miami Gardens, Florida. Though he began the speech by referring to Obama as "a friend of mine," he then laid into Obama for "throwing Jeremiah Wright under the bus" and said, "If you're gonna condemn the remarks every time someone shows you a transcript, you're gonna be throwing Negroes under the bus every week." He then added, "We ain't got to demonize 'us' to prove our loyalty to 'them.'"

Smiley questioned the Illinois senator's fundamental fealty to black people, reminding "all the Obama supporters in the room" that voting for Barack Obama for president wouldn't clear the historical slate over the country's racial past, "just as voting for Hillary won't do away with the legacy of sexism in America.

"The thing about the Jeremiah Wright situation that's so troubling to me is that you can't let other folk define the terms," Smiley said. "Some folk have learned to love this country 'because' . . . most of us in this room have learned to love this country '*in spite of,*' and we're still patriots. So I'm not gonna let Sean Hannity, or John McCain, or anybody else define for me what patriotism is. You've got to love your country enough to tell the truth." That, Smiley inveighed, is what it means to be a "free black man or woman."

Smiley closed his speech by asking an absent Obama: "If you're asking for black folks' support, do you love us? Will you tell the truth about our suffering?"

Cornel West was echoing this same critique in his own travels around the country. West had signed on as a surrogate to the campaign, but he continued to be such a consistent critic of Obama and the campaign that his fellow surrogate, Dyson, later said of West, "I don't think he understood what being a surrogate was."

Obama was being battered in mainstream circles for not being definitive enough in either explaining or severing his ties to Wright, while Smiley and West were beating him up for not being loyal enough to his black pastor, and by extension, to the cause of social justice for African Americans. Smiley's assault also came before he had even heard what the candidate would say in Philadelphia.

On March 18, Barack Obama delivered the speech he'd written—one the campaign hoped would be his final word on the Jeremiah Wright affair. Titled "A More Perfect Union," it was both a rebuke of Rev. Wright and an embrace of him. It explored Obama's own biracial, multicultural roots and the complex alchemy of America's racial history, from slavery through to Obama's own family, in a depth not previously heard in public discourse, let alone in a presidential campaign.

"I have already condemned, in unequivocal terms, the statements of Rev. Wright that have caused such controversy," he said. "For some, nagging questions remain. Did I know him to be an occasionally fierce critic of American domestic and foreign policy? Of course. Did I ever hear him make remarks that could be considered controversial while I sat in church? Yes. Did I strongly disagree with many of his political views? Absolutely— just as I'm sure many of you have heard remarks from your pastors, priests, or rabbis with which you strongly disagreed."

Obama called Wright's words "not only wrong but divisive . . . at a time when we need unity; racially charged at a time when we need to come together to solve a set of monumental problems—two wars, a terrorist threat, a falling economy, a chronic health-care crisis, and potentially devastating climate change; problems that are neither black or white or Latino or Asian, but rather problems that confront us all."

He spoke of his attraction to Trinity and its ministry, and praised Wright as "a man who helped introduce me to my Christian faith, a man who spoke to me about our obligations to love one another; to care for the sick and lift up the poor. He is a man who served his country as a U.S. marine; who has studied and lectured at some of the finest universities and seminaries in the country, and who for over thirty years led a church that serves the community by doing God's work here on Earth—by housing the homeless, ministering to the needy, providing day care services and scholarships and prison ministries, and reaching out to those suffering from HIV/AIDS."

Obama declared, "I can no more disown him than I can disown the black community. I can no more disown him than

I can my white grandmother—a woman who helped raise me, a woman who sacrificed again and again for me, a woman who loves me as much as she loves anything in this world, but a woman who once confessed her fear of black men who passed by her on the street, and who on more than one occasion has uttered racial or ethnic stereotypes that made me cringe."

"These people are a part of me," Obama said. "And they are a part of America, this country that I love."

The speech was widely praised and was compared to addresses by John F. Kennedy and Martin Luther King Jr., though Obama could never mollify his most adamant conservative critics, who accused him of throwing his white relations overboard in the service of his campaign.

In the end, Obama's message of racial balance won the day. The speech enraptured the media and cooled the histrionic coverage of the Wright sermons. At the same time, the uproar tightened Obama's grip on black public opinion, as the growing sense of siege against an African American candidate by the media, the Clinton campaign, and conservative critics drove even skeptical black voters to his defense.

On April 3, Hillary Clinton addressed the Wright imbroglio for the first time, telling the *Pittsburgh Tribune Review,* "You don't choose your family, but you choose what church you want to attend." There had been a debate inside her campaign over what to do with the Wright controversy. One faction, led by Mark Penn, wanted to use it, to try to keep the narrative and questions about Obama's "real beliefs" alive in the press by keeping surrogates actively talking about Wright and further exploring what went on inside Trinity. The other thought it should be allowed to develop on its own, arguing that it was Clinton's public image that took a hit when she swung too hard at Obama. In the end, the latter view prevailed.

On April 11, Smiley announced on the air that after twelve

years he was leaving the *Tom Joyner Morning Show*. No reason was given, but colleagues speculated it was due to listener complaints about Smiley's constant criticism of Obama, who by that time enjoyed the overwhelming support of black voters—and of Joyner.

Two months before, Smiley had again rejected Obama's proposals to send Michelle to the State of the Black Union symposium, being held in New Orleans that year. The feud with Obama now metastasized to the popular radio host, who privately and increasingly publicly was lashing his onetime protégé Smiley as little more than an Obama hater, whose envy at the senator's meteoric rise was getting the better of him. Smiley's constant critiques were also roiling Joyner's listeners, who were increasingly vocal in their objections to his continuing platform on the show. Joyner spent four hours every morning taking the pulse of black America on the air. He knew, intrinsically, that Smiley no longer had his finger on it. As a longtime friend of both men explained, "Tom made the decision that, 'Tavis, I just can't have you on anymore.' It wasn't just what Tavis was saying. The listening audience was calling in and saying, 'You shouldn't have him. This brother's lost his mind. Why is he so angry?' . . . So Tom said, 'Tavis, you're done.'"

Indeed, black Americans had arrived at a full turn, from utter skepticism of Obama—the Harvard-educated, exotic enigma from Chicago by way of Hawaii—to profound hope, that the dawn of a real first black president was near. Smiley's criticisms felt small and petty and too personal in that moment. He seemed to be throwing a roadblock in front of not just Obama but the very hopes of African Americans, seemingly because those hopes hadn't traveled through him and through other members of the black intellectual, political, and civil rights elite. There would be a time when criticism of Obama and his manner of dealing with black suffering would break into the open among black folk.

But in the spring of 2008, Smiley's attacks felt jarring and out of place. Moreover, Smiley was known to have close ties to the Clinton camp, and senior campaign members said they expected he would eventually become a surrogate for Hillary. This was known to Obama World at the time and further stained Smiley's critiques with the scent of self-interest.

Barack Obama was on the cusp of securing the Democratic nomination and making history, having fought Hillary Clinton state by state to an insurmountable delegate lead. He had vanquished the party's most formidable political family and mastered the contradiction between embracing the aspirations of black Americans and avoiding the pitfalls of racialized politics in America, wherein a black candidate was often little more than a candidate for black voters. And there was no turning back.

Smiley and West, and Bob Johnson and Cathy Hughes, and the luminaries that commanded the stage to proclaim the State of the Black Union, had become rhetorical Don Quixotes, tilting at black America's hopes and dreams. They had, in a very real sense, missed the Obama moment, and now the windmill was spinning on despite them. A prominent civil rights leader later recalled having warned Smiley: "You're standing on the tracks, in the path of a freight train, brother, and all you're focusing on is the conductor."

CHAPTER 7

Father's Day

How many in this generation are we willing to lose to poverty or violence or addiction? How many?

—Barack Obama, Father's Day speech at Apostolic Church of God in Chicago, June 15, 2008

BY JUNE 2008, SENIOR STRATEGIST DAVID PLOUFFE HAD CALCU-
lated that the campaign needed to focus Obama's attention on swing voters. As one member of the senior staff said, "[Plouffe] figured, 'We're going to be ninety-plus with African Americans, so we don't need to spend much time there. But it was tough to endure going through it, and the residual is still there. It's why you still have rough going with most of the CBC, the black mayors, legislators, and key influencers around the country who still don't feel they get that love."

As a result, black staffers on the campaign complained privately about not being able to make the senator visible, in the barbershops, beauty shops, and black churches, as he'd done in South Carolina. Even in that state, at one point senior campaign adviser Valerie Jarrett had to fly in to mediate the black campaign team's concerns about access to the candidate for black elected officials, churches, and audiences.

The campaign even faced a minirevolt by black newspaper and radio outlets that complained about scant media buys compared to the outlays for general and Hispanic media. But the senior staff was right not to be worried about a lack of drive among black voters. Black voters were more than energized for the November election. "Our problem," one senior Florida strategist said, "was how do we get *my* people, white people, to do the right thing."

Still, the needed shift to court the electorate outside the coalition of liberal white and black (and increasingly, brown) voters, the candidate's natural drive toward broad inclusiveness, and his tendency to deliver Old Time Religion to black audiences continued to rankle some members of black academia and media.

Obama's Father's Day speech at Apostolic Church of God, on the South Side of Chicago, a church he and his family visited a week after officially severing their ties to Trinity Church, drew a fresh round of criticism from those quarters when he chose to discuss fatherhood. He had been defined, in many ways, by his father's absence. His first book, *Dreams from My Father,* was an elongated discourse with a man he barely knew, but whose rejection of family life molded his son in countless ways. Obama was a deliberate, involved father to his daughters and in some ways, a puritan. He spoke from the pulpit about black men, encouraging them to fully embrace the responsibilities of fatherhood, and warned of the social consequences their absence was visiting on black communities.

Ron Walters, a renowned black history scholar and a professor of politics and government at the University of Maryland, flatly replied, "We're not electing him to be preacher in chief," and said Obama should "give more speeches about how he would help black communities." In the online editions of *Ebony* and *Jet*, writer Eric Easter accused Obama of making the kind of political calculation Bill Clinton had when he rebuked Sister Souljah.

"By choosing that moment to castigate Black fathers," Easter wrote, "some worry that Obama gave public voice to what white people whisper about Blacks in their living rooms and cemented his image as a post-racial savior at the expense of Black men. Whether that was Obama's intention or whether he just figured it was Father's Day so why not do the absent Father stump speech again is impossible to know, but the event smacked of calculated political expediency that troubled more than a few people."

Even Michael Eric Dyson was critical, writing in *Time* magazine, "On father's day [*sic*], when Barack Obama assailed absent fathers as a critical source of suffering for black communities, he sought two political advantages for the price of one. He embraced a thorny tradition of social thought that says black families are largely responsible for their own troubles. And he was seen in a black church not railing at racism but rebuking his own race. Obama's words may have been spoken to black folk, but they were also aimed at those whites still on the fence about whom to send to the White House."

The campaign was frustrated by the persistence of Obama's critics, though debates over the causes and cures for black suffering were not new, as in the divide between W. E. B. DuBois and Booker T. Washington, or the wrangling over the Moynihan Report.

"Clinton got the same grief," one consultant to the Obama effort said. "As much as there has been tension between these two families, I always felt in 2008 that Barack Obama was more the heir to the Bill Clinton legacy and the product of the Clinton legacy than Hillary was. The things about them: the single mothers in and out of their lives, [being] raised by grandparents. And the politics that [Obama] was talking about—the politics of getting over old divisions, and trying to find a way forward, were very reminiscent of what Bill Clinton was talking about when he ran in 1992."

But the unkindest cut of all would come from a familiar foil of Democratic campaigns: Jesse Jackson.

On July 9, Al Sharpton was in the middle of his radio show when his cell phone rang. A senior Obama campaign staffer was on the line, asking him to go to break, because the staffer needed to tell him something.

The campaign had a clip of Jackson during a commercial break on Fox News, with a still-open mic, whispering complaints about Obama's Father's Day address to Dr. Reed V. Tuckson, a health executive. Jackson could be seen and heard leaning in and telling Tuckson, "See, Barack's talking down to black people, on this faith-based . . ." and then, after trailing off, "I want to cut his nuts out."

Tuckson, the brother-in-law of one of the Obama campaign's legal advisers, Eric Holder (their wives were among the seven siblings of Vivian Malone Jones, who came to the nation's attention in 1963 as one of two black students to integrate the University of Alabama when that state's governor, George Wallace, made his infamous "Stand in the Schoolhouse Door"), had come to *Fox & Friends* to talk about the need for African Americans to get health screenings for high blood pressure; a conversation that quickly turned to the role of faith-based versus government institutions. His reaction to Jackson's words was silence and bewilderment.

The Obama campaign wasn't worried that Jackson could deenergize black voters, as he'd done to Walter Mondale and Michael Dukakis. But they weren't leaving anything to chance and wanted Sharpton to appear on some prime-time shows to refute Jackson's contention that the senator was belittling black men when he admonished them to be present in their children's lives. Sharpton had himself booked on shows with CNN's

Anderson Cooper and Fox News' Sean Hannity, with whom Sharpton at the time enjoyed a surprisingly cordial relationship. While Sharpton was in an SUV on his way to CNN's studios on July 9, Jackson called: "You know how these mics are," Jackson said, according to Sharpton aides. Sharpton reminded Jackson that he'd spent nine years hosting his own program on CNN and Sharpton couldn't understand how the "hot mic" moment had happened to a seasoned TV host.

"What are you doing?" Sharpton asked.

Jackson wanted his onetime protégé to remind people about his forty years of work in the movement. Sharpton agreed that those years deserved respect, and he had already defended Jackson in this way after it was revealed that Jackson fathered a child out of wedlock. And though people close to Sharpton believed he was tiring of coming to the aid of his onetime mentor, he felt a deep loyalty that endured despite their growing differences. But the comments, and their vulgarity, left little room for explanation.

On CNN, Sharpton defended Obama as "running for president for all Americans, not just African Americans," and admonished people not to "segregate Senator Obama and impose some litmus test that is unfair and unproductive."

After CNN, as Sharpton was on his way to his next interview, another call came in, this time from Hannity. "It's your favorite conservative," Hannity said, according to Sharpton aides, to which Sharpton replied that he was pulling up to the building and would be on time for the show.

But Hannity wasn't calling to ask where Sharpton was. He was calling to warn Sharpton not to get out too far on a limb in Jackson's defense. Only part of the hot-mic tape had been aired by then; Fox would likely release the next part the following week, Hannity warned, and it included Jackson referring to Obama with a racial slur.

Sharpton hung up and called Jackson, an aide said, and repeated what he had just heard. Jackson at first denied it, saying you can't believe everything you hear on Fox News. Sharpton did the interview, sparring during the show with Maryland's African American Republican lieutenant governor, Michael Steele, one of the three unsuccessful black statewide Republican candidates in 2006. Sharpton offered Jackson a measured character reference, saying the civil rights leader had "done a lot of great things in his life" and that "I think that anyone would say this is not his greatest moment." Sharpton staunchly defended Obama's speech. "I'm glad Rev. Jackson apologized," he said. "I'm glad Senator Barack Obama accepted. I happen to think that talking about parenting is not talking down to black people."

Jackson issued a written statement apologizing for the remarks and held a press conference reiterating his contrition. He declared that his support was "wide, deep, and unequivocal" for Obama's historic campaign, and the campaign publicly accepted his apology even as Jesse Jackson Jr. denounced his father's words in unsparing terms: "His divisive and demeaning comments about the presumptive Democratic nominee—and I believe the next president of the United States—contradict his inspiring and courageous career."

But within days, rumors were flying that dovetailed with Hannity's warning, that there was more to the tape than the outrageous clip already in circulation. Blogs and news websites were teeming with speculation, leaked by unnamed staffers at the conservative network, that producers for Bill O'Reilly's nightly program had left out of the edited version of the Jackson clip the fact that Jackson had called Obama a "nigger"—perhaps even a "no-good, half-breed nigger." After nearly a week of speculation, the transcript of the full clip, taken secretly by a production assistant, leaked in full to a media website. The transcript contained the full quote, in which Jackson said Obama was "telling niggers how to behave."

Jackson was forced to apologize again, and he did so profusely, in multiple cable television appearances and in a phone call to the campaign. He chalked the incident up to "trash talk" and insisted that it hadn't affected his relationship with Obama, which by that time was already paper-thin, having been damaged by Jackson's criticism a year earlier of Obama's reticence to jump headlong into the conflagration over the arrests of the six black students in Jena, Louisiana. Now a fresh controversy cemented Jackson's isolation from the campaign, which had never thought him particularly necessary, despite the web of history that connected Obama and the Democratic Party to Jackson like an umbilical cord.

Indeed, the legions of black voters activated by Jackson's 1984 and 1988 campaigns directly aided Bill Clinton's 1992 victory, and that voter registration model was in place for Barack Obama to build on in crucial southern states like Georgia, Virginia, and North and South Carolina.

Before Jackson, no black candidate had made a serious run at the presidency or achieved success beyond a small number of heavily gerrymandered congressional districts, plus a pittance of Senate seats. It was Jackson's showdown with the party, after carrying one-fifth of the popular vote into the 1984 convention but receiving fewer than 10 percent of the awarded delegates under the party's "winner-take-all" primary system, that made it possible for Obama to bleed away the vaunted Clinton advantage in the primaries and caucuses. Under the new rules of proportionality that he demanded as the price for throwing his full support to Walter Mondale in 1984, Jackson boosted his own take to more than 1,200 delegates four years later—second only to Michael Dukakis—on the strength of a thirteen-state romp in which he garnered nearly a third of the popular vote, an unprecedented achievement for an African American political candidate. Jackson's gains forced the party to change its very structure, even as his campaigns brought a generation of newly minted African American voters into the Democratic fold, literally creating the math that allowed Obama to overtake Hillary Clinton in 2008 by racking up small-state victories to claim the Democratic nomination despite losing big states like New York, California, and Florida.

Still, whatever his historical debt to Jesse Jackson, Obama had built a solid wall of black voter support without Jackson, and without the political infrastructure of black officialdom. This included local elected officials whose presence had vindicated the aims of the Voting Rights Act, and the political fixers, ward leaders, and voter turnout machines who'd helped elect black mayors in Philadelphia, New York, Baltimore, Seattle, Kansas City, and Denver; nearly all of them had backed Hillary Clinton. He'd done it without the broad support of the other civil rights leaders of Jackson's era, and over the objections of much of the black intellectual elite. For Obama, the support from black America had been belated, but it was organic and seemingly unshakable. He didn't need validation from the traditional wellsprings of black power to retain the loyalty of black voters. Simply by becoming the nominee, and surviving the crucible no black American had come close to traversing, he already had it.

And the campaign and the candidate knew it.

ON AUGUST 20, A WEEK BEFORE THE OPENING DAY OF THE DEMocratic National Convention, word reached Washington that Stephanie Tubbs Jones was dead. She had been spotted by a police officer the evening before, driving erratically through her Cleveland Heights neighborhood. When her car finally stopped, a police officer found the congresswoman breathing, but unconscious, behind the wheel. She had suffered an aneurism, causing her brain to hemorrhage. She died the next day at Huron

Hospital in her beloved Cleveland, as a stream of stunned political and religious leaders made a pilgrimage to the bedside of the fifty-eight-year-old firebrand.

Statements of shock and sympathy poured in, from Ohio governor Ted Strickland, from Tubbs Jones's fellow members of Congress, from the House leadership on both sides of the aisle, and from former presidents George W. Bush and Bill Clinton. Tubbs Jones's death was especially hard on Hillary Clinton, for whom the Ohioan had been a stalwart, fierce combatant for her campaign, but for far longer than that, a dear and faithful friend.

The convention was set to begin in Denver, and the Obama campaign was working assiduously to court Clinton supporters, and in the words of one senior campaign operative, "to make it easy for them to come home." Issues of women's representation and Hillary's voluminous campaign debt swirled around the negotiations, as did what roles she and Bill Clinton would play at the convention. There was little time for immediate mourning.

Even after Hillary's concession in June, when Obama returned to Washington with a small contingent of staff to meet with his colleagues in the Black Caucus, the mood had been tense. Obama had opened his remarks by suggesting it was time to get over the campaign and whatever raw feelings it had left behind and pull together toward November.

"Get over it?" Diane Watson of California, a Hillary supporter from early in the primary, shot back. "With all due respect, Senator, don't come in here telling me to get over it."

Obama aides said Tubbs Jones was among the most recalcitrant, with one attendee describing the congresswoman as "addressing Obama like her houseboy."

"We were stunned by the attitude," said one Obama aide. "We walked into that meeting, where ninety percent of the members who attended had been for Hillary and not for us. But the attitude in the room was not 'Oh, hey, you're the first black major party nominee, let's go off and make history together.' It was more, 'What are you gonna do to get our support?'" As for Obama, the aide said, "He didn't say it out loud, but his attitude was like, wait a second . . . ninety percent of your constituents just voted for me—why exactly do I need y'all?"

A sharp contrast was Obama's growing bond with John Lewis, whom a former Obama aide called "a statesman throughout" the campaign. "I thought that he handled the transition from the Clintons to Obama expertly," the former aide said. "And I think his humanity always came through, in every interaction. He got it. He helped to frame it, even when he wasn't with us. He's a special human being."

Beyond Lewis, bringing the Clinton and Obama camps together was a painstaking process. Below the leadership level, "the contact on the staff level was bitter," one Clintonite recalls, though that bitterness was rarely on display with the principals themselves.

"Fortunately, every organization gets their conditioning and approach from the top down," the former Obama aide said. "And though Barack was clearly personally wounded by how he had been treated by the Clintons, he was a pretty big guy. He was magnanimous, and he understood the challenges that were in front of him in the general election."

"He never got as giddy as the rest of us about beating the Clintons," said a former senior aide and longtime friend. "He understood that he was a black guy with an African name, running to make history in this country, and that it would get harder and not easier. And though sometimes he can make his political job harder than it needs to be by holding people at arm's length, in that period he knew that he had to pull people in. And he wanted to sue for peace immediately, and that filtered out through the leadership of the campaign, and folks got that we had to have a different tone."

With the fights over delegates behind them, the Obama

campaign prepared to welcome Hillary Clinton and the former president to Denver. They had not yet seen President Clinton's speech, and they wouldn't until just hours before it was delivered. The delay punctuated the nervous energy in the convention center, but the campaign anticipated a moment of clarifying unity for their party.

On August 27, Hillary Clinton interrupted the delegate roll call to place Barack Obama's name into nomination by acclamation, a dramatic touch meant to heal the party by sheer force of theatrical will. Earlier that day she had formally released her delegates to vote for the Illinois senator.

"On behalf of the great state of New York, with appreciation for the spirit and dedication of all who are gathered here, with eyes firmly fixed on the future, with the spirit of unity," Senator Clinton announced, bathed in a sea of supporters who flanked her at close quarters, nearly drowning her small frame in bodies and news cameras, "let's declare all together with one voice right here and right now that Barack Obama is our candidate, and he will be our president!"

She was seconded by Nancy Pelosi, who'd broken a glass ceiling of her own as the first female Speaker of the House. The convention hall broke into chants of "Yes we can!" while the O'Jays' "Love Train" exploded from the loudspeakers inside the Pepsi Center.

That night, Bill Clinton lauded Obama in his speech to the convention, declaring that "everything I learned in my eight years as president, and in the work I have done since in America and across the globe, has convinced me that Barack Obama is the man for this job." As a report in the London *Telegraph* exclaimed: "The Bill Clinton who had called Obama's opposition to the Iraq war a 'fairy tale,' who had belittled his success among African American voters, was gone. The venerated Democratic elder statesman was back."

And yet the former president remained personally bruised by the just-ended primary gauntlet. He had lost something tangible during the campaign, and he wanted it back. And he was keenly aware that fully supporting the Obama project—and being seen to do so robustly—was a key step along the path. If Obama was going to lose the White House, it would not be because of the Clintons.

Two days after the convention, the Clintons and Obama were together again, sharing the stage at Stephanie Tubbs Jones's funeral. Given the campaign's rancor, the invitation by Tubbs Jones's family was a further sign of a party yearning to repair its greatest breech since Teddy Kennedy challenged the sitting president, Jimmy Carter, to a primary showdown in 1980.

The service stretched on for four hours. Besides the Obamas and the Clintons, the sanctuary was filled with luminaries of the Democratic Party: Jill and Joe Biden, now the vice presidential nominee; Congressman Kendrick Meek, for whom Tubbs Jones had been like a godmother; Cleveland mayor Frank Jackson; and the legendary Louis Stokes, whom Tubbs Jones had succeeded in the House of Representatives.

Obama spoke of Tubbs Jones's hard work and unfinished business in the Congress, and praised her "grace and compassion." But he also alluded to Tubbs Jones's stalwart support of Hillary Clinton's candidacy for president. Obama said that when he'd met her on the trail, the congresswoman said simply, "'This is what it means to be a friend for me.' And all I could say is, 'I understand.'"

Hillary described Tubbs Jones as a fierce legislator, a proud member of the Delta Sigma Theta sorority, and a woman she wistfully remembered as "a real girlfriend" and sister, with whom she'd expected to share diet tips, recipes for southern cooking, and laughter as they both grew old.

Bill Clinton talked about Tubbs Jones's skill at cards, and at politics; but he also gave a nod to the history Obama was set to make in November. He spoke of a little boy, all of six years old, whom he'd met in Cleveland during the campaign. The boy had expressed surprise that Clinton could be a president and still be alive.

"I mean, you know, he thought the president was George Washington, Thomas Jefferson—he thought the president was a dead white guy," Clinton said, turning to Obama. "Thanks to you, Senator, no one will ever think that's the definition of a president again."

The assembled crowd cheered them all: the Clintons and the Obamas. The mourners stood on their feet as each one took the stage.

When the service was over, Hillary Clinton and Obama embraced, and he planted a kiss on her cheek.

Obama and Bill Clinton would meet again on September 11, for a tense lunch arranged by a Washington éminence grise whose connection to the elder man was as a friend, and the younger as a would-be mentor. The lunch consisted mostly of small talk, and a thick veil of tension hung overhead. As men, Clinton and Obama couldn't be more different. Obama seemed to revile the forced intimacy of politics—the constant gamesmanship, false joviality, and political glad-handing. Clinton reveled in it. As one mutual acquaintance put it, "If you play a round of golf with President Obama, at the end of the game you've played a round of golf. If you play a round with Bill Clinton, at the end of the game you've signed on to a whole bunch of policies, and promised to vote for things you hadn't even thought about when you got on the green."

Fundamentally, Obama couldn't give Clinton what he wanted most: a vow of public absolution from any taint of racism, on his part and Hillary's, for comments during the primary. Though Obama assured Clinton that neither he nor his supporters believed the former president was a racist, the senator, still flush with the thrill of the convention, wasn't sure Clinton could give him anything at all.

Clinton, celebrated as his generation's most able campaigner, had entered his wife's campaign unprepared for the age in which it was being fought. "I think [it was] because he was rusty," a former aide said. "He hadn't been in a national campaign in a full-time way since 1996, and campaigning had changed so much. . . . But now with Facebook and Twitter and the Internet and talk radio," one verbal slip and "it's all over the country. Just the speed and the velocity were unfamiliar to him."

And the Clintons, Bill Clinton in particular, were not prepared to wage a political fight against the very African American base that since his days as Arkansas governor had been endemic to the success of white Democratic politicians, particularly in the South. The percentage of registered black voters in the southern states had been growing at an increasing velocity since 1965, from 46 percent in the year the Voting Rights Act passed, to 66 percent by the time Jimmy Carter got elected in 1976, accelerating further after the massive voter registration campaigns of 1984 and 1988, and reaching just under 70 percent by 2008, second only to non-Hispanic white voters at 73.5.

"I think there were things that he said that were racially tinged that were more about the emotion of the moment, that kind of got away from him just because of the vortex he was in," the former aide, who is African American, said. "One thing I've never seen with Bill Clinton was any sense of second-class status about black people. But sometimes the language just gets away from you."

Friends said the Clintons took the attacks on African Americans who supported Hillary personally and were angered that longtime African American friends didn't feel free to stand by their preferred candidate without reaping retribution from within the black body politic, once it was clear that Obama was viable. And Bill Clinton in particular blamed the Obama campaign for fanning the flames of black anger against him.

But for all the pain and divisiveness of the campaign, people who knew both Bill Clinton and Barack Obama thought they had more commonalities than differences. Aides to both men believe they view the world from fundamentally similar vantage points, where pragmatism outweighs ideology, and that they cleave to the same formula for moving the country beyond its historic racial and class differences. "I think had Hillary not run, Bill Clinton would have been one of [Obama's] biggest supporters," the former Clinton aide said. "Obama was the embodiment of everything he wanted his own legacy to be."

The Clinton-Obama lunch resolved little between the two men, but both came away from it confident that they could get past their personal feelings to fight the real battle in November. Clinton wanted the victory almost as badly as Obama himself.

THE 2008 GENERAL ELECTION WAS THE CULMINATION OF THE demographic forces that had been reshaping the political parties since the 1960s, especially in the South.

In defeating Republican John McCain, Obama won a commanding 95 percent share of African American voters, a larger percentage than any Democrat since Lyndon Johnson claimed 94 percent in 1964, and far exceeding the mandate delivered by black voters to Bill Clinton in 1992. Black and Hispanic voter turnout was historic, setting records not seen since 1996.

Obama's triumph with black voters vindicated fifty years of civil rights organizing and dogged voter registration, fulfilling the great expectations of a community that had widened its gaze with every electoral advance, from Fannie Lou Hamer's rejection at the hands of the party of LBJ to Jesse Jackson's 1984 and 1988 convention gains to Clinton's multiracial bridge to the twenty-first century.

But Obama's sweep of African American votes was deeply rooted in his early success with white Democrats during the primaries. "He ended up getting solid black support *after* Iowa," voting rights expert David Bositis said. "He wouldn't have gotten the nomination without the strong black support that he got. But where he really defeated Hillary, was that he went in to the totally white caucus states—Idaho, Wyoming, Colorado, Montana, where Hillary and her people thought, 'There's no black people there, he's not going to win.'"

Obama's performance in the general election with white voters exceeded expectations for a Democrat. He won a larger share of white voters than any Democrat since Jimmy Carter in 1976, even as he fell well short of a majority, losing white voters nationwide, by 12 points—55 percent to 43 percent. But that deficit wasn't universal and it reflected the new, great racial cleavage in the electoral map. Obama won a majority of white voters in nineteen states, and got 30 percent or better in Arkansas, Tennessee, North Carolina, Kentucky, Virginia, West Virginia, and Florida, where he received 42 percent. Obama's candidacy was soundly rejected in the states of the Deep South. He got just 10 percent of the votes of white Alabamans, 11 percent in Mississippi, 14 percent in Louisiana, and between 22 and 26 percent in Georgia, Texas, and South Carolina.

And yet, for Democrats, even that was an improvement. Obama had outperformed John Kerry and Bill Clinton with white voters overall. But white voters were slowly shrinking as a share of the total electorate, making it increasingly possible for a Democrat to win the White House without a majority of them. (Obama himself would be able to regain the White House four years later without meeting his own high-water mark with the white electorate, and while losing catastrophically among white voters in the South.)

"Every four years the country as a whole becomes two percentage points less white working class," Bositis said. "So not only do you have the white population declining relative to the minority population, you have an increasing number of college-educated whites as opposed to working-class whites. So that the group that was dominant in the 1950s, who made up sixty percent of the vote, the white working-class voters, that percentage keeps getting smaller and smaller."

Indeed, in the four years since George W. Bush's reelection, 5 million new voters had gone to the polls, 2 million of them black, 2 million Hispanic, and 600,000 Asian. Obama got 8 in 10 of their combined votes. Meanwhile, the white voting population remained unchanged.

Obama's campaign also benefited from extraordinary support from an energized swell of young voters, those ages 18 to 29, a group already more ethnically diverse than any of the generations before them. They gave Obama 66 percent of their votes compared to 32 percent for John McCain. Those ages 30 to 44 chose Obama over McCain, 52 to 46 percent. And Obama even edged McCain among voters ages 45 to 64.

And despite all of the hand-wringing about the ultimate fate of Hillary stalwarts, particularly after McCain selected a woman, Alaska governor Sarah Palin, as his running mate, Obama triumphed with women, besting McCain 56 percent to 43 percent. The votes of women had been both overwhelming and decisive, since women made up 53 percent of the electorate. It was a stronger performance with women than by any presidential candidate since Ronald Reagan in 1984. The gender gap with McCain was on par with John Kerry's performance in 2004 and larger than McCain's advantage among whites.

Obama's victory was broad and deep. In the end, 69.5 million Americans voted for Obama, nearly 10 million more than chose McCain. Obama won a majority of independents, and nearly 10 percent of Republicans. The Democratic ticket won more than 70 percent of gay and lesbian voters and more than 70 percent of Latinos. Obama won surprise victories in North Carolina and conservative Indiana, whose proximity to his home media market in Illinois paid dividends. And he won the crucial swing states of Florida and Ohio, thanks in part to a flood of early votes. No Democrat had won a simple majority of the popular vote since Jimmy Carter. (Bill Clinton won three-way contests in 1992 and 1996.) And Obama bested John McCain by a decisive 7-point margin.

The election had turned on the nation's weariness with the Iraq War, the panic over the spiraling economic recession, and widespread fatigue with the Bush administration. The opportunity to elect the nation's first black president, who vowed to heal the divisions of North versus South, black versus white, and red versus blue, ultimately redounded to Obama's favor. The raw venom coursing through the McCain-Palin campaign rallies, where the name of the Democratic candidate was spat out like a curse—*Barack . . . Hussein . . . Obama*—and where accusations by Palin that the senator from Illinois was "palling around with terrorists," amid shouts of "traitor!", "off with his head!", and even "kill him!" repulsed white suburban voters, leading *Time* columnist Joe Klein to denounce the "sewage" emanating from the Republican campaign.

IN 2008 HILLARY CLINTON HAD SEEN HER POLITICAL DREAMS, and those of millions of women who had supported her, deferred. But Obama's victory had, in some sense, been hers, too, and Shirley Chisholm's, and Fannie Lou Hamer's; it was built on a foundation of hope and civic ambition that each of them had helped to build.

But the sense of euphoria, among Democrats and among some in the media, that the nation had turned an historic corner in its racial history, toward a post-racial future, was premature at best. Obama's moment in the sun of seeming racial reconciliation would be brief, and the transition to the darkness of racial division would be wrenching for the new president, for his party, and for the country.

CHAPTER 8

Post-Racial

The irony of Barack Obama is this: He has become the most successful black politician in American history by avoiding the radioactive racial issues of yesteryear . . . and yet his indelible blackness irradiates everything he touches.

—Ta-Nehisi Coates, "Fear of a Black President," 2012

THE OBAMAS ARRIVED IN WASHINGTON TO A CRUSH OF EXPEC-tations and excitement not seen in Washington since the Kennedys and the Reagans. The Washington press seized on the parallels to Camelot—from the couple's young children to the fashion designers clamoring to dress the new First Lady and the way black women adored and related to Michelle to the couple's celebrity friendships (George Clooney! Oprah! Jay-Z and Beyoncé!). But the media also fixated on echoes of Lincoln, on whether the "team of rivals" approach that brought Hillary Clinton into the cabinet as secretary of state would yield cooperation or conflict, and whether Obama's entry into the White House marked the beginning of the "post-racial" future that

Lincoln's bold stroke of emancipation was supposed to have set in motion so long ago.

Placing Hillary in such a powerful role sent a strong signal to women in the United States and abroad, and brought the public narrative of bitterness between Clinton World and Obama World to a close. But a sense of cynicism ran deep within parts of the Clinton camp. "He was brilliant for picking her," said one Clinton ally, calling the choice "from Obama's standpoint one of the smartest decisions he ever made," while adding sardonically, "What better way to shut down Bill Clinton for the next four years so he couldn't criticize you?" Friends cautioned the former First Lady to keep her eyes open. "Make sure you know him well enough that you can trust him, that he's not gonna throw you under the bus," one old Washington friend and longtime Clinton hand recalled telling her. "But boy, what a great opportunity to do good." Apparently, Bill Clinton had given her the same advice.

Hillary's ascension as a loyal member of the Obama cabinet brought an end to any lingering public anger at the former president among African Americans, who soon shifted their focus to the new administration and the possibilities it held for reversing the intense economic suffering of the country, which was being felt even more acutely by communities of color. For African Americans, the start of the new administration seemed like the beginning of a golden age.

Obama came into office with high approval ratings, across the racial divide. He installed a handful of African Americans in prominent, "first in history" positions in his administration. Patrick Gaspard was named political director; Susan Rice, the Clinton-era State Department official and a foreign policy adviser to the campaign, was appointed United Nations ambassador; and Eric Holder was nominated as attorney general. But no one in the administration would have more influence than Valerie Jarrett.

Jarrett was from the rarefied upper echelons of black Chicago, linked by birth to three of the city's storied black families: the Dibbles, the Bowmans, and the Taylors. Her father, James Edward Bowman, was a renowned geneticist. Her mother, Barbara Taylor Bowman, was a University of Chicago trustee whose father, Robert Rochon Taylor, once managed the historic Rosenwald Building on Forty-Sixth Street and South Michigan Avenue. It was built in the 1920s by Sears, Roebuck & Company president Julius Rosenwald as affordable apartments for middle-class black Chicagoans in the segregated city, and was once frequented by the likes of W. E. B. DuBois, Langston Hughes, and Quincy Jones, who as a child lived in the building, where his mother became the manager, and his father was a carpenter. Taylor rose to become the first African American to lead the Chicago Housing Authority, lending his name to what would become a notorious sprawl of housing projects on the city's South Side. Jarrett's great-grandfather Robert Robinson Taylor, the son of a white slave owner and a black mother from Tuskegee, Alabama, was the first black graduate of the Massachusetts Institute of Technology. Her cousin Ann Dibble is married to civil rights icon, Clinton friend, and urbane elder statesman Vernon Jordan.

A veteran of the Daley and Harold Washington administrations in Chicago, Jarrett, as Mayor Richard M. Daley's deputy chief of staff, had in the early 1990s hired the then Michelle Robinson, who brought her fiancé, Barack Obama, along to their first dinner to size Jarrett up. She became a friend and mentor to Michelle, and increasingly an adviser and friend to Obama as well. She introduced the couple to Martha's Vineyard, the summer vacation haunt of upper-middle-class black families for a century, where their children could escape the world of segregation and isolation and be together on Inkwell Beach in quiet Oak Bluffs, among their racial and social peers.

The Obamas built their own alliances in Chicago, to be sure.

"Michelle Obama's friendships and connections got that man into power," one close observer of the couple said. Among her circle were the children of Rev. Jesse Jackson and John W. Rogers Jr., who was the son of Jewel Lafontant and Tuskegee Airman John Rogers Sr., ex-husband of the first family's social secretary, Desiree Rogers, and a key Obama fund-raiser and friend. And Barack Obama had, over time, cultivated a multiracial circle that included judges and professors at the University of Chicago, his state senate mentor, Emil Jones, and elements of Chicago's mon-eyed class. Judge Abner Mikva, a former legal counsel to President Clinton, tried to hire Obama out of law school; Chicago billionaire Penny Pritzker became a friend when her children played basketball at the YMCA where Michelle's brother was the coach; and Bettylu Saltzman, the daughter of a shopping mall tycoon who was also part owner of the Chicago Bulls, sought Obama out after meeting him as he stumped for Project Vote, while she was volunteering on Bill Clinton's campaign. Saltzman believed he had what it took to become the first black president and she financially supported his subsequent runs for office.

But Jarrett opened the door to a wider world of important Hyde Park donors and political advisers who were key to Obama's success once he decided to run for office. She became a key adviser on his presidential campaign, where she was placed in charge of "constituency groups"—a political euphemism for the minorities, the LGBT community, and other out-groups inspired by the Obama project, but who often found themselves on the back burner in Democratic campaigns that for decades had placed more emphasis on winning over blue-collar white Democrats and independents. Black, Latino, and gay staffers relied on her to intervene with the senior staff in Chicago when their complaints that the senior leadership was too reticent to take the campaign into the heart of the black community or to spend money with black media and political consultants fell on deaf ears.

She arrived in Washington as senior adviser to the president, and the one member of the administration with equal influence in the East and West Wings. Other top staffers, including Rahm Emanuel, Obama's new chief of staff, and later William Daley, his successor, were made to understand in no uncertain terms that, to paraphrase one former Obama cabinet member, Valerie reported to no one but the president. "She's a family member. She's not a staffer," the former cabinet member said. "And I think people underestimate her."

Jarrett occupied a rare space, as both friend and gatekeeper, "testing the waters" for Obama on policy matters and enjoying the couple's complete trust. The position didn't always make her popular inside the White House, particularly with Emanuel, a fellow veteran of Chicago's bare-knuckle politics whose irascible manner made for caustic moments in the West Wing and on Capitol Hill. Jarrett's closeness to the family even confounded some longtime political insiders in Chicago, who groused that Jarrett was more Daley acolyte than consummate insider within traditional black political circles, and that in her role as granter and denier of access, she was freezing out Obama's black Chicago allies, too.

Even people who had been close to Obama in Chicago and to the campaign were being told, including by Barack Obama, "if you need anything, just call Valerie." In addition to her policy portfolio, Jarrett was tasked with interacting with the governors and with black political, media, and civil rights leaders. Said one longtime Obama ally from Chicago of the indirect route to conferring with the new president: "It was a waste of time."

If the arrangement was painful for some of Obama's old allies, it proved helpful for some of the new. Sharpton, whose bona fides with the new president, and with Jarrett, were solid, and black media figures such as D.C. radio veteran Joe Madison and then CNN host Roland Martin, the former editor of the black *Chicago Defender* weekly newspaper, quickly found a comfortable seat at the table. But others, including members of the Congressional Black Caucus, felt frozen out. They had waited more than a decade for the Democrats to return to the White House, and many never believed they'd see a black president in their lifetimes. Jarrett was often the first point of contact for Black Caucus staffers, and sometimes the last, as entreaties for face time with the president went nowhere. Emanuel was viewed by many as dismissive and the president as distant. The new White House was viewed as opaque by many on Capitol Hill, and in particular by Black Caucus members and civic leaders who had sided with Hillary Clinton in the Democratic primaries.

Worse, for some, was the fact that while the administration was filling up with veterans of the Clinton administration, including people like Rice, Gaspard, and Holder, who'd broken ranks with the Clintons during the Democratic primary, black Clintonites who'd stuck with the First Lady were being passed over.

"The perception was that the white Clinton people were brought in, while the black Clinton people felt that they were given a scarlet letter," said one prominent African American civic leader. "They felt that the white Clinton people—Larry Summers, Hillary Clinton, Rahm Emanuel—a whole host of these people got . . . well . . . absolution."

The Obama team saw it differently, believing that early tensions with the Black Caucus and with black civic leaders stemmed not from presidential snubs, but from a dearth of personal, staff-level relationships.

"None of them really knew our camp," one former Obama adviser said. "It was a challenge managing expectations from the community and elected leaders and influencers because their reference was always the Clintons and how good they were at team building."

Others on the Obama team viewed the frayed relationship as stemming from lingering resentment toward, not from, the incoming administration, particularly among members of the Black Caucus.

"The first year in the White House, they didn't seize the moment in the way that I thought they could have," said another ex–White House staffer, referring to Hillaryites within the Black Caucus. "There was never a coherent approach to how they handled the Obama moment, to how they pivoted as a group."

Indeed, with a handful of exceptions, members of the caucus felt an untenable distance from the new president, and that caused them to be alarmed about issues that were front and center in their districts—from the alarming rates of black poverty and unemployment in black communities to gaps in educational attainment and racial profiling by police. Many believed they were confronting the ultimate historical irony: that even with a black president and a euphoric black body politic, African Americans in Congress had precious little influence at 1600 Pennsylvania Avenue.

Washington veterans began to suggest to the new White House team, and to the president, that they reach out to caucus members, but the entreaties seemed to go nowhere. And members complained that Emanuel showed open disdain, not just for the Black Caucus, but for Democrats on the Hill, and particularly the party's liberal wing. This new administration appeared uninterested in the hand-to-hand grappling with Congress that Bill Clinton had so reveled in, and that had produced important legislation that could be felt on the streets.

Part of this simply was the president's personal style. Obama had no intention of going out of his way to court the denizens of Capitol Hill. The days of frequent golf outings with members and dinner invitations to the White House or to Camp David, common in the Clinton years, were not going to be repeated.

The kind of glad-handing that fuels Washington politics was just not in Obama's personality. "And that filters down to the staff," said one former staffer. "No one wants to be the skunk at the garden party pushing him to do these things, even if at the end of the day it would help to get the work done."

The Black Caucus met for the first time with the new president in late February 2009. It would be a year before the major national civil rights leaders would do the same, though Jarrett's office continued to be a valve for contact. Some significant donors to the campaign found their calls going unreturned.

"I talk to a lot of people who gave a lot of money" to the Obama campaign, one D.C. insider said. "And they tell as many tales of woe, of giving a whole bunch of money and not being able to get on the phone, not being able to get a picture with [the president], not being invited to the White House, never being invited to a State Dinner . . . the stories just go on and on. Take the chair of the Democratic Party of—pick a state—and you run into them and they say, 'I haven't been in the White House since Bill Clinton left.'"

Left most conspicuously on the outside were Obama's harshest critics during the campaign, most notably Rev. Jesse Jackson. Some blamed the rift on the older man's tic of criticizing Obama's approach to African Americans during the campaign. Others said Jackson had been reluctant to acknowledge Obama's ascendancy as a genuine movement. Sharpton surmised that civil rights leaders might get to have a special relationship with just one president. DuBois and William Monroe Trotter had their parries with Woodrow Wilson over the scourge of lynching; Walter Francis White, T. Arnold Hill, and Mary McLeod Bethune engaged with Franklin Roosevelt; Dr. King and other civil rights leaders had their jousts and collaborations with Kennedy and Johnson. For Jackson, for better and for worse, his presidential relationship had been with Bill Clinton.

And though Obama held a level of respect for Jackson, aides said he simply didn't give the relationship much thought, though they said others, including Jarrett, did keep accounts.

"Valerie is very much a protector of Obama's dignity," a former staffer said. "And so with Jesse Jackson, where some folks would want to say, 'let's let him back in,' she's like, 'no, you can't say you want to cut his nuts off and then come in.'"

The Obama team was not anxious to make peace with critics who they didn't think had a broad enough standing to move significant masses of African Americans away from Obama or who they felt had been disrespectful or extreme. That left black critics like Cornel West and Tavis Smiley on the outside, too.

Bill Clinton's approach toward them would have been very different, former aides to both presidents said. He would have told them off in colorful fashion and then listened to what they had to say. But according to one early adviser, "The new-school way is deafening silence. In the new-school way, nobody talks to Tavis."

The administration had little time to worry about hurt feelings. They'd inherited an economy in free fall, including collapsing housing and banking markets, and an opposition party that was determined from the beginning to undermine the new president at all costs, and to cut short the nation's euphoria at having crossed a key Rubicon in its racial history. Vice President Joe Biden would later say that more than a half dozen Republican colleagues told him, as early as the transition, that their marching orders from Senate Minority Leader Mitch McConnell were specific and damning: no cooperation with the administration, on anything, ever. Biden recounted to writer Michael Grunwald that Republican friends had described it as "our ticket to coming back."

The administration spent most of the first year focused on two goals: wresting the economy from the depths of the Great

Recession and getting a universal health-care bill through Congress; the latter goal was met with deep skepticism by Emanuel but fully supported by Jarrett, who viewed it as key to Obama's governing as the man he'd run to be.

But health care and the economy were not destined to be the president's only first-year legacies. It wouldn't be long before the new president and the country would be reminded that the notion of a "post-racial" America, and one in which the first black president's race was incidental to the conduct of his office, was a beautiful delusion, one that had been exposed long before Barack Obama and his family moved into the White House.

DATING BACK TO THE EARLIEST DAYS OF THE CAMPAIGN, A DARK vein of resistance to Obama's candidacy due to his race arose periodically. There was former Democratic vice presidential candidate Geraldine Ferraro's comment that Obama would never have been in a position to defeat Hillary Clinton had he not been black. Republican congressman Geoff Davis of Kentucky said, "That boy's finger does not need to be on the button." A California Republican women's group issued gag currency they called "Obama bucks"—food stamp send-ups with Obama's head on the body of a donkey, surrounded by spare ribs, Kool-Aid, and fried chicken. And Buck Burnette, a University of Texas Longhorns lineman, updated his Facebook status after the election to declare: "All the hunters gather up, we have a nigger in the whitehouse [sic]."

Michelle Obama, so celebrated in the national press, was subjected to the basest racial distortions. She was depicted in online memes as an unfeminine brute and beast, derided in conservative columns as a dangerous, "whitey"-hating, America-loathing radical. The term "Obama's baby mama" was used on Fox News, and National Review called her "Mrs. Grievance."

The attacks didn't end with the election, and even the Obama girls, just seven and ten years old when their father took the oath of office, wouldn't be spared. But the new president found himself under a microscope calibrated to detect any hint that he was reacting to the slings and arrows of national politics from the perspective of a black man. The attacks on him and his family had to be borne with a special type of dignity. Every president before him had borne some measure of ridicule, parody, and hatred, the reasoning would go. Why not him? Why should attacks on him be especially scrutinized for racist intent?

Barack Obama had burst onto the national stage by "transcending" race and by practicing consistent and convincing racial ecumenism. The onus was on him and his African American first family to represent America's racial progress and to be the *Cosby Show* Huxtables in real life. Even Mrs. Obama's mother, Marian Robinson, who in 2009 moved from her Chicago home to the White House to help care for the couple's young daughters, a move not without precedent, from the mother-in-law of President John Tyler to the father-in-law of Benjamin Harrison to multiple family members of Andrew Jackson, was under constant scrutiny.

One false policy move, untoward word, or flash of anger would snap the hair trigger of skepticism about whether the *real* first black president truly did represent all Americans, and not just "his own people." Any black politician elected outside a safely black district knew "the Rules" for staying racially neutral. They had been around for decades, though this was the first time they were being applied to a president of the United States.

One month into the nascent administration, Eric Holder broke the Rules.

On February 18, a cartoon in the *New York Post* lampooned the nearly $1 trillion economic recovery package, rejected by Republicans and passed almost entirely by Democrats. The *Post* cartoon referred to the horrific news story of a Connecticut woman who had been mauled by a pet chimpanzee. In the cartoon, two police officers stand over the body of a blood-spattered, dead primate. "They'll have to find someone else to write the next stimulus bill," the caption read.

The cartoon drew immediate outrage as it flew across the Internet. Rev. Sharpton issued a statement denouncing it as "troubling at best, given the historic racist attacks [on] African Americans as being synonymous with monkeys." New York governor David Patterson called on the paper to explain. The *Post*, owned by conservative mogul Rupert Murdoch, whose international media empire includes Fox News, was a longtime opponent of Democrats, local and national, and had sparred with Sharpton for decades. Its editor vigorously defended the comic as mocking the stimulus package and not the president. But for African Americans, it read as the kind of bestializing that black men and women had been subjected to for centuries, written off as comedy to many on the right, but touching a deep vein of ugly historic memory in black minds and souls.

On the day the cartoon ran, Holder was giving his first Black History Month address to the staff at the Justice Department. His speech touched on historic memory, too, and on the inability of black and white Americans to confront it equally.

Holder, a former judge and deputy attorney general during the Clinton administration, had joined other Clinton veterans, such as David Wilhelm, Susan Rice, and Patrick Gaspard, in choosing Obama over Hillary in the Democratic primaries. He became a senior legal adviser to the campaign of a man he'd met roughly a year before.

UNLIKE OBAMA, WHO PROCEEDED ON MATTERS OF RACE WITH cautious deliberation, Holder, the son of Barbadian parents who raised their two boys in the mostly black, middle-class suburb of Elmhurst, Queens, had the bearing of an activist. Ten years older than Obama and with a New Yorker's pugnaciousness, he often recounted the time he was stopped by police while sprinting through an upscale neighborhood with a friend, trying to make the start of a movie. At the time, he happened to be a federal prosecutor.

Holder's Justice Department speech was expansive, touching on the fiftieth anniversary of the Supreme Court decision in *Brown v. Board of Education,* integration, affirmative action, and the broad civil rights movement. He spoke of his late sister-in-law, Vivian Malone Jones, one of the two black students to face down Governor George Wallace to integrate the University of Alabama in 1963. And he talked about the need to heal communities long scarred by crime and mistrust with police. But Holder began his speech with a damning assessment of the state of interracial dialogue; it landed like a fully armed rocket when it reached the national media.

"Though this nation has proudly thought of itself as an ethnic melting pot," the attorney general said, "in things racial we have always been and continue to be, in too many ways, essentially a nation of cowards."

Holder went on to explain that unresolved issues of race remain front and center in America's politics and culture, though "we, average Americans, simply do not talk enough with each other about race. It is an issue we have never been at ease with and given our nation's history this is in some ways understandable. And yet, if we are to make progress in this area, we must feel comfortable enough with one another, and tolerant enough of each other, to have frank conversations about the racial matters that continue to divide us."

Within hours, conservative blogs were denouncing Holder and trying to use his presence as the attorney general and Obama's as president—and even Martin Luther King Day—as proof that the nation had paid its racial debts. But these were some of the same voices insisting that a monkey cartoon lampooning the first black president was just a monkey cartoon.

The White House was caught off guard by the outcry over Holder's speech. The new administration had no intention of wading into racial conflict, preferring to keep the president focused on the needs of all Americans, and principally on the economy. Anything that "racialized" the Obama presidency was unwelcome in the West Wing.

Asked about Holder's comments by *New York Times* reporter Helene Cooper in early March, Obama said that had he been advising his attorney general, "we would have used different language." Obama concurred with the underlying point of Holder's speech, saying, "We're oftentimes uncomfortable with talking about race until there's some sort of racial flare-up or conflict," and as a country, "[we] could probably be more constructive in facing up to sort of the painful legacy of slavery and Jim Crow and discrimination." But Obama was quick to pivot to a focus on the nation's progress. "I'm not somebody who believes that constantly talking about race somehow solves racial tensions," he said. "I think what solves racial tensions is fixing the economy, putting people to work, making sure that people have health care, ensuring that every kid is learning out there. I think if we do that, then we'll probably have more fruitful conversations."

WHATEVER THE PRESIDENT'S ANNOYANCE OVER THE BLUNTNESS of the attorney general's words, Holder had exposed a truth that to black Americans seemed both obvious and glaring: their countrymen too often ease their discomfort over racial disparities by ignoring the subject of race altogether, except on those occasions when it sputters and spills out in ugly e-mails and Facebook posts, gag food stamps with Barack Obama's picture on them, ugly rally signs, and unfortunate newspaper cartoons. His speech earned him widespread acclaim among African Americans, who quickly took notice of the attorney general. And Holder had strong supporters inside the White House, including Gaspard and Jarrett and the president himself. He had no intention of walking his comments back. On the contrary, Holder would continue to be a lightning rod.

From the start, the new attorney general had stated his determination to revive the Justice Department's Civil Rights Division, which had become moribund and dispirited under the previous administration. There had been large numbers of resignations as pressure mounted to pursue mythic voter fraud and what many longtime division lawyers viewed as politicized, partisan cases. Holder put an end to that quest in a bid to revive what he saw as the department's original mission: safeguarding voters from impediments to access to the polls, vigorously responding to alleged violations of the Voting Rights Act as the country headed toward a new census and a fresh round of federal and state gerrymandering. An admirer of Nicholas Katzenbach—Robert Kennedy's successor who as attorney general brought federal troops to Alabama and personally faced down Governor George Wallace to break the infamous "stand at the schoolhouse door"—Holder saw his role as grounded in Katzenbach's example: protecting vulnerable citizens from the caprice of state power by bringing federal authority to bear.

Holder had his critics on the left who thought he and the president did not vigorously pursue the titans of Wall Street who had brought about the collapse of the economy. They also blamed him for not surmounting congressional opposition to the closing of the prison camp at Guantánamo Bay, and for his failure to secure federal prosecution for accused terrorists imprisoned there. Those criticisms were a source of deep frustration for Holder, who determined early on that there were no strong cases to bring against Wall Street bankers. But for civil rights leaders, he was an immediate friend.

By the summer of 2009, Democrats had claimed their sixty-vote majority in the Senate, after resolving the seat in Minnesota, where a lawsuit by his opponent forced Al Franken to wait until July 7 to take his seat, and once Biden and Obama's seats in Delaware and Illinois were filled (the latter ended in the indictment of the state's governor). However, Republicans had honed their strategy of total obstruction, calling upon the same device segregationist Democrats once used in order to stall civil rights legislation: the filibuster. It was in those months that the health-care bill—an Obama priority since the campaign—was making its way, slowly, painfully, and publicly, through the Senate.

The president's opponents soon had the perfect vehicle to exploit the tortured process for political gain.

The day after Holder's "nation of cowards" speech, a former hedge fund manager and commodities trader from Chicago, Rick Santelli, launched into an extended rant on CNBC, denouncing what he saw as Obama's mortgage bailout, in which the financial industry would be forced to write down the amounts due on mortgages that had ballooned far beyond the value of the homes they were tied to. The policy, called "cram down," had been a key request of the administration from progressive and civil rights groups. The big banks, not surprisingly, were vehemently opposed.

"How many of you people want to pay for your neighbors' mortgage that has an extra bathroom and can't pay their bills? Raise your hand!" Santelli raged, vilifying "deadbeat" home-owners. "President Obama, are you listening!?"

The rant went viral, punctuated by Santelli's call for a July Fourth "Chicago tea party." The swelling opposition from the Right to everything the president was doing, from financial reform to health care, now had a name. And while the origins of the "tea party movement" had roots in Chicago's libertarian movement dating back to 2002, Santelli popularized it and aimed the laser straight at Obama.

Coincidentally, the president's chief economic advisers, Timothy Geithner and Larry Summers, were counseling the White House away from the actions the financial industry was so up in arms about, and as a result the president was getting heat from the Left because he seemed to avoid progressive solutions to the housing crisis. Liberals were learning that they may have underestimated the extent to which Obama's pragmatism outweighed his idealism.

As the White House and Democrats in Congress moved toward passage of the health-care bill, the road got increasingly ugly as town hall meetings turned raucous. Tea party protesters claimed the president was secretly planning "death panels" to discard the elderly and disabled, cried "socialism!" and carried homemade signs equating Obama with African witch doctors and Adolf Hitler.

In the midst of it all, the president followed Holder into the thicket of racial outrage.

On July 16, a Cambridge, Massachusetts, police officer arrested Henry Louis Gates Jr., an Obama friend and the head of Harvard's Department of African and African American Studies. Gates had accidentally locked himself out of his home and was attempting to gain entry when a neighbor called 911 to report a possible break-in. Gates became angry when Sergeant James Crowley didn't believe he lived in the home and removed him from his porch in handcuffs. And though the Cambridge Police Department later dropped disorderly conduct charges against the professor, the officer refused to apologize, saying he had followed proper procedures. The local police union stood firmly behind Crowley, even as Gates threatened to sue.

At a July 22 prime-time press conference, Obama responded to a question about the incident. "Now, I don't know, not having been there and not seeing all the facts, what role race played, but I think it's fair to say, number one, any of us would be pretty angry; number two, that the Cambridge police acted stupidly in arresting somebody when there was already proof that they were in their own home; and, number three, what I think we know separate and apart from this incident is that there's a long history in this country of African Americans and Latinos being stopped by law enforcement disproportionately. That's just a fact."

President Obama was speaking off the cuff, and as Gates's friend. But he had broken the rules of comportment, particularly for a man who had billed himself as a practitioner of racial healing, not racial confrontation. His comments set off an immediate firestorm. Conservative commentators accused the president of race-baiting and of an outrageous attack on law enforcement. For the first time in his political career, Barack Obama was discovering what it was like to be Al Sharpton.

The speed and vehemence of the uproar shocked the White House. They had come to Washington prepared to fight on the familiar ground of spending and taxation, and to engage in the battles that were necessary to pass health-care reform. But Obama had not intended to light any bonfires on race as president. In an attempt at healing, a "summit" was hastily arranged for the next week, in which Crowley and Gates would sit for a photo opportunity in the Rose Garden with the president and Vice President Biden, who during the fall campaign served as a key validator for Obama with white, blue-collar voters. The goal of this "beer summit," as it came to be known, was to create a patina of national healing. The "teachable moment" was punctuated by exhortations about "disagreeing, without being disagreeable."

As political theater, it was pure Barack Obama—the very picture of midwestern moderation and probity. But the damage was already done. A Pew poll taken five days after the press conference showed that Obama's approval rating among white Americans had slipped from 53 percent to 46 percent, while the approval of nonwhite and/or Hispanic Americans *climbed* 11 points, from 63 to 74 percent.

African Americans thought Obama had spoken truth to a power many found onerous and omnipresent: the police. He'd also exposed the reality of racial profiling, even of a man who'd done everything right, becoming educated and successful and affluent. And Obama had done the exposing from the pulpit of the presidency, which gave his exhortations a power they had never known. It was cathartic, particularly coming from a man who up to this point had been so measured in his public pronouncements on race.

The Pew poll also found that white Americans blamed Gates more than Crowley for the incident by 7 percentage points, and overwhelmingly disapproved of the president's handling of the incident, by a margin of 2 to 1. Of those white Americans who heard a lot about the incident, the level of disapproval was 70 percent versus 23 percent approval. It was just six months into his presidency, and Obama's racial honeymoon was over. His opponents on the right felt this proved that Obama was no racial healer. He was just another "race hustling" divider, who never had any intention of being everybody's president.

The White House team absorbed a lesson that Bill Clinton had learned a generation earlier with the uproar over his "apologies" during his African trip: For even a "post-racial" president, touching the electrified rail of race bears exquisite peril. It was a lesson that would reverberate within the administration for years to come.

ON AUGUST 26, 2009, SENATOR EDWARD "TED" KENNEDY DIED, ending a life and career that were the stuff of Greek tragedy and Democratic Party legend. The last of the Kennedy brothers, whose every movement had enthralled the national press for fifty years, he had been preceded in death by his sister, Eunice

Kennedy Shriver, by just two weeks. With his death, Democrats lost a portion of their collective soul.

Kennedy had been perhaps the most important of Obama's endorsers during the campaign, draping the young senator in the mantle of Camelot so badly desired by the Clintons and making a triumphant appearance at the Democratic convention to reprise his most famous words from the gathering in 1980: that "the work goes on, the cause endures, the hope still lives, and the dream shall never die." Kennedy had long been a champion of the kind of universal health care Obama was seeking. Now, as president, Obama would give the eulogy at the seventy-seven-year-old's funeral mass in Boston. Earlier that month Obama had awarded the Presidential Medal of Freedom to the man deemed the Lion of the Senate, with the honor received by Kennedy's daughter on his behalf.

Kennedy's funeral mass was grand, attended by four presidents: Obama and Bill Clinton, George W. Bush, and Jimmy Carter. The Obamas and Clintons sat together, as they had at Walter Cronkite's funeral a month before. And Barack Obama was seen wiping away a tear as he stood outside Our Lady of Perpetual Help Basilica in Boston, where he had taken a private meeting with the senator's widow, Victoria.

Most observers believed that when Kennedy was at full vigor, he would have been able to will this health-care reform through the upper house. But in Obama's Washington, where he was the object of almost otherworldly scorn by the Right, Kennedy's loss did nothing to tamp down the opposition. Two weeks after Kennedy's death, at a massive tea party "march on Washington" led by Fox News host Glenn Beck, some protesters mocked the late Senator with preprinted signs supplied by the anti-abortion American Life League that read: BURY OBAMACARE WITH KENNEDY. Beck had already declared on his Fox News program that Obama was a "racist," who "hates white people, and the white culture."

The health-care fight had taken on racial as well as class dimensions, with wealthy talk show hosts causing their fans to believe the reform's main tenets involved stealing the tax dollars of the successful and redistributing the proceeds—free medicine, free doctor's visits, and a new, insidious form of welfare—to minorities and "illegal immigrants" who refused to work. Back in February, radio host Rush Limbaugh had told his audience the health-care bill involved "income redistribution" and was "a civil rights bill" that included "reparations."

On September 9, President Obama addressed a joint session of Congress, making a national pitch for health-care reform before an audience of 32 million television viewers.

"I am not the first president to take up this cause," he said, noting a century of trying that began with Theodore Roosevelt and continued through Bill Clinton. "But I am determined to be the last."

But as the president sought to refute the claim that illegal immigrants would benefit from the proposed law, the words "You lie!" rang out from Republican congressman Addison Graves "Joe" Wilson, of South Carolina. At various other points in the speech, there were other shouts of "Not true!" as the president vowed that no federal health-care funds would fund abortions, and there were other cries of "Shame!" and "Read the bill," along with derisive laughter. Texas congressman Louie Goehmert wore a sign that said, WHAT BILL?

Wilson's eruption, punctuated by the word *lie*, drew particularly scathing condemnation. Few could recall a similar display during a presidential address to Congress, and Wilson was roundly denounced by his colleagues, Democrat and Republican alike: including Minority whip Eric Cantor, fellow South Carolinian Jim Clyburn, and Senate Minority Leader Mitch McConnell. Democrat Patrick Leahy of Vermont was fuming as he left the chamber, and told reporters that in his thirty-five years in the Senate, he had never heard such an outburst. Even Obama's recent opponent, Republican John McCain of Arizona, said the eruption was "totally disrespectful." Wilson soon apologized and even telephoned the White House and delivered his apology to Emanuel. But by the next day, Wilson was using his status as a conservative folk hero for fund-raising.

For African Americans, the "you lie" moment spoke to a fundamental lack of respect for the black man who now held the White House, and put a coda on the summer of angry tea party rallies over health-care reform. Wilson's words, which he called spontaneous, were read by African Americans as a robbery: of the stature normally afforded a president, of a moment granted by tradition and design to the country's sole, nationally elected leader, and of the political norms that had been in place before the election of the forty-fourth president.

On March 20, a warm Saturday in the nation's capital, tea party groups held one of their most vociferous public protests against the proposed health-care law as the House prepared to debate a revised version of the bill. As Democratic House members, including Speaker Pelosi, Majority Leader Steny Hoyer, Florida congresswoman Debbie Wasserman Schultz, and House Whip Jim Clyburn, along with several black lawmakers, including Emanuel Cleaver and John Lewis, were entering the Capitol for the final vote, they were forced to walk past a gauntlet of angry hecklers screaming, "Kill the bill!"

On the balconies overhead, Republican self-declared "tea party congressmen," led by Michele Bachmann of Minnesota, whipped up the crowd below as they waved KILL THE BILL signs and screamed venom. One protester warned Pelosi, "You're going to burn in hell!"

As the black lawmakers passed through the raucous crowd, Cleaver noticed he had been spat upon, and wiped the spittle from the side of his face. An ordained minister, the congressman first appeared ready to roll up his sleeves and fight, as he turned to confront the man who'd spat on him, and who was continuing his angry tirade. But Cleaver moved past instead, sending a Capitol Police officer in his place. In the end, Cleaver declined to press charges, but he, Clyburn, and Lewis would recall hearing the word *nigger* hurled at them from the crowd. Clyburn said it was language he hadn't heard since his days as a young civil rights organizer in South Carolina.

Barney Frank of Massachusetts, who entered the House in 1981 and eight years later survived a humiliating sex and prostitution scandal to become one of just two openly gay members of Congress at that time, reported being called a "faggot" as he entered the Capitol vestibule. It was a frenzied week. At least ten members of Congress sought added police protection, and more than a hundred Democratic lawmakers in the House held a closed-door meeting with the Capitol Police and the FBI, citing serious concerns for their safety. Around the country at Democratic congressional offices, bricks and rocks thrown through windows left shattered glass and shattered nerves among staffers.

When a brick was thrown into the Niagara Falls, New York, office of Democratic congresswoman Louise M. Slaughter, a "threatening voice-mail message referring to sniper attacks" was also left there. Bart Stupak, the conservative Democrat from Michigan whose last-minute negotiations to reinforce the ban on abortion funding through health-care reform helped secure the bill's passage in the House, received a fax with a drawing of a noose and an anonymous voice mail saying, "You're dead. We know where you live. We'll get you."

Tea party supporters, including Republican members of Congress, angrily distanced themselves from these acts, as did conservative media. But the anti-health-care protests were building to a seemingly uncontrollable fever pitch.

The voice mail at John Lewis's district office was filled

with hateful messages, including one he released in April that denounced "that goddamned nigger" in the White House and warned, "Don't tell me I gotta get some goddamned health insurance, I ain't payin' no goddamned fine" and "I ain't gettin' no goddamned mandatory health insurance." The angry caller railed against the "niggers" and "white trash honkeys" who voted for "that nigger Obama," and dared the president, presumably, to "come and put my ass in jail if he don't like it."

John Boehner, the House minority leader, went on Fox News and said, "Violence and threats are unacceptable. That's not the American way. We need to take that anger and channel it into positive change. Call your congressman, go out and register people to vote, go volunteer on a political campaign, make your voice heard—but let's do it the right way."

On March 21, 2010, in that climate of chaos, anger, and fear, the House passed the reconciled health-care bill. Every Republican voted against it. In the Senate, Majority Leader Harry Reid forced passage of the final bill with just 51 votes, using a parliamentary procedure called reconciliation. Republicans denounced the maneuver as "Chicago-style politics" and vowed repeal even though reconciliation had been used before, including to pass Republican George W. Bush's 2001 and 2003 tax cuts.

On March 23, President Obama signed his signature health-care bill. As he repeated his left-handed signature twenty-two times so he would have a pen for each special guest, he was surrounded by a group of lawmakers including a beaming Pelosi, Reid, Vice President Biden, Clyburn, Rangel, and John Dingell, the longest-serving U.S. senator, who had seen many attempts at creating a universal health-care plan come and go. Also present was Senator Max Baucus, who had managed the ugly and unenviably public process in the Senate Finance Committee, Ted Kennedy's son Patrick, then a congressman from Rhode Island, and the late senator's widow, Victoria. Also there was an eleven-year-old African American boy, Marcellus Owens, who'd lost his mother to cancer for lack of insurance, and whom the White House had made a symbol of the importance of the bill.

Barack Obama had achieved his party's century-old dream of enacting comprehensive health-care reform, however flawed the process and bitter the road.

For Bill and Hillary Clinton, it was a moment to give Obama his due. Soon after the signing ceremony, President Obama took two congratulatory phone calls: from Hillary, who had labored so hard, and in vain, to craft a health-care bill in the early days of her husband's administration, and from Bill, who understood like few others what a hard-fought and rare achievement it was.

"One of the great things about Clinton," said a longtime Clinton adviser, is this: "I'm sure he recognized that Obama did something that he couldn't do, in the health-care space." He understood it as a genuine accomplishment—and he was glad it had gotten done.

CHAPTER 9

Backlash

The dream was not to put one black family in the White House,
the dream was to make everything equal in everybody's house.

—Rev. Al Sharpton, May 2, 2010

FOR THE PRESIDENT AND HIS PARTY, THE CELEBRATION OVER
health-care reform's passage was short-lived. Anger on the right
over the Affordable Care Act had not ebbed, and Republicans
were preparing to use it as a battering ram in the midterm elections, which were just six months away. And some of the president's supporters worried that even as the outcry over health care
took on an outwardly racial tone, the president and his team
either couldn't or wouldn't see it, and worse, were refusing to
take it on.

The vilification of health care, the hysteria over it in some
quarters, seemed to be summed up in a sign hung on the door of
a Mount Dora, Florida, urologist in April that read: "If you voted
for Obama . . . seek urologic care elsewhere. Changes to your
healthcare begin right now, not in four years." The doctor who

hung it, Jack Cassell, was fifty-six years old, white, and relatively affluent, and as such was in the demographic median of the tea party movement. His hostility to health-care reform, and to the president who pushed for and signed it, was replicated across a wide swath of voters, including a growing majority of white baby boomers and New Dealers, who in another era would almost certainly have been Democrats. And that's what Barack Obama's party feared the most.

Republicans were portraying health-care reform as just another extension of LBJ-style welfare that would be abused by shiftless minorities and illegal immigrants, robbing the successful and the thrifty and consigning seniors to a bleak future by allegedly cutting Medicare (which while untrue, was particularly potent). Polls showed the narrative was having an effect. One month after the bill passed, a rising star in the Republican Party, Governor Bob McDonnell of Virginia, kicked off April by reviving the state's celebration of Confederate History Month, with nary a mention of slavery as the driving cause of the Civil War. McDonnell recanted after an uproar by the state and national NAACP, but the denunciation of health care was reflected in rising hostility toward the man in the White House, and not just in the states of the former Confederacy.

Vulnerable Democrats, rather than touting a legislative victory that had eluded their party for nearly a century, began a wholesale retreat away from both "Obamacare" and Obama himself.

Among the president's African American supporters, some worried that the White House, flush with victory over health care and preparing to move on to the next item on the president's agenda—a comprehensive budget agreement that would raise taxes on the wealthy and bolster the slowly rebounding economy—was ignoring the headlights of the electoral locomotive barreling toward the Democrats in November.

Ben Jealous was among those who were worried. At thirty-five, he was the youngest NAACP president in the organization's history. Prior to holding the position, he had been many things: an NAACP voter registration volunteer, a Rhodes scholar, a reporter at a black weekly newspaper in Mississippi, the head of the black newspaper publishers association, an investment manager and prodigious fund-raiser, and at every turn, an activist.

The son of a prominent, white New England family on his father's side and the descendants of slaves on his mother's, Jealous could be impatient, and he was leading an organization beset with problems in need of patience, from its staid reputation and tendency toward bureaucratic responses to local crises, to an aging, dwindling membership.

He'd made his public debut as head of the NAACP at Harlem's Abyssinian Baptist Church a month after Barack Obama's inauguration, telling the congregation and its pastor, Rev. Calvin Butts, "I'm here like most of you with my head in the clouds of January 20 . . . but with my feet firmly planted in January 21. My generation was told that all the great battles were over. And we emerged the most murdered people in the country, and the most incarcerated group on the planet."

Jealous, Marc Morial of the National Urban League, and Rev. Al Sharpton held their first formal meeting in the White House with the president in February, as a record snowstorm shuttered the Capitol. (Civil rights pioneer Dorothy Height, age ninety-seven, was to attend but could not make the trip due to the storm. Obama would eulogize her two months later, at Washington's National Cathedral. He noted that Height, in her trademark brightly colored hats, had visited the White House twenty-one times and met with every president since Dwight Eisenhower.)

The three civil rights leaders had come armed with an agenda: to focus the administration on the plight of black communities, rural and urban, who were continuing to struggle, even though the nation had passed through the worst of the Great Recession. Jealous in particular believed it was imperative that the president be seen to overtly and visibly combat the economic crises facing black communities, both as a moral matter and to ensure that the president's most ardent supporters didn't become dispirited and disengaged, with a census year midterm looming. Though Jealous now led a nonpartisan organization, those close to him said he was a political animal, and he privately voiced frustrations to colleagues that the new president was ignoring his black and liberal base.

Black unemployment had spiked to 16.5 percent by April, even as the overall jobless rate had dropped to a still high 9.9 percent. The stimulus was beginning to work its way through the economy, but for black communities, the foreclosure and jobs crises were continuing to spiral out of control. The unemployment rate for black men that month was 20.2 percent, versus 9.6 percent for white men, so high that a coalition of advocacy groups, including the National Employment Law Project, submitted an April complaint to the United Nations.

The president surprised and perplexed some aides at the February meeting by striding into the room in a casual shirt and khakis, while his three guests were decked out in suits and ties. But Jealous, Morial, and Sharpton found his presentation was formal indeed. He firmly opposed the kind of racially targeted programs the activists and their allies in the Congressional Black Caucus wanted. Obama explained during the hour-long meeting that he believed his economic plans, including health care—which was to be broadly distributed to all struggling Americans—would especially aid black households due to their disproportionate suffering. That had been his stance since the start of his term, despite growing criticism from black writers and thinkers, and members of the Congressional Black Caucus. And he maintained it now.

Jealous, colleagues said, came away from the meeting unsatisfied, though afterward, Sharpton told the reporters assembled outside the White House, "I think he [Obama] was very clear that he was not going to engage in any race-based programs. But at the same time, he was determined that going forward we can correct some of the structural inequalities that are currently in place." Jealous confirmed that the conversation focused less on race than on the many economically hard-hit areas of the country. "The reality is that poverty has been greatly democratized by this recession," he said. "What all Americans have in common is that they are hurting and struggling and want to see the pace of progress quicken."

No photos were released, however, because some African American White House aides were worried the president's casual attire would send the wrong impression to black communities. Friends said Jealous was particularly frustrated, not by what the president wore, but by what he viewed as a lack of urgency on the president's part, to confront either the specific economic ills of black communities or the conservative fringe that even a month before the health-care bill was signed were massing to kill it and to blunt the impact of the historic 2008 election.

If the White House wouldn't be proactive, Jealous determined that he would, and he began pushing the NAACP, through protests and direct action and online, to do more to confront the tea party head-on—particularly after they held their second annual "tax day" rallies in April, with more than a thousand protests nationwide.

On July 10, the NAACP opened its 101st annual meeting in Kansas City, Missouri, with the delegates calling on the tea party movement to repudiate the racism within its ranks, including the offensive signs at rallies and ugly statements directed at the president online and in conservative media. Also listed were the taunts, spittle, and epithets directed at black and gay members of

Congress during the ugly last walk to passage of the Affordable Care Act back in April.

In his address to the more than two thousand assembled delegates, Jealous declared that the tea party movement "must expel the bigots and racists in your ranks or take full responsibility for all of their actions."

The St. Louis Tea Party immediately responded by passing its own resolution: "We settle our disputes civilly and avoid the gutter tactic of attempting to silence opponents by inflammatory name-calling." Also, "The very term 'racist' has diminished meaning due to its overuse by political partisans, including members of the NAACP."

Sarah Palin, the former Alaska governor and vice presidential candidate, and a favorite of tea party groups, lashed out at the NAACP on Facebook, writing, "the charge that Tea Party Americans judge people by the color of their skin is false, appalling, and is a regressive and diversionary tactic to change the subject at hand."

Four days later, on the morning of July 19, firebrand conservative political commentator Andrew Breitbart posted two heavily edited videos titled "Video Proof: The NAACP Awards Racism—2010." It claimed that Shirley Sherrod, the director of the U.S. Department of Agriculture's Georgia Office of Rural Development, had admitted, during a speech at the Georgia NAACP's 20th Annual Freedom Fund dinner on March 27, four days after President Obama signed the national health-care law, that she had discriminated against a white farmer, deciding that he should get help from "one of his own kind" and referring him to a white attorney.

The clip was immediately picked up by right-wing media, online, on talk radio, and on Fox News. The Right reveled in the opportunity to accuse an Obama administration official of hypocrisy and "reverse racism."

The Obama administration found itself in an untenable position. With the midterms just four months away, they could ill afford to hand the tea party and the Republicans ammunition in the form of a federal staffer who appeared to have endorsed discrimination against whites, particularly with the tea party whipping up a frenzy among white voters, and particularly white seniors, over health care. And the administration had been made hypersensitive to race-related incidents by the increasingly racialized debate over the Obama presidency, from the "beer summit" to "you lie."

Alarms were going off inside the White House personnel office. Fox News producers were calling for comment, and aides were preparing to brief President Obama on the Sherrod affair the next day. Taking no chances, and doing no due diligence, Secretary of Agriculture Tom Vilsack, through staff, let Sherrod know she should resign, immediately, in the hopes that her resignation would blunt the controversy.

As news of Sherrod's resignation broke, Speaker Newt Gingrich, during an appearance on Sean Hannity's program on Fox News, praised Vilsack in loaded terms: "You know, you can't be a black racist any more than you can be a white racist."

The phones at the NAACP national headquarters were ringing off the hook, too. Jealous, having mounted high profile attacks on the tea party for which he and his organization were reaping the whirlwind, joined Vilsack in acting too soon. When word of Sherrod's resignation came, with the videotape of her full remarks still making its way from Georgia to Washington via FedEx, and without speaking to her himself, Ben Jealous fired off a blistering statement joining in the condemnation of the now former USDA employee. The statement was quickly posted to the NAACP website and mailed to several journalists, and Jealous tweeted it under his personal Twitter handle.

Sherrod was angry at the Agriculture Department, at the

NAACP, and at the president and his administration, whom she believed had been frightened into submission by Fox News and the right wing. She began accepting requests to be interviewed, including by CNN, where she recounted her biography and explained the full context of her remarks. Sherrod recalled growing up in Baker County, Georgia, where when she was seventeen years old, her father, a Baptist church deacon, was shot to death in 1965 by a white farmer over a livestock dispute. An all-white grand jury declined to indict the farmer, and Sherrod noted that the circumstances of her father's death and the lack of justice that it entailed had made her initially reticent to aid the white farmer and his wife, but that she soon realized that what was important was not race, but taking the opportunity to help a fellow human being. The farmer in question, Roger Spooner, appeared on the cable network, too, with his wife, Eloise, calling Sherrod a lifelong friend who had truly saved their farm. The story had been one not of racism but of redemption.

When the full video was finally posted to the NAACP website, it had become horrifically clear that the organization, and Sherrod's employers in Washington, had made a grave mistake.

Jealous quickly reversed course. A new statement was released, saying that after viewing the entire speech, the organization believed they had been "snookered by Fox News and Tea Party activist Andrew Breitbart" into promoting a false tale that upended the meaning of racial bias. Breitbart was still defending himself Tuesday night, saying he was simply hitting back against NAACP charges of tea party racism.

"I could care less [*sic*] about Shirley Sherrod," Breitbart told Sean Hannity. "This is not about Shirley Sherrod."

By Wednesday, Sherrod was fielding apologies, from Vilsack, from the NAACP, in qualified fashion from Bill O'Reilly, and eventually from then CNN correspondent Roland Martin, who, before the full tape was released, had also joined in the condemnation—and from the White House. Press Secretary Robert Gibbs, in the daily briefing, declared: "I think without a doubt Ms. Sherrod is owed an apology. I would do so certainly on behalf of this administration."

Vilsack publicly took the blame for the firing, indemnifying the White House and offering to bring Sherrod back. She didn't accept.

By Thursday, the full judgment of the media descended on the White House, with the *New York Times* declaring: "The Obama administration has been shamed by its rush to judgment after it forced the resignation of a black midlevel official in the Agriculture Department who was wrongly accused of racism by the right-wing blogosphere." And Sherrod herself told NBC's *Today* show that she'd like to "have a conversation" with the president, "to help him understand the experiences at the grassroots level." The conversation came that night, when Obama telephoned Sherrod.

For some in the African American community, the Sherrod affair revived the sting of Lani Guinier's ouster during the Clinton years. Worse, it seemed to bespeak a troubling reflex within the White House to protect itself so thoroughly on racial matters, and to distance itself so instantaneously from racial conflict, that it would sooner jettison a black woman accused of racial offense than take the time to find out who she was, or to confirm what she supposedly had done. Black critics of the White House said the incident had exposed the administration's Achilles' heel: a dearth of personal contacts within the wider body of black politics, and an unwillingness to reach out to those old hands who might help the president and his staff know more.

"They didn't know who [Sherrod] was," one civil rights leader lamented. "What you had were junior staffers who heard snippets of her comments, taken out of context, and reacted based on what they heard without a clear impression. They went for the bright, broad bait."

They should have called someone, the lament would go. *They should have called John Lewis, or Vernon Jordan,* who was from Georgia and had been the NAACP field director there in his younger days, *or David Scott,* who sat on the House Agricultural Committee. *They should have picked up the phone before throwing Shirley under the bus.*

But if the administration had been too quick to act and too slow to consult, so, too, had the NAACP.

Jealous flew to Albany, Georgia, and with a contingent of NAACP staff met Sherrod in the lobby of the Hilton hotel. He apologized without reservation, saying he had acted before receiving all the information.

"He pretty much came out of the NAACP president role and became a humble man," said Larry Nesmith, head of the Coffee County, Georgia, NAACP branch, which had hosted the event at which Sherrod spoke. "He said, 'I made a mistake, I'm sorry.' He did it with emotion, because he knew the damage that had been done. He apologized to not only her, but to her husband as well. I really respected him for that."

For Sherrod, forgiveness came right away. The group shared lunch at Old Times Country Buffet. They talked about fishing.

As the 2010 midterm elections approached, the White House was being battered by serial storms: a deepwater oil spill in the Gulf of Mexico in April, WikiLeaks's July release of tens of thousands of classified documents on the war in Afghanistan, an ongoing humanitarian crisis following a devastating earthquake in Haiti, and a pernicious, worldwide flu pandemic in August. The last thing the Obama administration needed was a march on Washington.

Still, that's just what the NAACP and dozens of labor and civil rights groups—the SEIU, AFL-CIO, and United Auto Workers unions, the Leadership Council on Civil Rights, the Sierra Club, the National Council of La Raza, and others—had been planning since August. They scheduled an October rally on the National Mall that they dubbed "10-2-10." It was the kind of ground-level activism Ben Jealous hoped would propel the NAACP out of the boardroom and onto the front lines.

In some ways, the White House seemed almost to be at war with parts of its own base, or at least with what spokesman Robert Gibbs derided as the "professional left" in an August 10 interview with the *Hill*. A chorus of liberal critics were battering the administration over the president's stated personal opposition to gay marriage (which few liberal activists believed was genuine), his refusal to order the military to stop enforcing the "Don't Ask, Don't Tell" ban on open military service for gays and lesbians, the lack of a public option in the health-care law, and the failure to close the prison camp at Guantánamo Bay. The fact that Congress had authority over the latter two matters did little to deter Obama's critics on the left, who, Gibbs sneered, "will be satisfied when we have Canadian healthcare, and we've eliminated the Pentagon."

Gibbs charged that those comparing Obama to George W. Bush "ought to be drug tested. I mean, it's crazy," he said.

But the critics, led by liberal libertarian bloggers, many of whom had opposed Obama from the start, were undeterred. They charged that Obama had not earned the continued support of liberal voters. He hadn't done enough or fought Republicans hard enough.

The vitriol "was what I expected from the Right," said one prominent African American leader. "I didn't expect it from some of the liberal whites. It always amazes me, how under pressure a lot of people you thought were our friends would be the first ones to jump ship, and do it with hostility."

Some progressives occasionally pointed out that the president's pragmatism was necessary in an atmosphere in which Republicans had vowed total obstruction. But the story line of liberals angry with the progressive president was almost irresistible for the D.C. media.

As the election approached, it became increasingly clear that the threat of electoral rout was real. Democrats up for reelection were fleeing from the health-care law, and from the president. Conservatives, emboldened by the Shirley Sherrod dustup and leaning more aggressively than ever into the charge that the president and his allies were the embodiment of *true* racism, with white Americans the victims of a "gangster" president, even launched a "Rally to Restore America," held provocatively on the date of the forty-seventh anniversary of the 1963 March on Washington. Right-wing host Glenn Beck, Sarah Palin, and Alveda King, a niece of Dr. King and an ardent conservative, declared themselves and the tea party to be the true "people of the civil rights movement."

As Sharpton, Jealous, Marc Morial, Avis Jones-DeWeever, who had succeeded Dorothy Height at the National Council of Negro Women, Martin Luther King III, and others, flanked by Secretary of Education Arne Duncan, led a five-mile "Reclaim the Dream" march from Dunbar High School in Northwest Washington in outraged response, Glenn Beck boldly declared of his 9/12 movement: "We are the ones that must stand for civil and equal rights, justice, equal justice. *Not special justice, not social justice.* We are the inheritors and protectors of the civil rights movement. They are perverting it."

And while the president appeared on black media outlets, and while he and the First Lady barnstormed the country in the late summer and fall, calling on African Americans and women to vote to defend the gains of the previous year and a half, it was apparent that the election of 2010 would be nothing like 2008.

Speaking at the Congressional Black Caucus Foundation's annual legislative conference gala on September 18, President Obama acknowledged that "a lot of people may not be feeling that energized or that engaged right now," but he implored the members and their constituents to "go back to your neighborhoods, to go back to your workplaces, to go to churches, and go to the barbershops, and go to the beauty shops, and tell them we've got more work to do."

The White House enlisted Bill Clinton to rally support among Democrats, too, and the former president dutifully hit the road, but it wasn't enough.

Democrats suffered a fulsome defeat, made to sting more by the fact that it was a census year, with not just the legislatures and governorships and congressional seats on the line, but also a decade of redistricting, with its power to cement Republican House and statehouse majorities for a decade.

Republicans retook the House, picking up sixty-three seats and snatching the speaker's gavel from Nancy Pelosi's hands. In the Senate, Republicans grabbed five seats, leaving Democrats with a slim majority. Republicans grabbed a half dozen swing state governorships, including Florida and Ohio, and the GOP finally completed its takeover of every southern legislature.

House Democrats lost white voters by 24 points, where their losing margin had been just 4 points in 2006, at the nadir of George W. Bush's popularity. Winning 9 in 10 black voters, 7 in 10 Hispanics, and 6 in 10 Asian Americans was not enough in a shrunken midterm electorate that was all but devoid of the younger, more racially diverse voters who helped put Obama in the White House.

Instead, facing a smaller, older electorate, Democrats posted their worst performance with white voters since World War II.

For African Americans, the election was tantamount to political Armageddon. As David Bositis, then the lead researcher on the black electorate at the Joint Center for Political and Economic Studies, would later write, the election ushered in the "resegregation of southern politics," all but completing "the 46-year transition from a multiracial Democratic political dominance to a white conservative Republican political dominance."

Racially polarized voting meant that, particularly in the South, white voters, even those who called themselves Democrats, voted overwhelmingly Republican—just as overwhelmingly, it turned out, as African Americans supported Democrats, with both giving 9 in 10 votes to their preferred party.

For black state legislators, 98 percent of them Democrats, that meant near-total isolation in the minority party across the South for the first time since the passage of the Voting Rights Act.

The defeats meant a complete loss of control, or even influence, over the coming redistricting process. And as Columbia University journalism professor Thomas Edsall would point out, "Republicans in control of redistricting have two goals: the defeat of white Democrats and the creation of safe districts for Republicans. They have achieved both of these goals by increasing the number of districts likely to elect an African American. Black voters are gerrymandered out of districts represented by whites of both parties, making the Democratic incumbent weaker and the Republican incumbent stronger."

In Washington, the loss of black electoral power was nearly as thorough. Black Democrats who had swept into power with Bill Clinton and were now elder statesmen in the House had held an unprecedented number of chairmanships, including the gavels of the powerful House Judiciary and Ways and Means committees, wielded for years by John Conyers of Michigan and Charlie Rangel of New York, plus the Homeland Security chairmanship held by Congressman Bennie Thompson of Mississippi. Now all were gone, along with a dozen subcommittee chairmanships. For Rangel, Waters, and other Black Caucus members, ethics trials would replace committee hearings during the coming lame duck session.

Black voters in 2010 shed 3 percent from their share of the

2008 electorate, a performance that was stronger than the other Democratic constituencies, who ignored the midterms in droves. What sank the party's prospects was the staggering decline among white voters, who if they didn't stay home, coalesced to drive the Democrats from power in the House.

Obama described the election as a "shellacking," but during the lame duck session in December, Democrats made the most of their remaining time in power: passing a full repeal of "Don't Ask, Don't Tell"; extending unemployment benefits to beleaguered Americans; belatedly compensating first responders who toiled at the base of the destroyed World Trade Center in 2001; and ratifying a new nuclear START Treaty with Russia. The session led political scientist Larry Sabato to declare, via Twitter: "It's official. Like it or not, this lame-duck session is the most productive of the 15 held since WWII."

More triumphs for the administration would come in the new year, when on May 2, President Obama announced that a U.S. Navy SEAL team had killed Osama bin Laden in Pakistan. Celebrations erupted outside the White House at the news.

But the president's war with parts of his base would linger, as Cornel West told Tavis Smiley on Smiley's Public Radio International program within days of the bin Laden announcement: "You and I take seriously the legacy of Martin Luther King. . . . It means then that we must be dissenting voices in the middle of a moment of such self-celebration and self-congratulation, to say quite explicitly that justice does not come out the barrel of a gun."

Smiley and West were mounting a growing crusade against the president, accusing him of paying insufficient attention to the poor, and to African Americans. Fourteen days after the bin Laden announcement, West called the president a "black mascot of Wall Street" and a man who has "a certain fear of free black men."

West was roundly condemned for the comments, including by longtime friends, who privately wondered if the eccentric professor had lost his mind. West claimed, in his own defense and echoing Smiley's own complaints, that he had been shut out by the White House; he said his calls went unreturned and invitations were not forthcoming. According to friends and a former White House staffer, West was even nursing a grudge over Obama's inauguration: A bellman at his Washington hotel had received tickets to stand on the platform and West's tickets were "merely" for the front row. (His repeated complaints eventually annoyed the president enough that Obama confronted West, as the professor stood on a rope line at the 2010 National Urban League annual meeting. According to a former staffer, "Obama said, 'I can't believe you keep telling these lies. You know I personally sent you and your mother inaugural tickets.' Then the president and a couple of people with him walked to the back, and Obama spat out, 'Did you hear him? This is why I don't deal with these people.'")

It was a bizarre and increasingly personal descent into demagogic warfare that led some of West's fellow black public intellectuals, including MSNBC host Melissa Harris-Perry, who like West was a former Princeton professor, to deride West in her column in *The Nation* as "President Obama's silenced, disregarded, disrespected moral conscience," and to label his lamentations a "self-aggrandizing, victimology sermon deceptively wrapped in the discourse of prophetic witness."

The irony of West's critique is that it echoed a small but growing body of black thought that saw the president as not sufficiently forward-leaning on matters of race and woefully inattentive to African Americans who remained locked in a cycle of unemployment and economic want. Still, the president had his defenders, who were determined to stand between him and his fiercest critics on the left and the right.

"Obama is not the president of Black America," Marc Morial of the Urban League said. "He's not a civil rights leader. That job is taken, by the leaders of groups like the NAACP, the Urban League, and the National Action Network." It was a view that Sharpton repeated often, including in sharp ongoing clashes, on camera and off, with West.

The rumblings of discontent came as the president prepared to hold his second formal meeting with the Black Caucus, on May 13, and as caucus members prepared to launch a multi-state summer tour to dramatize the African American joblessness crisis. At the White House meeting, the members again pressed for economic policies targeted toward black communities, and the president continued to resist, insisting that his overall policies on education and health care would produce the most meaning-ful solutions for black economic progress.

Obama had his friends in the caucus, and he had his de-tractors. His staff worked closely with some members, and not with others. The caucus pushed hard on some issues, like revising administration education policies to avoid harming historically black colleges, and gave the White House a wide berth on others.

To White House aides, the narrative of African American critiques of the president became overly reductive and simplistic when translated by the D.C. media. "It's either, we love him or we hate him," a former staffer said, adding, "with any leader, particularly the first black president, it's going to be complicated. Yes we love him and by and large most people see areas where they want him to shift and do things differently. He has tremen-dous respect for" the caucus members, "but he's not going to agree with them every time and he has other stuff on his plate."

In the end, the president's conflict with members of the Af-rican American community was less daunting than what was taking place outside of Washington, where the Right was suc-cessfully building a racial narrative designed to drive a wedge between the president and white Democrats. Even members of the Black Caucus who were critical of the president's policies said that dynamic informed the way they talked about the president and his administration.

One member of the caucus commented that though the members were unhappy about some things not being done, "[w]e're not going to aid and abet the haters, because the moment we jumped in it would be used by the extreme right to further dismantle the legitimacy of this president."

Indeed, when Obama addressed the caucus's annual gala in September 2011 and enjoined black voters, "Take off your bedroom slippers. Put on your marching shoes," and "shake it off. Stop complainin'. Stop grumblin'. Stop cryin'. We are going to press on. We have work to do!" most of those assembled cheered, even as Emanuel Cleaver, then the caucus president, told McClatchy Newspapers that had Bill Clinton similarly failed to address black unemployment as part of his economic recovery plan, "[w]e probably would be marching on the White House."

That reticence rankled some Obama critics among black intellectuals. Columbia University professor and author Frederick C. Harris said that even though African Americans were certain to overwhelmingly support the president's reelection in 2012, "for those who had seen in President Obama's election the culmination of four centuries of black hopes and aspirations and the realization of the Rev. Dr. Martin Luther King Jr.'s vision of a 'beloved community,' the last four years must be reckoned a disappointment." Harris, in his book *The Price of the Ticket,* concluded that the Obama presidency had "already marked the decline, rather than the pinnacle, of a political vision centered on challenging racial inequality." Harris added, "The tragedy is that black elites—from intellectuals and civil rights leaders to politicians and clergy members—have acquiesced to this decline, seeing it as the necessary price for the pride and satisfaction of having a black family in the White House."

Harris and others noted that Obama rarely talked directly

about race, and that when he did within the black community, it was often in the guise of a racial scold. At the Congressional Black Caucus gala, Obama rallied black voters to the cause, not with promises of direct aid to black communities, but with an appeal toward the collective responsibility to redeem the history of black struggle for the right to vote. The only concrete promise on the table was that his broad and untargeted economic agenda would lift black Americans, too.

But many African Americans and some white Obama supporters sensed that if there were those on the right who either couldn't or wouldn't fully accept Barack Obama as president, and who sought to mark his time in office with the asterisk of failure; some on the *left* would remain stubbornly unsatisfied no matter what the president accomplished. "I don't recall you folks asking Clinton for his black agenda," Rev. Sharpton, who began hosting a news/commentary program on MSNBC in January 2011, said when confronted by Obama critics like Smiley and West.

Those who remained in Obama's corner saw him as a man marching into serial battles with the thinnest rear guard, and they tried to be his guardians, on social media, in fierce online commentary, and soon, at the ballot box.

ANY DESIRE OBAMA HAD TO STEER CLEAR OF THE ROCKY SHOALS of race and to hold his party's interracial coalition together ahead of his 2012 reelection came crashing to the shore on February 26, 2012.

The NBA All-Star Game had returned to Orlando, Florida, for the first time in twenty years, and in Sanford, a small city just twenty-seven miles away from where the big game would be held, seventeen-year-old Trayvon Martin took a fateful trip to a convenience store in the rain, leaving the gated community where his father's fiancée lived, to get her ten-year-old son some candy and a drink for himself before the game. He wouldn't return.

Instead, Martin, who had been sent to stay with his father for a few weeks after getting into trouble at school in Miami, was shot dead by George Zimmerman, a neighborhood watch volunteer who spotted the teen walking in the drizzling rain, talking on his cell phone. Zimmerman, when questioned by the responding officers, claimed that the teen had attacked him out of nowhere, as he left his truck in the dark and rain to try to spot the young stranger while he called the police nonemergency line. The shooting remained a minor local news story for thirteen days, causing little notice outside of Sanford, whose only previous brush with national renown was as the city that once refused to let Jackie Robinson practice on its segregated baseball fields.

By March, Martin's family had hired attorneys to sue the Sanford Police Department and demand the release of 911 calls from the night of the shooting. They held press conferences, demanding Zimmerman's arrest. As days turned into weeks, with Zimmerman still free and a police department that appeared to be more sympathetic to the shooter than to the victim investigating the case, Martin's anguished parents traveled to Sanford. They called Rev. Sharpton for help and also contacted Benjamin Crump, a civil rights attorney from Tallahassee who was known for taking cases involving the violent deaths of black men and boys. A storm was gathering over Sanford; age-old racial tensions gripped the town where a railroad line separated the main city limits from Goldsboro, the impoverished historically black neighborhood it once annexed.

The national rallies began on March 22 as Sharpton organized a march that attracted thirty thousand people to Fort Mellon Park, near Sanford City Hall. The growing controversy over Zimmerman's continued freedom forced the resignation of the police chief that morning and put the anguish of Martin's parents on national display.

Trayvon Martin's boyish face, forever frozen in time in iconic black-and-white, staring out from a gray hoodie like the one he was wearing when he died on the wet grass, alone, was gaining national attention as young black men took to the airwaves and to online forums, declaring that their lives have value.

On the day of the Sanford march, Congressman Bobby Rush was escorted off the House floor after walking to the podium to speak and removing his suit jacket to reveal a gray hoodie underneath. The aging congressman, who remained the pastor of a Chicago church, pulled the hood over his head, launching into a protest sermon that began with the words "Racial profiling has to stop, Mr. Speaker. Just because someone wears a hoodie does not make them a hoodlum." He proceeded to recite a biblical verse, Micah 6:8:

> *He has shown you, O mortal, what is good.*
> *And what does the Lord require of you?*
> *To act justly and to love mercy,*
> *And to walk humbly with your God.*

Rush ended with a blessing on Trayvon Martin's soul, as the acting chair, Republican Gregg Harper of Mississippi, pounded the gavel and ordered, "The gentleman will suspend!"

In the early weeks, the national outrage over Martin's death was both universal and bipartisan, with both front-runners in the Republican presidential primary, former Pennsylvania senator Rick Santorum and former Massachusetts governor Mitt Romney, calling the shooting "tragic," and the lack of an immediate prosecution "chilling." Former House Speaker Newt Gingrich said Zimmerman was "clearly overreaching" in his role as a neighborhood watch volunteer, while Senate Minority Leader Mitch McConnell, former secretary of state Condoleezza Rice, and even Florida tea party congressman Allen West made statements calling for an investigations into Martin's killing.

Inside the White House, Obama was following the story along with the country. Sharpton's involvement gave the president and Valerie Jarrett a direct line to what was happening in Sanford, where the local prosecutor recused himself, leading the Florida governor, Rick Scott, to appoint a special prosecutor. The Justice Department dispatched investigators to Sanford to search for any evidence of a hate crime. And the president's personal circle was percolating with the same questions and concerns as the country at large.

And yet, for the White House, the politics were deeply uncertain.

Obama's previous foray into public commentary on matters of race had met with singular scorn, and immediate backlash. With a reelection campaign ahead, the White House could ill afford to wade into an issue so heavily freighted with questions of gun rights and violence and racial identity. Zimmerman was white and Hispanic. Pro-gun activists were championing his cause. Prosecutors were using Florida's version of the controversial, National Rifle Association–endorsed "Stand Your Ground" law—which protects an individual's right to defend his life with deadly force if he feels threatened—in not charging Zimmerman.

And yet, with the national outcry over the case growing, touching off a country-wide conversation about the status of black men and boys in a society that often fears them, the nation's African American president seemed conspicuous in his silence. Friends said that as a father, Obama was deeply disturbed by Martin's death. Despite the objections of his senior communications staff, he resolved to speak out.

And so just after 10 A.M. on the day after the Sanford march, with Hillary Clinton and Tim Geithner standing on either side of the podium in the White House Rose Garden for the announcement of the nominee to head the World Bank, President Obama took a single, expected question.

"Mr. President, may I ask you about this current case in

Florida, very controversial, allegations of lingering racism within our society—the so-called . . . Stand Your Ground law and the justice in that? Can you comment on the Trayvon Martin case, sir?"

Obama began by noting that as head of the executive branch, and with Eric Holder's Justice Department in an open investigation, his remarks required care. He called Martin's death an obvious tragedy and said that when he thought "about this boy, I think about my own kids."

Obama said every parent should understand why the case had to be thoroughly investigated in order to prevent future tragedies and called on the nation to "do some soul searching to figure out how does something like this happen," including examining "the laws and the context for what happened, as well as the specifics of the incident." It wasn't a call to review the nation's gun laws or for activists to take to the streets.

And then Obama directed a message to Trayvon Martin's parents. "If I had a son, he'd look like Trayvon," he said. "And I think they are right to expect that all of us as Americans are going to take this with the seriousness it deserves, and that we're going to get to the bottom of exactly what happened."

It all seemed innocuous enough. The president hadn't mentioned race as a root cause or even a factor in the shooting. He hadn't criticized the legal process in Sanford, or its police force. Given that he is a black man, it seemed self-evident that if Barack Obama had a son, he, too, would be black, like Trayvon was.

Conservative media had largely sat out the national conversation on the shooting that was enthralling liberal media outlets and thought leaders. But Obama's Rose Garden statement gave them a fresh opportunity to draw blood, and by the time he was appearing on Sean Hannity's 3 P.M. radio show, Newt Gingrich had changed his mind, making a sharp U-turn from his remarks as recently as earlier that day. Now he rushed head-first into the breach, calling Obama's comments "disgraceful," accusing the president of dividing the country by race, and asking provocatively, "Is the president suggesting that if it had been a white who had been shot, that would be okay because it didn't look like him?"

It wasn't long before the national shock over Trayvon Martin's killing turned into a polarized showdown, between black supporters of Martin's family and a growing number of white Americans who dismissed the marches, news conferences, and demands for justice as merely the latest in a history of racial taunts by Al Sharpton and other black leaders, designed to hold white Americans guilty and black Americans inviolable, forever. In that vein, the "national dialogue on race" that activists were calling for was most unwanted.

Soon, Trayvon Martin was being demonized in some right-wing quarters as an archetypal "thug"—particularly once attorneys for Zimmerman pushed to make public his text messages, which were filled with a teenager's bravado. Conservative blogs seized on any kernel of information injurious to the dead teenager and his family, and Sean Hannity taped a sympathetic interview with George Zimmerman, which prosecutors, confounding legal watchers, would play back in lieu of his testimony during a belated trial.

And just as happened in the Henry Louis Gates incident, polls soon showed black and white Americans, and Republicans and Democrats, decamping to opposite ideological silos as the case hurtled toward a Sanford courtroom and the country headed for another polarized presidential election. The ongoing process of "racializing" Barack Obama had received another gear.

CHAPTER 10

Victory

Victory has a thousand fathers, but defeat is an orphan.

—John F. Kennedy, April 21, 1961

FOR THE 2012 ELECTION, THE REPUBLICAN PARTY PROVIDED Democrats the perfect foil in Mitt Romney, the patrician former venture capitalist and the son of the late, moderate governor of Michigan. As the governor of Massachusetts, Romney signed the progenitor to the Affordable Care Act, derided by conservatives as "Romneycare," which allowed Romney's opponents on the left and the right to skewer him as a health-care hypocrite. Meanwhile, Romney's record as the head of Bain Capital opened him up to a portrayal by his foes in both parties as a job-canceling Simon Legree. The latter image was cemented in September when *Mother Jones* posted on its website a surreptitiously recorded cell phone video of Romney at a Boca Raton, Florida, fund-raiser, commiserating with the similarly well-heeled about the "forty-seven percent" of Americans who, as government dependents and self-declared victims, would vote for Obama "no matter what."

Romney chose as his running mate Wisconsin congressman Paul Ryan, the author of serial House Republican budgets that proposed to strip away funding for programs aiding the poor, institute vouchers for Medicare, and give generous tax cuts to the wealthy.

Despite the continued scourge of unemployment, black voters remained incredibly motivated to support the president's reelection. Polls showed African Americans evincing higher degrees of optimism about the economy than the general public. It was clear that whatever the economic or political headwinds, blacks were determined that Barack Obama's presidency would be seen as more than a mere accident of history by being consigned to a single term.

And there was the math, which, as pointed out by veteran journalist Ron Brownstein, suggested that even if white voters didn't shed another 2 percent of their voter population share (which they did, dropping from 74 to 72 percent of the electoral pool), Obama would triumph so long as he received votes from 80 percent of minorities and just 40 percent from white Americans; on the Republican side, Romney needed an historic 61 percent of white ballots, a performance on the order of Ronald Reagan or Dwight Eisenhower.

By the summer of 2012, Bill Clinton had become the leading surrogate for the Obama reelection campaign. His singular purpose was to go into white, rural, and blue-collar communities and translate the Obama presidency into terms that Reagan Democrats could accept. Clinton at times seemed to desire Obama's reelection almost as badly as Obama did—a development that delighted the Washington media and triggered the cynicism of some in and around the Clinton orbit.

"Immediately after the [2008] election, in my view, the Clinton operatives and particularly Bill and Hillary Clinton themselves began looking at 2016," one longtime member of Congress said. "And what better way to embed your operatives than to go ahead and cooperate" with Obama's reelection.

"Hillary and Bill aren't dumb," said a former Clinton staffer. "I think they know they had to do that for their own reputations." Clinton's administration had been the incubator for key members of the Obama team, from Rahm Emanuel to Eric Holder to Susan Rice. And while Obama's Chicago branch ran the politics, the Clinton wing was fully represented in the policy arena, from John Podesta at the Center for American Progress, to Leon Panetta at the Defense Department and Hillary Clinton at the State Department.

Although Obama had undone key Clinton compromises on gay rights, his "evolution" allowed the Clintons to move left on those very issues, with the former president renouncing his signature on "Don't Ask, Don't Tell" and walking away from the Defense of Marriage Act. The Clinton and Obama wings of the Democratic Party had found an accommodation that could replace the New Democrat ideal and would better position Hillary with young and emerging voters in the future.

"Lincoln's team of rivals was the classic example," the longtime member of Congress said. "JFK and Lyndon Johnson couldn't stand each other," but Johnson understood that his own legacy was intertwined with Kennedy's. Friends of the Clintons saw the same dynamic, as Bill continued to plot a political comeback for his wife.

At the Democratic convention in Charlotte, North Carolina, on September 5, Bill Clinton took the stage and launched into an expansive defense of the Obama era and the president's economic policies, leading the forty-fourth president to label the forty-second as the "the Secretary of Explaining Stuff." Afterward, the two appeared onstage together, seeming with one walk down a prefabricated stage to heal years of Democratic dissonance.

Clinton declared that he came to Charlotte to nominate a

man who was "cool on the outside but who burned for America on the inside . . . who believes with no doubt that we can build a new American dream economy driven by innovation and creativity . . . and by cooperation . . . and who had the good sense to marry Michelle Obama."

It was Clinton at his best, and the former president would do more, hosting a series of fund-raisers to "shake the money tree" among liberal Democrats who, by the fall of 2012, were less enamored of Barack Obama, but who, as Democrats, wanted to see him reelected.

And when Obama was reelected on November 6, the victory was resounding.

He beat Romney by some 5 million votes—winning every state he'd won in 2008, except North Carolina and Indiana—taking a commanding 332 electoral votes and a 51 percent showing in the popular vote. He had confounded pundits and Republican operatives, who had gone into the election certain that Mitt Romney would be the next president.

The origins of the victory were clear. Obama was presiding over a party that had fundamentally changed: It was more black, more brown, and more Asian; and those groups now represented a golden share of the presidential year electorate, at 28 percent. Romney had 60 percent of white voters in his corner, but that simply couldn't get him to a majority without winning more than a nominal share of black and particularly Hispanic voters.

For the first time in the country's history, African Americans voted at a higher percentage than their white counterparts. Their determination to defend the president and his legacy was just one factor in their electoral zeal. Another, and palpably so, was the cascade of voter laws that sprang up after the 2010 elections.

In the wake of that midterm triumph, Republican-controlled legislatures had unleashed a flurry of laws, some using model legislation crafted by the American Legislative Exchange Council, a veritable conservative bill factory. In Ohio and Florida, the Republican-led legislatures set out to decrease the period for early voting, and state legislatures in red and newly red states sought to erect stricter criteria for voting applications that in some cases invalidated the registrations of voters who had gone to the polls without incident for decades, or made it harder for students to vote in the states where they attend school or for women who had changed their surnames after marriage or divorce to vote.

The tea party movement was declining in popularity, but the Right's core activists remained fiercely devoted to the idea that restricting access to the ballot was the way to win back the White House. Groups like True the Vote, funded through grants by the Bradley Foundation and other conservative nonprofits that were less ostentatious than the notorious Koch brothers but no less enthusiastic, paid for billboards that warned of legal consequences for "fraud" at the polls in Ohio and Wisconsin. They also dispatched volunteers to "observe" polling locations in majority-black precincts in key states nationwide. At True the Vote's national summit in Houston in April 2012, Bill Ouren, the group's national "elections coordinator," said that voting under the watchful eye of the tea party–allied group should feel "like driving and seeing the police following you."

By June 2011, ten states had enacted strict voter ID laws, including five in the South—Alabama, South Carolina, Tennessee, Virginia, and Mississippi—along with Kansas, Texas, Rhode Island, Wisconsin, and the strictest of them all, Pennsylvania, where a Republican state representative, Mike Turzai, boasted that the law would ensure a Romney win.

The Pennsylvania law was eventually struck down by a federal judge, and a spate of lawsuits filed by Eric Holder's Justice Department and its busy Civil Rights Division slowed the rush toward nationwide voter ID laws, which civil rights organizations viewed as a slide backward toward Jim Crow. But as the

2012 election dawned, news about the efforts by the Right to enact these laws clearly aimed at making it more difficult for minorities to vote triggered a virtual stampede of black and Hispanic voters to the polls.

"I don't think even the mainstream *Democratic* politicians understood how voter ID and voter suppression would be a galvanizing issue," Marc Morial said, adding that had Republicans run this "through the lens of common sense and intuition" they might have predicted the depth and breadth of the backlash among not only black but also Hispanic voters.

Many had predicted that black voters would sit out the election out of disaffection with the economy, Obama's failure to fulfill some campaign promises, or even his "evolution" into an official supporter of gay marriage, which some thought would sink him with black evangelicals.

Instead, despite lines that in some states stretched on for hours, 1.8 million more African Americans went to the polls than did so in 2008, while 2 million fewer white voters cast ballots. Obama lost the white vote by a catastrophic margin, but the electorate was infused with a share of black, brown, Asian, and white urban voters that was large enough to counterbalance the lowest share of white voters, at 39 percent, that any Democrat had claimed in a generation.

President Obama's second inauguration, on Martin Luther King Jr. Day, was punctuated by a call to national unity, and by cultural notes that spanned generations. There was the invocation, delivered by Myrlie Evers-Williams, widow of slain civil rights leader Medgar Evers; and the administration of the vice presidential oath by the Supreme Court's first Latina justice, Sonia Sotomayor. There was the president's speech, which offered the first ever inclusion in an inaugural address of gay and lesbian Americans in the American pageant, and the oath of office taken on a pair of Bibles: one that had been owned by Abraham Lincoln, the other by Martin Luther King Jr. The secular hymnal of the country—from "America the Beautiful" to "The Star-Spangled Banner"—were sung by an eclectic range of voices, from James Taylor to Kelly Clarkson to Beyoncé.

As THE PRESIDENT ENTERED HIS SECOND TERM, REPUBLICANS were more determined than ever to neutralize him by repealing his health-care law and stripping away hated policies like financial reform. Just as they had in 2010, moderate and red-state Democrats would flee from the reelected president as they focused on the 2014 midterms. Key U.S. Senate races were to be waged largely in the South, which was now hostile territory to the party that once ruled it unilaterally. The South had become the home to two political parties: one black and Democratic and the other Republican and white. Democrats on Capitol Hill, faced with the choice of validating Barack Obama, as Bill Clinton had done, or spurning him to curry favor with increasingly conservative white voters, were choosing the latter.

In February 2013, more than a dozen civil rights leaders gathered in the White House for a meeting with the president. The groups represented included the NAACP, National Action Network, National Urban League, National Coalition on Black Civic Participation, National Council of Negro Women, Joint Center for Political and Economic Studies, and the Leadership Conference on Civil and Human Rights, along with Washington, D.C.'s historic Nineteenth Street Baptist Church, whose pastor attended. They called for aggressive administration policies to halt black unemployment, which had declined to 13.8 percent while the nation's total jobless rate had fallen to below 8 percent. They also wanted the president to attack disparities in the criminal justice system and education. But mostly they'd come to talk about voter ID and the other laws that challenged the belief that every American of age should have free access to the ballot.

Obama didn't disagree about the laws' pernicious intent. But he cautioned the group not to make voter ID the "be all and end all," telling those assembled that "if people want to vote they can," and "you can't assume you can't vote and not meet the test that's set up by the state and then claim you've been disenfranchised," one participant recalled, adding, "And there's some truth in that."

"There are clearly examples where he has shied away from matters of race and examples where his team overreacted, like with Shirley Sherrod, who I believe they threw under bus, but in this instance he was just trying to calibrate things," the participant recalled. "I think depending on who heard it, it came off differently, but he was not denying the significance of the issue" of voter ID.

Still, some in the group were surprised by Obama's comments, and not pleasantly so, having gone all out for months to fight against voter ID laws. Now the president seemed to be saying that if people want to vote badly enough they could, and that his reelection and the long lines of black and Hispanic voters around the country had demonstrated as much.

"He said we had to get over it," another participant said, recalling that the president even mentioned polls showing broad support for voter ID laws. "I was sitting there just still kind of completely sapped of energy from crisscrossing the country firing up our people to stop voter suppression so that he could become president [again] and then we all sit down in the White House and he thanks us by telling us to get over it. . . . I was just thinking, *You've got to be fucking kidding me.*"

Some in the room worried that Obama, ever the pragmatist, failed to see the peril not just for his presidency but also for his most loyal constituency. Voter ID was just one weapon Republican state legislatures and governors could use against minority voters. States were also busy restricting early voting days and hours, making it harder for working-class Americans to make it to the polls before they closed, and particularly targeting the Sunday before elections, known in black churches as "souls to the polls Sunday," for closure in key states like Ohio and Florida.

"If you're a senator from Illinois you can get over voter ID," the second participant, a younger movement activist, said. "But if you're the president of the United States, leading the Democratic Party that has been targeted by voter suppression, let alone the first black president, when blacks are being targeted, then you shouldn't be saying 'get over' any aspect of voter suppression; the only thing you should be saying is 'fight, fight, fight!'"

"I think he's against it," a third participant in the White House meeting said of the president's views on voter ID. "I think he understands it in political terms related to his own [re]election," that when you try to suppress voters, they turn out more. The problem, the participant said, is that many of those who work in the White House "don't know anybody without a driver's license."

The meeting ended with the group and the president largely agreeing to disagree, and with several participants concerned that the White House wasn't going to fight hard enough to protect the votes of the very people whose enthusiasm had helped make him president twice, with another potentially disastrous midterm looming.

"Our view [was that] the interests we hold dear wouldn't be served by having McConnell leading the Senate, so we were trying to do everything we [could] to increase black turnout," the first participant said.

In 2013 THE NATION MARKED THE FIFTIETH ANNIVERSARY OF John F. Kennedy's momentous civil rights speech, and remembered his assassination; the martyrdom of Medgar Evers; George Wallace's stand in the schoolhouse door; Dr. King's letter from a Birmingham jail and the March on Washington; and the children who paid, with their fire-hosed and dog-bitten bodies and with their lives, for the Birmingham campaign. The nation paused to remember four little girls who today could perhaps be grandmothers had they not been destroyed by bombs and fire with the 16th Street Baptist Church.

In addition to the country having reelected its first African American president, a bronze bust of Isabella Baumfree, the former slave who fought both for abolition and the rights of women and who at the age of forty-six renamed herself Sojourner Truth, now stood in the Capitol visitors' center. A granite monument to Dr. Martin Luther King Jr. peered out onto the National Mall, carved into the Stone of Hope, separated by a small expanse from the Stone of Despair.

And yet Barack Obama was still engaged in an ongoing dialogue with members of the black intellectual class, who parsed his every word and keynote and commencement speech for evidence of the hated dogma of "respectability," which for many equated to blaming the victims of a house fire for getting burned.

Obama's insistence on pursuing the Responsibility Gospel with black men, continually admonishing them to be better fathers, and the black community to get its young men off the street and into college classrooms, while refusing to adopt explicitly targeted policies to alleviate black economic suffering—hadn't hurt him a whit with black voters, who, like many members of the Black Caucus, seemed to subordinate private concerns to their determination to protect the Obama presidency from its right-wing foes. Many African Americans believed members of the Right were openly disdainful of the president at least in part due to his race. With polls showing the president's approval ratings remaining high with African Americans, if not at the stratospheric levels of the beginning of his term, the White House was not about to give in to demands from Capitol Hill, or from the pages of *The Atlantic,* or from Ebony.com, that he fix his policies with a black label. The White House team insisted that fixing the overall economy, along with broadly targeted health-care and education reform, was the best way to address the economic and health disparities in black households, who suffered disproportionately from both. It wasn't necessary to launch a "Mashall Plan for Black America," as some black lawmakers were calling for.

The difference of opinion rankled some in the black community who'd watched as the president championed specific remedies for discrimination against gays in the workplace and the military, women in terms of equal pay, and the Latino community with immigration reform. Some of them wondered, *Why not African Americans?*

Obama was slated to give the commencement address at Morehouse College on May 19, a singular honor for the school that was the alma mater of Dr. Martin Luther King Jr. and a jewel in the crown of the nation's historically black colleges and universities. But Obama's arrival was upstaged in advance by an editorial from a Morehouse alumnus, Rev. Kevin Johnson, the pastor of Bright Hope Baptist Church in Philadelphia; he was scheduled to speak ahead of the president. The column, in the black newspaper the *Philadelphia Tribune,* was titled, "A President for Everyone, Except Black People." It referenced a recent letter to Obama from the incoming chair of the Congressional Black Caucus, Marcia Fudge, the former Ohio small-city mayor who'd succeeded the late Stephanie Tubbs Jones into the House. Fudge's letter chided the White House for a lack of diversity in the president's second-term cabinet, citing the implications for African Americans.

Johnson had a clear and familiar reference point for his criticism: the administration and diverse cabinet of William Jefferson Clinton.

"While having African Americans in senior cabinet positions does not guarantee an economic agenda that will advance Black people," Johnson wrote, "it at least is a starting point and puts us in the driver's seat. With President Obama, we are not in the driver's seat or even in the car." His critiques were echoed by Douglas Wilder, once an Obama supporter, who began publicly blasting the president over the predominantly white and male cast of his administration, and over the lack of targeted policies to address black economic pain.

With the op-ed gaining traction online, Johnson was promptly disinvited from the commencement by Morehouse's president, prompting an outcry from liberals as well as conservatives, including an op-ed in *National Review* denouncing the college's actions. Johnson's speaking engagement was restored, but he would address the graduates during an earlier event, separate from the president's appearance.

On the podium, Obama launched into his now-familiar admonitions to black men, confessing to the "bad choices" of his own youth, when he sometimes "wrote off my own failings as just another example of the world trying to keep a black man down.

"But one of the things you've learned over the last four years," the president said, "is that there's no longer any room for excuses. I understand that there's a common fraternity creed here at Morehouse: 'excuses are tools of the incompetent, used to build bridges to nowhere and monuments of nothingness.' We've got no time for excuses—not because the bitter legacies of slavery and segregation have vanished entirely; they haven't. Not because racism and discrimination no longer exist; that's still out there. It's just that in today's hyperconnected, hypercompetitive world, with a billion young people from China and India and Brazil entering the global workforce alongside you, nobody is going to give you anything you haven't earned. And whatever hardships you may experience because of your race, they pale in comparison to the hardships previous generations endured—and overcame."

Writing on *The Atlantic*'s website, Ta-Nehisi Coates called Obama "the scold of black America" and charged that "taking the full measure of the Obama presidency thus far, it is hard to avoid the conclusion that this White House has one way of addressing the social ills that afflict black people—and particularly black youth—and another way of addressing everyone else."

The speech touched off a rollicking debate among black and white intellectuals, who on one side consisting almost exclusively of black writers and thinkers, blasted Obama's "responsibility gospel" as a blame-the-victim approach to struggling communities, and on the other, racially mixed side, pointed to the administration's concrete accomplishments and their real and lasting implications for African Americans, who would disproportionately benefit from improved access to private health care, expanded Medicaid, the protection from abuse by predatory lenders and credit card companies included in financial reform, and the easing of federal sentencing disparities between black and white defendants. Easing those concrete burdens on everyday life would mean more than a day's restraint from the familiar church homilies on responsible behavior, Obama's defenders, including respected writers like Jonathan Capehart and Jonathan Chait, contended. It was the age-old argument between behavior and outcomes, symbolism and targeted investment, outside forces and internal fortitude, and the power of each to enforce or alleviate systemic suffering. Obama had long since come down on one side of that debate, and it was not the side that many of the leading black writers and intellectuals of the day—Ta-Nehisi Coates, Melissa Harris-Perry, Jamelle Bouie, Jelani Cobb, Mychal Denzel Smith, Michael Eric Dyson, and others—were on.

Obama's defenders argued that his black critics failed to recognize the breadth and depth of Republican resistance, not just to Obama's agenda, but to his very being, and the tight restrictions around the explication of race that the country's first black president operated under. For the nation's first black president to announce a series of programs targeting his own racial community would only deepen Republican resistance, the argument went, and make Obama more politically toxic than he already was, not just to Republicans, but to moderate Democrats on the Hill. That would make getting any semblance of an agenda through Congress impossible.

"To expect the president to introduce an explicit and definable 'black agenda' in a Congress filled with people who believe him to be a socialist destroying the country while illegitimately occupying the Oval Office is seriously naïve," Jonathan Capehart wrote in the *Washington Post,* a point echoed by Al Sharpton, who continually pointed out to these critics that Obama's challenge when it came to maintaining his influence over American politics was to not only *be* the president of all Americans, but to be *seen* as such.

The president's defenders pointed to Valerie Jarrett's status as the president's closest and most powerful adviser, and her careful consideration of issues facing black institutions. Civil rights leaders pointed to Anthony Foxx, the former Charlotte mayor appointed as transportation secretary; Mel Watt, the former congressman from North Carolina whom Obama tapped to head the Federal Housing Finance Agency , whose appointments were partly credited to Representative Fudge's prodding; and the three nominees the president would announce in June, to fill vacancies on the U.S. Court of Appeals for the District of Columbia Circuit, which reviews most federal regulations, including those impacting the Affordable Care Act.

In October, Jeh Johnson would be nominated to lead the Department of Homeland Security, making the face of the country's federal law enforcement apparatus—from the attorney general to counterterrorism, to the Bureau of Alcohol, Tobacco, Firearms and Explosives, headed by B. Todd Jones—the face of black men. The president would tap a rising Latino political star, Julián Castro of Texas, to lead the Department of Housing and Urban Development, and fill the open seat at the Consumer Financial Protection Bureau, which had been the brainchild of newly elected Massachusetts senator Elizabeth Warren, with Richard Cordray, a favorite of civil rights leaders.

The president bristled at suggestions that he didn't care enough, or do enough, for African Americans, members of his team said. From the administration's point of view, Obama was providing both a living example of progress, and tangible access to it, from the health-care law, to education fixes to shore up black students and better prepare them to go to college, to an improving economy that was directly alleviating suffering.

In public forums, and in private discussions with African American members of the media in particular, administration officials like Valerie Jarrett and Anton Gunn, the deputy state director of Obama's 2008 campaign in South Carolina, who went on to lead the external affairs office at the U.S. Department of Health and Human Services, stressed continually that if Republican governors and legislatures across the South had not rejected the health-care law's expansion of Medicaid, nearly 5 million more Americans would have had access to insurance that would enable them to afford to see a doctor. Half of them were black and Hispanic, and the remainder were among the white working poor.

Obama was presiding over a country that was as politically and racially polarized as it had been in decades. Or perhaps simply more overtly so. And while Democrats blamed the far-right tea party and its growing stranglehold on the GOP, conservatives just as vehemently blamed the president and his administration for stoking, rather than alleviating, the racial divide.

In August 2013, conservative writer Ross Douthat, in a *New York Times* blog post, said Democrats had "embraced and furthered the trend" toward "racial polarization of the parties." He accused the Obama campaign team of abandoning the

Clinton-era strategy of wooing anti-abortion, pro-coal, working-class whites who were skeptical on matters of immigration and hawkish on matters of crime. He said the campaign had alienated swing voters who once made the notion of a North Dakota, West Virginia, or Arkansas Democrat possible. Douthat and other conservatives laid the blame squarely at the White House door, for pushing away religious, blue-collar white voters through their pursuit of marriage equality, abortion rights, gun control, and the secularist marginalization of God.

While Obama in 2008 had slightly improved upon previous Democratic presidential candidates' performance with white voters, in 2012 his reelection was attended by a near collapse of white support for him and his party, particularly in the South. The turn among white voters had begun during the first months of Obama's presidency and it had been swift and sharp, resulting in a steep decline in the president's approval ratings in 2009. By 2010, researchers at Brown University and the University of California, Los Angeles had determined that attachment to the two political parties was becoming "increasingly polarized by both racial attitudes and race, as a result of Obama's rise to prominence within the Democratic Party," and that the most resentful white voters had fled the fastest and most furtively toward the GOP.

Despite a tendency toward conciliation that some of his liberal supporters found maddening, and a studious avoidance of race-centered conflict, President Obama had been unable to prevent the relentless narrative tide on the right, which stoked deep-seated opposition to everything from the health-care law to immigration reform, primed by a broad discomfort, particularly among older Americans, with the sweeping demographic changes overtaking the country, whose white majority was shrinking with every presidential election.

For many Americans, their country was being forcibly changed, whether by a perceived "invasion" of "illegal" migrants pouring across the southern border, through a corrupted voting system that was robbing Republican candidates of their rightful victories, or by an "imperial" president who was ignoring the will of congressional Republicans and thus the "true" will of the American people. Obama was the exotically named, racially mixed cipher for their deepest fears. Also, his occasional digressions from the constant reminders—required of every American politician, including any politician of color who sought broad support—of the country's inherent goodness and progress and exceptionalism made him an enemy.

Stoked by conservative media, aggrieved Americans found evidence of the president's alleged infidelity to defending the lives of its citizens in such tragedies as the failed, Bush-era anti-gunrunning program code-named "Fast and Furious," in which a U.S. Border Patrol agent died, and the terrorist raid on two American diplomatic and intelligence compounds in Benghazi, Libya, in September 2012, in which four Americans were killed, including the U.S. ambassador to Libya, J. Christopher Stevens. They agitated for investigations of the IRS's reviews of tea party and liberal organizations seeking tax-exempt status, and encouraged the never-ending scrutiny of Obama's birth certificate.

If the 2010 election, which handed swing states like Ohio, Pennsylvania, Michigan, and Wisconsin over to Republicans in a census year, was the first blow by the Right against the coalition that placed Obama in the White House, the second came on June 25, 2013. On that day the Supreme Court's five-member conservative majority ruled in the case of *Shelby County v. Holder* that Section 4 of the Voting Rights Act of 1965—which provided the formula for determining which geographical areas must have their voting laws reviewed by the federal government or federal courts—was unconstitutional, and remanded to a hopelessly gridlocked Congress the job of updating it. Justice

Clarence Thomas, filing a separate, concurring opinion, stated that he would have struck down any requirement to preclear state voting laws.

"Our country has changed," a triumphal Chief Justice John G. Roberts Jr. wrote in the majority decision, citing the large black voter turnout in the recent presidential elections in which Barack Obama was on the ballot, swelling the ranks of black participation. He wrote specifically about the southern states that once were home to the most trenchant resistance to black registration, as proof that federal oversight of those states was arcane, unfair, and no longer necessary. History, Roberts wrote, "did not end in 1965."

Opponents of the ruling cried that history didn't begin in 2008, either.

The decision ripped the heart out of the 1965 law, passed in the wake of "Bloody Sunday" during Dr. King's Selma marches, to patch the holes in the Civil Rights Act, which, for all its breadth in sweeping aside impediments to black daily life, had failed to address the ongoing barriers for blacks at southern voting booths.

Legal experts said the decision was a brazen renunciation of judicial restraint and a bold move to free the former Jim Crow states from federal scrutiny, and would be felt all over the country. Civil rights groups also noted that when Roberts was a deputy solicitor general in the Reagan administration, he opposed strengthening the Voting Rights and Fair Housing acts and "urged undoing policies aimed at achieving racial diversity in employment, education, and broadcasting through affirmative action," while casting doubt on the right to privacy for women seeking abortions and referring to the "the purported gender gap."

In dissent, Justice Ruth Bader Ginsburg cited current barriers to voting access, including gerrymandering that still remained heavily freighted by race. Ginsburg proclaimed that the majority's decision was full of "hubris" in ignoring Congress, which had renewed the Voting Rights Act as recently as 2006, and said they had relied simply "on increases in voter registration and turnout as if that were the whole story.

"Throwing out preclearance when it has worked and is continuing to work to stop discriminatory changes is like throwing away your umbrella in a rainstorm because you are not getting wet," Ginsburg's dissent continued. "The sad irony of today's decision lies in its utter failure to grasp why the VRA has proven effective. . . . The Court appears to believe that the VRA's success in eliminating the specific devices extant in 1965 means that preclearance is no longer needed. . . . With that belief, and the argument derived from it, history repeats itself."

Indeed, within two hours of the court's decision, Greg Abbott, the Texas attorney general, announced that his state would immediately implement a voter ID law that a federal court had previously prevented. In turn, the attorney general of Alabama, where the Shelby County litigation began, put in place a law that required proof of citizenship in the form of a birth certificate or passport to legally vote.

Within forty-eight hours, six of the nine states once covered by preclearance, all in the heart of the South, had tightened their voting laws. For voters in Mississippi, Arkansas, South Carolina, Texas, Alabama, and Virginia, the impact of the Supreme Court's decision would be felt as early as the next election.

Within weeks, North Carolina enacted the most tight-fisted law of them all: It shortened the time for early voting, tightened restrictions on acceptable identification—for example, ID from the state's colleges was insufficient to vote—ended same-day voter registration and preregistration of sixteen- and seventeen-year-olds in the state's public schools, forbade provisional ballots for anyone who goes to the wrong precinct, and barred county clerks from extending voting hours, even in cases of emergency.

Protests broke out at the state capitol—dubbed "Moral Mondays" by Rev. William Barber, the head of the North Carolina NAACP—compounded by the governor's refusal to expand Medicaid under the national health-care law.

Even states that had been beyond the reach of the Voting Rights Act, since they had not previously been required to preclear their election laws, moved to take advantage of the ruling, eliminating same-day voter registration in Wisconsin, and slashing the early voting period in Ohio.

Civil rights organizations began filing suits. The NAACP Legal Defense Fund and groups like the Advancement Project and the Lawyers Committee on Civil Rights Under Law geared up for a fresh round of legal battles, from state to federal courts. Eric Holder's office at the Justice Department was remanded to the front lines and he announced that his Civil Rights Division was joining the lawsuits in Texas and North Carolina. Holder stated, "We will not allow the Supreme Court's recent decision to be interpreted as open season for states to pursue measures that suppress voting rights."

Holder had become the man conservatives hated nearly as much as the president. He had already been held in contempt of Congress for allegedly refusing to disclose Justice Department documents on Operation Fast and Furious. In the first year after the Supreme Court's *Shelby County v. Holder* decision, the Justice Department would take the states of Ohio, Wisconsin, and Pennsylvania to court. Conservatives were furious. Texas governor Rick Perry accused the Justice Department of mounting an "end-run around the Supreme Court [that] undermines the will of the people of Texas, and casts unfair aspersions on our state's common-sense efforts to preserve the integrity of our elections process.

"Once again," Perry said, "the Obama administration is demonstrating utter contempt for our country's system of checks and balances, not to mention the U.S. Constitution."

Perry was joined by Texas senator John Cornyn, who accused Holder of running a "politicized Justice Department bent on inserting itself into the sovereign affairs of Texas." He declared, "[W]e reject the notion that the federal government knows what's best for us."

Greg Abbott, the state's attorney general, doubled down on his state's intent to "prevent illegal votes," adding for good measure that "Eric Holder's outrageous claim that voter ID is a racist plot to disenfranchise minority voters is gutter politics and is offensive to the overwhelming majority of Texans of all races who support this ballot integrity measure."

On July 13, a Saturday, two weeks after the Supreme Court's landmark decision, a Sanford, Florida, jury, which included only one nonwhite member, acquitted George Zimmerman for killing Trayvon Martin, touching off nationwide protests, from Times Square to Miami. The conservative media rejoiced. Zimmerman had become a cultural hero of the Right, whereas for many black Americans he had become a chilling emblem of the metastasizing power of the gun, wielded not just by police officers, but even by fellow citizens, whose deadly actions reflected the still-commonplace visceral fear of black men.

Rev. Al Sharpton, who had stood with Martin's family and led mass protests calling for Zimmerman's arrest, denounced the verdict as an "atrocity" and a "slap in the face to those that believe in justice in this country."

The next day, the president released a statement that called on Americans to "respect the call for calm reflection from two parents who lost their young son," and admonished his fellow countrymen to "ask ourselves if we're doing all we can to widen the circle of compassion and understanding in our own communities . . . if we're doing all we can to stem the tide of gun violence that claims too many lives across this country on a daily basis . . . and . . . as individuals and as a society, how we can prevent future tragedies like this." He added, "That's the way to honor Trayvon Martin."

For many, the first president who had experienced American life in brown skin had released an overly studious missive that was devoid of personal reflection and seemed hollow and insufficient. Michelle Alexander, a law professor at Ohio State University whose book *The New Jim Crow* had become a bible for those engaged in the struggle against mass incarceration and the disproportionate weight of the criminal justice system on black lives, accused Obama and Holder of promoting "frank conversations about race" but showing "relatively little in terms of actual initiative and leadership . . . around issues of racial justice." Alexander expressed her hope that "in the months that follow the Trayvon Martin tragedy, . . . we will see much more courage and bold leadership coming from the Justice Department."

Civil rights leaders, including National Urban League president Marc Morial, challenged Obama to use this moment to arrest the economic decline in black communities, while Rev. Jesse Jackson, on CNN, urged the president to offer "moral leadership," noting that "the heat will continue to rise."

Even the president's strongest supporters pleaded with him not to let the crisis pass. Sharpton publicly and privately pressed Obama to speak out, whatever the political consequences. Cornell Belcher, an African American whose polling firm aided Obama's 2008 and 2012 campaigns, called the verdict "an opportunity for us not to kick the can down the road again," and "a chance for the president to get larger than the regular politics and the racial riffs would dictate . . . an opportunity to create an understanding. A lot of white America doesn't seem to understand the hurt that's in the African American community today."

In a *Washington Post* op-ed, Janet Langhart Cohen, a black author and former television journalist who is married to Clinton-era defense secretary William Cohen, lamented Obama's sober call for "calm reflection": "Few expected the president to denounce the verdict or call upon people to take to the streets in protest, but we did expect him to speak in a way that touched the heartbreak, despair and quiet rage that so many of us feel at this moment."

Langhart Cohen wrote,

> On multiple occasions, Obama has asked blacks to understand the high wire he is forced to walk on the subject of race. He has pleaded that we cut him some slack. Most have done so even as conditions in the black community have become more desperate. We have waited and watched the president address issues of importance to women, gays and lesbians, Latinos and the security of our allies. We praised his boldness in speaking to the issue of sexual orientation during his visit to Africa. For the past four years, we have remained silent; some have been satisfied that Obama being the first black president was reason enough to seal our lips and muffle our voices. But most were convinced that, once he entered his second term, Obama would be liberated from the racial harness that politics forced him to wear.

Citing Dr. King's "fierce urgency of now," and noting that white presidents, including John F. Kennedy and Lyndon Johnson, had spoken forcefully on matters of race, Langhart Cohen expressed the "hope that President Obama will speak not just to black people or just to white people but to the good people in America." She added, "We can never have racial reconciliation without discussing the truth."

Protests and vigils were flaring around the country. In Tallahassee, Florida, more than a dozen members of a coalition of young activists calling themselves the Dream Defenders, who had marched to Sanford in the early days of the Trayvon Martin uproar, staged a sit-in inside the governor's office, demanding a change in the state's Stand Your Ground gun law. Three days after the verdict, on July 16, Holder told the NAACP's annual national convention in Orlando, less than a hundred miles from where Trayvon Martin was killed, that Martin's death was "tragic and unnecessary." The case "provides yet another opportunity for our nation to speak honestly—and openly—about the complicated and emotionally charged issues that this case has raised," Holder said. He went on to declare: "It's time to question laws that senselessly expand the concept of self-defense and sow dangerous conflict in our neighborhoods . . . [by] allowing and perhaps encouraging violent situations to escalate in public."

On the same day Holder spoke out, Hillary Clinton did, too, telling the fourteen thousand women assembled at the fifty-first annual convention of the black sorority Delta Sigma Theta in Washington that "no mother, no father, should ever have to fear for their child walking down a street in the United States of America."

Perhaps the fiercest pressure for Obama to speak more forcefully on the Trayvon Martin case came from within his personal circle. The people closest to him and Michelle were asking: If he, the nation's first black president, couldn't speak about the death of a young African American man with profundity, with depth, then what was the point?

Friends said Obama had indeed been profoundly shaken by Trayvon Martin's death, which one longtime mentor called "one of the most upsetting things in his lifetime." But he was always mindful of his delicate walk as president, as well as the minefields that constantly awaited him when he wandered into the arena of race. But ultimately he decided the people calling on him to say more were right. He would make a public statement, and he would not preview his remarks for his communications team.

On July 19, the president offered the most personal comments he'd made on the realities of race in America since his "Philadelphia speech" in March 2008 in the wake of the Rev. Wright controversy. That speech had been called "A More Perfect Union." Now, as president, Obama stood in the briefing room to lay out, with greater specificity, some of those imperfections.

He spoke for eighteen minutes, remarking on the grace and dignity of Martin's parents, and reiterating his sorrow for their loss. He said the Sanford jury had spoken. And then he began to talk about the context of the anguish reverberating across black America.

"You know, when Trayvon Martin was first shot, I said that this could have been my son," Obama said.

Another way of saying that is Trayvon Martin could have been me thirty-five years ago. And when you think about why, in the African American community at least, there's a lot of pain around what happened here, I think it's important to recognize that the African American community is looking at this issue through a set of experiences and a history that doesn't go away.

There are very few African American men in this country who haven't had the experience of being followed when they were shopping in a department store. That includes me. There are very few African American men who haven't had the experience of walking across the street and hearing the locks click on the doors of cars. That happens to me—at least before I was a senator. There are very few African Americans who haven't had the experience of getting on an elevator and a woman clutching her purse nervously and holding her breath until she had a chance to get off. That happens often.

And I don't want to exaggerate this, but those sets of experiences inform how the African American community interprets what happened one night in Florida.

And it's inescapable for people to bring those experiences to bear. The African American community is also knowledgeable that there is a history of racial disparities in the application of our criminal laws— everything from the death penalty to enforcement of our drug laws. And that ends up having an impact in terms of how people interpret the case. . . .

I think the African American community is also not naïve in understanding that, statistically, somebody like Trayvon Martin was statistically more likely to be shot by a peer than he was by somebody else. So folks understand the challenges that exist for African American boys. But they get frustrated, I think, if they feel that there's no context for it and that context is being denied. And that all contributes I think to a sense that if a white male teen was involved in the same kind of scenario, that, from top to bottom, both the outcome and the aftermath might have been different.

The president sought to moderate expectations about the Justice Department investigation, emphasizing the need to make something "positive" out of the tragedy rather than engaging in an endless pursuit of redress. He referenced racial profiling legislation he'd worked on in Springfield, and even posed a question on Stand Your Ground.

"For those who resist that idea that we should think about something like these 'stand your ground' laws," he said, "I'd just ask people to consider, if Trayvon Martin was of age and armed, could he have stood his ground on that sidewalk? And do we actually think that he would have been justified in shooting Mr. Zimmerman who had followed him in a car because he felt threatened? And if the answer to that question is at least ambiguous, then it seems to me that we might want to examine those kinds of laws."

The president characteristically ended his remarks on a hopeful note by saying that things were yet getting better. He said he believed the country was "becoming a more perfect union. Not a perfect union, but a more perfect union." He called on Americans to engage in more honest discussions about racial disparity in churches and workplaces and homes.

Charles Ogletree summed up the president's speech: "His point was, 'if Trayvon had the successes that I had and the mentors that I had and was able to break out of his youthful problems, look at what he could have done.' I think the Trayvon Martin moment was transformative for him."

Many had been calling for the president to launch a "national conversation" or a national commission on race, as Bill Clinton had done during the 1990s, but Obama declined. " 'I'm not going to lead it," he told friends. "I want people to meet [for] themselves, to decide what the priorities are and tell me what I need to do as president."

Obama's comments failed to mollify some of his more vociferous African American critics. Tavis Smiley called them "too little, too late." Cornel West went further, denouncing the president as a "Global George Zimmerman," with no moral authority, given the administration's continued use of drones to go after terrorist targets in places like Pakistan and Yemen. On Salon.com, writer Rich Benjamin contrasted Obama's remarks with Holder's more furtive address to the NAACP, wondering provocatively whether Holder was "Obama's 'inner nigger,' " and touching off a torrent of outrage, including from fellow critics of the president's approach.

Not surprisingly, the president's comments did nothing to assuage his detractors on the right, who immediately let loose on social media, radio, and Fox News, denouncing the speech as racially divisive. On his radio program, Rush Limbaugh harrumphed: "He represents the same damn stuff as Jesse Jackson. . . . I'm convinced of it now: There's no difference in Obama and Al Sharpton; there's no difference in Obama and Jesse Jackson. It's just Obama had a much better mask than those guys. *Those guys were argumentative and challenging, and Obama was pleasing and contrite."*

Polls, meanwhile, showed the repeat of a familiar pattern, with 49 percent of white voters satisfied with the Zimmerman verdict as of July 22, and 86 percent of black voters (along with 58 percent of Hispanics) opposed. In the same Pew poll, white respondents said the issue of race was "getting more attention than it deserved," by a margin of 60 to 28 percent, while by 78 versus 13 percent, black respondents said the case raised "important issues about race that need to be discussed."

On August 28, the nation paused to mark the fiftieth anniversary of the March on Washington, the civil rights era's transcendent moment, when Dr. Martin Luther King Jr. enunciated his "dream" in an address that a half century later had been rendered beautifully inert. It was now the stuff of greeting cards and slogans, devoid of its radical meaning, and, as expressed by King, its indictment of a nation that had, in the hundred years since emancipation, returned a check marked "insufficient funds" to its black citizens. The organizers of the event, keeping the Trayvon Martin tragedy in mind, made clear their desire not to blandly recite King's words, but to restart a movement.

The commemoration brought Dr. Martin Luther King Jr.'s sister, Christine King Farris, and two of his children, Martin III and Rev. Bernice King, to the steps of the Lincoln Memorial, along with Rev. Sharpton, Rev. Jackson, Andrew Young, Rev. Joseph Lowery, and Julian Bond, in a kind of civil rights class reunion. They were joined by activists old and young, and by speakers black and white, famous and not. The quarter million people who gathered on the National Mall heard from Caroline Kennedy and Lynda Bird Johnson Robb, the elder daughter of LBJ; from actor Jamie Foxx and Oprah Winfrey; from John Lewis and the Dream Defenders' Phillip Agnew. They were addressed by labor leaders and by members of Congress (who in an irony that pointed to the complete reversal of the parties' histories, included no Republicans). The families of Trayvon Martin and Emmett Till traveled to Washington to be a part of the events, along with the parents of Jordan Davis, shot dead at age seventeen the previous November in Jacksonville, Florida, as he rode in a car with friends, angering a white man with a gun who thought their rap music was too loud, and who a year later would be convicted of murder and sentenced to life in prison.

As a light rain descended over the Lincoln Memorial, there were three presidents onstage: Jimmy Carter, Bill Clinton, and Barack Obama—the sum of the Democratic Party's White House legacy since Lyndon Johnson declared that he would not seek a second term as president.

The civil rights movement celebrated its jubilee, and its inheritors marked the many miles ahead.

CHAPTER 11

Fracture

When an individual is protesting society's refusal to acknowledge his dignity as a human being, his very act of protest confers dignity on him.

—Bayard Rustin

BARACK OBAMA WAS ON MARTHA'S VINEYARD WHEN THE ST. Louis suburb of Ferguson went up in smoke.

The protests—punctuated by clouds of tear gas and police dogs trained on demonstrators with their arms raised, chanting "hands up, don't shoot"—began after eighteen-year-old Michael Brown was shot dead on Saturday, August 9, 2014, as he and a friend walked the short distance from a convenience store to Brown's grandmother's apartment, carrying two boxes of miniature cigars. A brief confrontation with a local police officer ended in a shooting that witnesses, the Brown family, and their attorneys called an execution.

For nearly four hours, Brown's body lay on the ground, his head oozing pools of congealed blood onto the pavement in front of the Canfield Green Apartments, as residents gathered behind yellow police tape near the scene. Bystanders were posting the grisly images to social media before the body was finally taken away in the back of a police SUV. As the images went viral that weekend, along with witness accounts posted on Facebook and Twitter, Michael Brown's death became an instant online cause in the growing "Black Lives Matter" movement, born during the Trayvon Martin saga.

Ferguson, a small city of twenty-two thousand residents, had gone from almost entirely white to two-thirds black during the white flight of the 1980s. The police force had only three African Americans on a force of fifty-three. The white mayor and a city council with only one African American among its six members presided over a city funded largely by the fees and fines disproportionately levied on black residents by law enforcement and the municipal court, for traffic and other violations large and small.

Protesters and black elected officials representing Ferguson and nearby communities in the Missouri statehouse immediately blamed the city's police chief, Thomas Jackson; the St. Louis County Police; Ferguson's seemingly hapless Republican mayor, James Knowles; and Missouri's Democratic governor, Jeremiah "Jay" Nixon, who'd been estranged from his state's black leaders since his days as attorney general. A year after being swept into that office in 1992 as Bill Clinton carried the state with 44 percent of the vote in the three-way presidential race, Nixon filed a brief proposing to end St. Louis's twelve-year-old school desegregation plan, by which black students in the city of St. Louis were being bused to the nearly all-white schools in the St. Louis County suburbs.

At the time, Nixon argued that the busing program was too expensive, but his opposition mirrored a shift in the Democratic Party away from support for busing as a remedy to segregated public schools, following decades of backlash from white suburban voters. Nixon's move created a lingering breach with African Amerericans, who comprised a fifth of the state's Democratic voters, largely concentrated in St. Louis and Kansas City. Five years later, in 1998, when Nixon ran for the U.S. Senate, members of the NAACP picketed his campaign events, with one chapter head deriding him as the reincarnation of George Wallace. Prominent black Democratic leaders like then Kansas City mayor and future congressman Emanuel Cleaver and Representative William "Lacy" Clay, whose district included Ferguson, sent campaign contributions to Nixon's Republican opponent, Christopher "Kit" Bond.

Nixon sailed into the governor's mansion after sixteen years as attorney general, despite Barack Obama becoming the first Democrat to win the White House without carrying Missouri (he lost the state by just over 3,900 votes), on a platform of "Independent. Experienced. The Change We Need." Nixon won the big cities, but he also outperformed his Republican opponent in the suburbs, which increasingly were where Missouri's power lay. He got more votes than John McCain did in the state and defeated his opponent 58.4 to 39.5 percent. And in a sign of the state's reddening, voters overwhelmingly approved a ballot measure making English the official language of Missouri and left the state's legislature firmly in Republican hands. As a Democrat who endorsed Barack Obama, Nixon had carried the black districts in the big cities, but that didn't translate into a significant thawing of relations with black leaders.

Six years later, Maria Chappelle-Nadal, the fiery state senator whose district included Ferguson, harshly criticized Nixon for taking days to cancel a trip to the Missouri State Fair so he could come within miles of Ferguson, and publicly called him a coward.

Pressure built as the police refused to release the name of the officer who fired multiple shots into Brown's body, including the fatal shot to the head. It was confirmed, however, that the officer was white. The already tense situation exploded when the large but peaceful early demonstrations were met with a mechanized and hyperkinetic response from police in riot gear, bomb-resistant assault vehicles, and military fatigues. By Monday night the city had degenerated into violence and sporadic looting, under the glare of an international media spotlight that likened the scenes out of Ferguson to the streets of war-torn Gaza.

On Tuesday, as protests continued and complaints that the president had failed to respond grew, the White House issued a written statement calling Brown's death "heartbreaking" and expressing sympathy for his family. The statement said the Justice Department would conduct its own investigation and called on Americans to "remember this young man through reflection and understanding," adding, "we should comfort each other and talk with one another in a way that heals, not in a way that wounds. Along with our prayers, that's what Michael and his family, and our broader American community, deserve."

The statement satisfied almost no one, and instead triggered complaints that the president had not been more personal; in contrast, earlier that day the White House had issued an emotional tribute to comedian Robin Williams, whose suicide that week shocked the nation.

The White House released photos of briefings that Eric Holder and Valerie Jarrett were giving the president, but Obama continued his schedule on Martha's Vineyard, which included golfing and even a party thrown by Vernon Jordan for his wife Ann's birthday. The party was also attended by Bill and Hillary Clinton, Jordan's dear, longtime friends.

Obama hadn't planned on going to the party but changed his mind after a phone call from Hillary Clinton, who was traveling to the island also to promote her sixth book, detailing her time as secretary of state. She wanted to clarify remarks in an *Atlantic* interview in which she appeared to take the president to task for not arming rebels fighting to oust Syrian dictator Bashar al-Assad; the rebels were not only losing momentum against Assad, but were losing ground to a lethal Islamist insurgency calling itself the Islamic State, or ISIS, which was spreading like a cancer from Syria to Iraq.

Now the media was buzzing over the Clintons and the Obamas on the Vineyard together and the prospect, floated by Secretary Clinton's staff, that she and Obama planned to "hug out" their differences at Jordan's party. In the end, the Obamas and the Clintons did more than hug at the party: They danced.

As the week went on, Holder was clamoring to leave Martha's Vineyard and fly to Ferguson himself, but the president and his senior advisers objected. They worried that sending in an administration official would only add to the drama on the ground and create a needless distraction, which in the country's hypercharged racial climate would likely make things worse. Obama instead called a press conference, going before the cameras and first providing an update on the military's progress against ISIS fighters before speaking about the unrest in Ferguson.

The president had been down this road before. Friends insisted that despite his outward cool, he was deeply disturbed, and particularly as a father, by yet another young black man being cut down before he'd had the chance to taste adulthood. But he had seen his political opponents use his seemingly innocuous words about the Trayvon Martin case to cast him as a racial demagogue, conspiring to side with black suffering and to indict white Americans. Some former Obama aides felt that his customary caution failed him in Ferguson, as it had with Trayvon Martin. He should have sent Holder, they'd say. He should have spoken out earlier and more forcefully. And "he shouldn't have gone golfing, either."

Still, the pressure was on for the president to give voice to the anxieties of African Americans. They had memorized the names: twenty-three-year-old Sean Bell, killed in the early morning hours on his wedding day by plainclothes police outside a Queens strip club in November 2006; Ramarley Graham, eighteen, shot dead in the bathroom of his grandmother's Bronx apartment on February 2, 2013, after police burst into the home without a warrant, and Grant allegedly tried to flush away a small bag of marijuana; Oscar Grant, twenty-two, shot and killed on New Year's Day 2009 by an Oakland, California, transit cop as he lay facedown on his stomach, hands behind his back (his story was told in the movie *Fruitvale Station* in 2013); Rodney King, Amadou Diallo, Patrick Dorismond, Arthur McDuffie, and decades' more names. Each story triggered its own microcosm of outrage. Most recently there was Trayvon Martin, whose name and likeness had become synonymous with a movement—while white America had quietly moved on. And now Michael Brown.

With Ferguson erupting in flames, something had to be said.

The president stood before a backdrop decorated with the presidential seal and reiterated his sympathy for Brown's family. He spoke about the responsibility of police to conduct a transparent investigation, then turned his attention to the conflagration in Ferguson, saying, "[T]here is never an excuse for violence against police, or for those who would use this tragedy as a cover for vandalism or looting," and likewise, "there's also no excuse for police to use excessive force against peaceful protests or to throw protesters in jail for lawfully exercising their First Amendment rights. Here in the United States of America, police should not be bullying or arresting journalists who are trying to do their jobs and report to the American people on what they see on the ground."

Obama called for a cooling of raw emotions, saying, "Let's remember that we're all part of one American family."

Activists in Ferguson, and their supporters around the country, were outraged that Obama had focused on the small number of looters, rather than taking on the issue of violence by police. On MSNBC, the president's old friend Michael Eric Dyson accused him of timidity and a lack of boldness that was letting the African American community down. CNN commentator Marc Lamont Hill accused the president of ignoring the obvious racial component in the Ferguson conflagration and not "leading the nation to a new level of understanding." He also said Obama prioritized calm over the legitimate expression of black anger.

"To be clear, I didn't have any unrealistic expectations for Obama," Hill wrote. "I didn't expect him to pump a black fist in solidarity or scream 'fight the power' from the makeshift press room. I didn't even need him to take a clear side on the issue. I did, however, expect him to tell the truth."

The president may have disappointed members of the black community, but he was being pilloried by law enforcement, including the head of the national Fraternal Order of Police, who derided as "unfortunate" the "incongruity of [the president's] evaluating police tactics from the comfort of Martha's Vineyard."

Holder continued to be restless, and made it clear during his daily consultations with the president and Valerie Jarrett that he wanted to go to Ferguson, even though the Justice Department had already ordered an independent autopsy of Brown's body and sent FBI agents to conduct their own investigation. But Obama, backed by Jarrett and other senior advisers, worried that sending Holder to Ferguson would only ratchet up the emotional stakes and focus undue attention on the administration without accomplishing anything concrete.

For the president, Ferguson also had an awkward political dimension.

Other than the city's mayor, most of the politicians involved in the growing shambles in Missouri were Democrats, including Governor Nixon, county prosecutor Bob McCulloch, and Jeff Roorda, the former cop and St. Louis Police Association spokesman who would become the lead opponent of any attempts to alter the system that protected police officers from the reach of law, as well as the chief antagonist of black lawmakers.

Nixon, who had deftly handled the aftermath of the deadly tornadoes that tore through the town of Joplin in 2011, had been considered a vice presidential prospect if Hillary Clinton ran for president in 2016. Obama publicly called him a "good man," though his stewardship of the Ferguson crisis was clearly wanting. Finally, Nixon turned security in Ferguson over to an African American captain in the Missouri State Highway Patrol, Ron Johnson, and displaced the local and county police command. The decision outraged McCulloch, who was refusing repeated calls that he recuse himself from the case—because of his close family and professional ties to police, as well as his father's death, allegedly at the hands of a black assailant. Finally McCulloch announced that he would turn the decision of indicting the officer who killed Michael Brown over to a grand jury, but not before publicly dressing down Nixon and daring the governor to use constitutional authority to sideline him.

The Johnson appointment touched off twenty-four hours of calm, even euphoria, as state police, shorn of tactical military gear, walked among the protesters, and Captain Johnson embraced mothers and sons and uncles in the city where he grew up.

It didn't last.

The next day, Friday, August 15, Ferguson police released the name of the officer who killed Michael Brown: Darren Wilson. But over vigorous objections by the Justice Department, Chief Jackson simultaneously released surveillance video and stills from just before the encounter with Officer Wilson that appeared to show Michael Brown and his friend Dorian Johnson taking two boxes of Swisher Sweets minicigars from a convenience store and shoving the store clerk aside on their way out the door. Police released the incident report related to the

alleged robbery, but no report detailing the circumstances leading to Brown's death. Brown's family and supporters accused
the authorities of trying to smear the dead teen to help ensure
Wilson's exoneration.

This caused the streets of Ferguson to explode again, prompting state police to declare a midnight curfew. Three days later,
Nixon called up the state's National Guard.

On Sunday, a week and a day after Michael Brown was
gunned down, Captain Johnson addressed thirteen hundred
people at Greater Grace Baptist Church for a service in Brown's
honor; thousands more gathered outside. Johnson told the crowd
about his "black son, who wears his pants sagging, who has his
hat cocked to the side, who has tattoos down his arms, but he's
my baby." He apologized to Ferguson's black community, saying,
"I am with you," and threw his fist into the air as he walked off
the dais to cheers.

Speaking after Johnson, Rev. Sharpton called for peaceful
protests to continue, irritating young activists in much the way
Obama had when he warned citizens against violence, rather
than warning police. "Don't loot in Michael's name," Sharpton said. "We're not looters. We're liberators! We're not burners.
We're builders!"

Sharpton thundered that no politician who wanted to be
president could avoid Ferguson. "This is the defining moment in
this country," he said. "All over the world, the debate is how the
rights of people are dealt with by the state." He insisted, "Ferguson and Michael Brown Jr. will be a defining moment on how
this country deals with policing and the rights of citizens to address how police behave in this country." It was a pointed rebuke
of two Democratic politicians who African Americans had noticed were being conspicuously silent: the Clintons.

"Jeb Bush, Hillary Clinton, don't get laryngitis on this
issue," Sharpton said, referring to two potential 2016 presidential

contenders. "Nobody can go to the White House unless they stop by our house and talk about policing!"

Indeed, more than two weeks into the Ferguson nightmare, with Michael Brown's funeral planned for August 25, neither Clinton had issued a public statement about Ferguson.

Obama's supporters, meanwhile, were keen to point out that no previous president had reacted more quickly to a fatal police shooting. George H. W. Bush had declared himself "horrified" by the videotaped beating of Rodney King nineteen days after the tape's release in 1991. It took Bill Clinton more than a week to speak out on the verdict in the O. J. Simpson case, which rent the country along racial lines in 1995. At the time, Clinton called on the country to "clean our house of racism." Whether Obama's statements were considered forward-leaning enough by black commentators, the president, his supporters insisted, had weighed in early. More important, his administration, through the Justice Department, was taking decisive action.

On Monday, August 18, the president arrived in Washington for three days of cabinet meetings and walked into the White House Press Briefing Room to make yet another dual announcement about the progress in Iraq and the situation in Ferguson. Obama had met earlier that afternoon with Attorney General Holder, who informed the president that he was going to Missouri to oversee the federal investigation; he planned to arrive by midweek, on the day the grand jury hearings were to begin. He would meet with the FBI agents, U.S. attorneys, and prosecutors on the ground. Whatever reticence the White House had had about the trip was immaterial now. Holder was visiting his team in the field, and needed no White House assent.

When asked if he would go to Ferguson, Obama demurred, saying he had to be mindful of putting his thumb on the scale, calling it important not just that justice was done, but that justice was *seen to be done;* there should be no perception that the president of the United States was taking sides against an individual police officer.

Supporters and old friends, including Harvard's Charles Ogletree, were urging him to be bold and to address the racial issues laid bare by Brown's death. But the president's demeanor remained cool. He called for "healing," and for Americans to come together and recognize their shared humanity.

The statement fell so flat that *Slate* writer Jamelle Bouie tweeted, "Barack Obama is either very tired, doesn't believe a single word he's saying re: Michael Brown, or both." *Atlantic* writer Ta-Nehisi Coates agreed, declaring on his Twitter feed that he felt "bad" for the president, "Not sarcastic pity. Like really feel bad." On Vox.com, former *Washington Post* columnist Ezra Klein declared that the Obama White House simply no longer believed in his ability to bridge divides.

In Ferguson, activists were equally frustrated, telling reporters that the president needed to stop talking and come to the scene, to "bring all this to justice." Being more direct, Tef Poe, a local rap artist and a leader of the Ferguson protesters, bluntly declared: "Fuck the White House. I'm never voting again. Another disenfranchised black male."

Obama had also touted his "My Brother's Keeper" initiative, a White House program launched in February 2014, on the anniversary of Trayvon Martin's death, that was designed to "unlock the full potential of our young people, including boys and young men of color." A cadre of black writers felt this was an outrageous non sequitur that unfairly redirected the blame for Brown's death onto the supposedly "broken" black family, even though Brown had a loving, involved father—as Trayvon Martin had—and even though Brown, despite getting into occasional trouble, was days away from attending community college.

Writing on her social media feed, Ebony.com writer Jamilah Lemieux spoke for the detractors. "Can we get a My Brother's

Keeper for the cops?" she tweeted. "They must not have dads, they keep killing people." During an extended rant, Lemieux echoed Marc Lamont Hill from days before, writing: "I don't expect President Obama to become a race man, I expect him not to reinforce notions of inherent Black deficiency. . . . And, also, not to bring up My Brother's Keeper when talking about a police killing."

For many, using Brown's death as an opportunity to tout a program about reforming black behavior was akin to grafting a titanium limb onto a rotting body; it may be an undeniable wonder, but it can do the corpse no good. The protesters and their legion of online supporters didn't want a new program to shore up black men—they wanted changes in policing that would keep more black men and boys alive.

Police in Ferguson, meanwhile, were angrily complaining that the media coverage was casting them in such a negative light they felt threatened on the streets. But the Justice Department issued scathing rebukes of officers who were patrolling with their name tags removed, some of them donning "I am Darren Wilson" bracelets.

Holder arrived in Ferguson on August 20 to the warm embrace of the African American community and the literal embrace of Captain Johnson. He met with the Brown family and visited local haunts, where he was received like a favorite son. Holder met with his FBI field agents and reassured local leaders and members of Congress during a closed-door meeting that the investigation was proceeding apace. With Holder in Ferguson, Obama returned to his family on Martha's Vineyard.

It had now been more than two weeks since Michael Brown was killed. And when Hillary returned to the Vineyard for a book signing on August 24, the day before Brown's funeral, she simply ignored questions about Ferguson as reporters volleyed them her way. Senator Clinton's camp refused comment when queried on the matter by MSNBC, the *Huffington Post*, and other news outlets. On CNN, Marc Lamont Hill called Hillary's silence "shameful."

"The Clintons have made so much of their political bones on the backs of black voters, getting black support, getting black love, identifying black causes," he said. "Hillary Clinton will go to Selma in 2008 and clap with black people and put on a fake southern accent and pretend to identify with black struggle and black pain. But now that real black issues are on the table, now that real black struggle is in the public eye, she has said nothing."

On August 25, Michael Brown was eulogized before thousands of mourners and family members at Friendly Temple Missionary Baptist Church in St. Louis, as throngs of media from around the world crowded outside. Rev. Sharpton delivered a fiery broadside against police brutality and a stinging rebuke to anyone who dared stay silent in the face of such an urgent national demand for action.

Three days later, Hillary Clinton finally spoke out, at the end of prepared remarks at a tech conference in San Francisco: "Watching the recent funeral for Michael Brown as a mother, as a human being, my heart just broke for his family because losing a child is every parent's greatest fear and an unimaginable loss. But I also grieve for that community and many like it across our country. Behind the dramatic terrible pictures on television are deep challenges that will be with them and with us long after the cameras move on."

Clinton may have been tardy with her remarks, but she displayed a freedom that Barack Obama seemed never to have, and she was able to directly address the seismic forces rending Ferguson, Missouri, and the country.

"Imagine what we would feel and what we would do if white drivers were three times as likely to be searched by police during a traffic stop as black drivers instead of the other way around," she told the nearly all-white audience. "If white offenders received prison sentences ten percent longer than black offenders for the same crimes. If a third of all white men—just look at this room and take one-third—went to prison during their lifetime. Imagine that. That is the reality in the lives of so many of our fellow Americans in so many of the communities in which they live."

Some black commentators marveled at how much bolder Clinton's remarks were than Obama's and that they were devoid of the mitigating language of respectability. Writing in *Slate,* Bouie pointed to polls showing that Obama began to lose the approval of whites after his comments on the Henry Louis Gates arrest during his first months in office.

"By siding with the black Gates against the white police officer," Bouie wrote, "Obama gave greater salience to his race. Put another way, Obama entered office as a president who was black, but ended that summer as a black president."

He quoted *The Atlantic*'s Ta-Nehisi Coates, who in an August 2012 essay titled "Fear of a Black President," posited that as president, Obama found himself having to be "twice as good and half as black." As president, he also had to be twice as careful with his words.

Hillary Clinton had no such constraints. There was no need for a white woman, speaking to a nearly all-white audience, to soften blunt truths about race and the disparate treatment of white and black Americans, including by police. Instead she could examine the exemption from the burdens of racial disparity that she shared with her Silicon Valley audience, and invite them to empathize, for a moment, with their fellow citizens. And then they could all go back to their lives.

Obama was not so lucky, and he found himself in the middle of another racially divisive case, which pit law enforcement against citizens, Right against Left, and according to polls, increasingly black against white. This could easily damage his political party, which was fighting to defend a half dozen Democratic Senate seats in deeply red and purple states. These Democrats wanted the president of the United States to do nothing more than to make himself inconspicuous in every way.

Late into the night of November 25, two days before Thanksgiving, prosecutor McCulloch announced that the grand jury in the Ferguson case declined to hand down an indictment against Darren Wilson. McCulloch had chosen to make the announcement at night, as crowds massed on the streets of Ferguson and tensions mounted. When he spoke, issuing what sounded like a lengthy defense of Officer Wilson, the streets of Ferguson erupted again.

The Congressional Black Caucus fired off a statement, signed by chairwoman Marcia Fudge that seemed to capture the depth of black despair. "This decision seems to underscore an unwritten rule that black lives hold no value. . . . This is a frightening narrative for every parent and guardian of black and brown children, and another setback for race relations in America."

President Obama went before the cameras one last time, pleading for calm and for respect for the rule of law. He called on the nation to focus on its vast racial progress, while noting that "what is also true is that there are still problems and communities of color aren't just making these problems up. Separating that from this particular decision, there are issues in which the law too often feels as if it is being applied in discriminatory fashion."

It was a measured and eloquent statement, full of plain and simple truths, but the fires of Ferguson had already been lit, and the city was engulfed.

Jarvis DeBerry, a black columnist for the *New Orleans Times-Picayune,* wrote after the president's press conference: "Which elected official disappointed more black people Monday night? Bob McCulloch, the St. Louis County district attorney who announced that there would be no trial for the police officer who killed a black unarmed teenager? Or Barack Obama, black man and president of the United States, who awkwardly illustrated the difficulty of speaking as a black man while being president of the United States?"

By December, the country was seeing a scattering of protests under the Black Lives Matter banner, each one touched off by seemingly limitless incidents reminiscent of the Ferguson saga: a grand jury declining to indict a New York City police officer in the chokehold death of a forty-three-year-old black man, Eric Garner, whose final words, "I can't breathe," were captured on cell phone video; the police shooting of twenty-two-year-old John Crawford III as he held a toy gun in the aisle of an Ohio Wal-Mart; a Cleveland police officer gunning down twelve-year-old Tamir Rice just seconds after emerging from his cruiser in response to a 911 call claiming a "man" was pointing what turned out to be a toy gun on a community center playground; and the shooting of twenty-eight-year-old Akai Gurley in the darkened stairwell of the Pink Houses projects in Brooklyn by a startled rookie cop, whose first call was not for help for Gurley but rather to his union rep.

At the end of the month, when two New York police officers were assassinated by a deranged black man who claimed to be avenging Eric Garner and Michael Brown, Republicans, including former New York mayor Rudy Giuliani, blamed Barack Obama. Whenever protesters chanted angry, and in some cases vicious, slogans at police, Obama was to blame.

Ironically, Barack Obama, for whom a strict fealty to interracial conciliation had paved a path to power, and who had long avoided the fate of black politicians and civic leaders who became marginalized as nonviable for statewide or national office by diving headlong into the "race issue," now joined Al Sharpton and Jesse Jackson and Eric Holder in the pantheon of accused racial provocateurs, cited by their conservative detractors as the true cause of racial strife and division in America.

BETWEEN THE BEGINNING OF THE FERGUSON CONFLAGRATION and its dismal conclusion, the United States held another election in November 2014. When it was over, an electorate smaller than any since World War II had given Republicans the Senate, and with it, total control of Congress.

The election all but eliminated the "blue dogs"—the centrist Democrats who swept into the party in the late 1980s and '90s with the goal of banishing the old New Dealers of the Johnson-to-Carter era. The Democratic Leadership Council had been shuttered since 2011. Two midterms had decimated the ranks of House Democratic moderates, who once had the power to force Nancy Pelosi to bargain on abortion to pass health care. In the Senate, southern Democrats were wiped out, conceding North Carolina and Arkansas, and in the ensuing wave giving up seats in Alaska, Montana, and Colorado, too, along with those of retiring stalwarts Tom Harkin in Iowa and Jay Rockefeller in West Virginia. Democrats failed to win the open Senate races in Georgia and South Dakota or to unseat Mitch McConnell in Kentucky.

In a final flourish, Mary Landrieu, the Louisiana senator from a family near synonymous with New Orleans, was defeated in a runoff, having reaped the whirlwind from Republicans for admitting in an interview that her state still struggles at times on matters of race. With her defeat, only one white Democrat remained in statewide office in the Deep South: Bill Nelson, senator from Florida and a former astronaut.

Democrats lost men, 58 to 42 percent, and white voters backed the GOP, 62 to 38 percent.

And while Democratic candidates received the lion's share of African American votes, they had done so for the most part by running without—and in many cases in contravention to—President Obama, the person with the most powerful claim on black voters. The large share of black voters siding with Democrats meant little in the end, with fewer black voters showing up at the polls. And the drop-off in turnout among black voters was minuscule compared to the near collapse of support for Democrats from white voters in the South, where so much of the midterm's Senate battles were fought.

It was a hard lesson for a party that in the South had been built in the modern era on a coalition of black party loyalists and blue-collar and rural white voters who remained culturally Democrats. It was the formula that propelled Jimmy Carter and then Bill Clinton to power. Now that coalition was gone. Much of the white part of that coalition had been slowly abandoning the party for decades. But Democrats themselves seemed to jettison what was left of it once Obama won the White House.

The party had once operated on a system of validation. It was what Lyndon Johnson gave to John F. Kennedy with southern white voters, and what Walter Mondale lent Jimmy Carter with northern liberals, and Joe Biden gave Barack Obama with working-class white voters in the Rust Belt in 2008 (and Rev. Sharpton gave to Obama with black ones). But by 2014, Democratic politicians in the South and West had all but abandoned the president, refusing to defend his policies and even pleading with the White House to keep him out of their states. In doing so, they gave what remained of persuadable white voters no reason to give Obama's party a second look and black voters little incentive to turn out in droves.

In Kentucky, a state that had a Democratic governor and was a rare southern state in fully benefiting from the health-care law, Democrat Alison Lundergan Grimes, the challenger to Senate Republican leader McConnell, refused to even say in successive media interviews whether she voted for Obama in the previous

election. Instead the Kentucky secretary of state declared her se-
crecy on whether she supported her party's nominee for president
"a matter of principle" regarding privacy at the ballot box, and
pronounced herself a "Clinton Democrat." It was emblematic of
a party that, particularly in red states, wanted nothing to do with
President Barack Obama, and that viewed the Clintons as the
figures whom their voters—read "white voters"—could identify
with.

The party that emerged from the elections of 2008 through
2014 was greatly changed from the one Lyndon Johnson had
wrapped around the mantle of civil rights. Now the Democratic
Party in the South was fundamentally a black party. What remained of white southern Democratic power was relegated to a
few liberal white mayors, in heavily black cities like New Orleans
and Columbus, Georgia, plus a smattering of city councilmem-
bers. It was almost a given that white politicians in the southern
state legislatures and congressional delegations were Republicans; any Democrats were nearly universally black. Redistricting
locked in this formula, creating majority-white districts that only
a Republican could win, and a small number of majority-black
enclaves winnable only by a Democrat. Ironically, having fought,
and in many cases bled and died to gain inclusion in the onetime
party of the South, African Americans in the southern states now
found themselves in full ownership of that party, but nearly as
politically powerless as they were in 1964.

As of January 2015, no state in the Deep South except Arkansas had authorized the Medicaid expansion under the Affordable Care Act, leaving nearly 5 million people, many black but
also rural, white, and poor, uninsured. Two states in the "upper
South"—Kentucky and West Virginia—had accepted Medicaid
funding, though under Democratic governors. Tennessee was
keeping the door ajar.

Though 2015 ushered in the largest Congressional Black

Caucus class in history—with 46 members—they still had precious little power in the House, with its 246 members of the GOP (including one black Republican, Mia Love) and two African American senators, one Republican—Tim Scott of South Carolina—and one Democrat—Cory Booker of New Jersey.

In many ways, though, the president was set free by the election, and by no longer having to confront and accommodate the political fears of the "blue dogs." He would show that liberation in some significant policy areas: an historic opening to Cuba and a proposed nuclear deal with Iran; executive action to protect millions from deportation, and an aggressive posture toward the new, Republican Congress, exemplified in a defiant post-election press conference in which the president vowed to push forward with his agenda, with Congress's cooperation when he could get it, or without it. "What I'm not going to do is just wait," Obama said, addressing immigration reform. "I think it's fair to say I've shown a lot of patience and tried to work on a bipartisan basis as much as possible, and I'm going to continue to do so. But in the meantime, let's see what we can do lawfully through executive actions to improve the functioning of the system." Newly elevated Senate Majority Leader Mitch McConnell described the press conference, and Obama's aggressive tone toward Republicans, as akin to "waving a red flag in front of a bull."

Obama had also been liberated to become more forthcoming on matters of race, speaking more freely and personally in interviews about his own experiences as a black man, though he had largely been unable to give black America the racial catharses it desired.

Eric Holder announced his resignation after the election, which set him free to wrap up federal investigations into the Michael Brown killing in Ferguson and Eric Garner's chokehold death in Staten Island, while a grand jury continued to quietly probe the Trayvon Martin affair.

In many ways, and despite the vitriol directed at him by his opponents, Obama had lost the Congress and won the day. The economy was sound, gas prices low, and unemployment and job creation and the stock market at levels not seen since the Clinton years, though growing income inequality tainted those gains. Barack Obama was destined to be viewed as a highly consequential president, not just for his race but because of his accomplishments in health care, ending two deeply unpopular wars, expanding the rights of gays and lesbians, opening doors to immigrants, salvaging the U.S. auto industry, and shepherding the country back from the economic brink.

But much had been lost in the Obama years.

The Supreme Court's conservative majority had hobbled the Voting Rights Act—the law that made the eventual election of a black president possible. And the Court's chief justice, John Roberts, couched the judicial repeal of one of the country's most revolutionary acts of racial progress in the faulty conclusion that racism had been consigned to the distant past, and that President Barack Obama himself was the evidence.

The Fair Housing Act was thought to be hurtling toward a similar fate, as the Court's conservative wing seemed determined to dismantle every pillar of the Johnson era, a goal long sought by conservatives, including some of the justices themselves. Antonin Scalia spoke scornfully from the bench about the Voting Rights Act, deriding its constant renewal over fifty years as little more than the enforcement of "racial entitlements." Clarence Thomas, the Court's lone black justice, believed the remaining core of the Voting Rights Act to be unconstitutional, period. And Thomas was known to have affixed a fifteen-cent price tag on his Yale Law School degree to denote his view of its true worth, having been "tainted" by affirmative action, a practice the Court invalidated in a 6–2 ruling upholding Michigan's ban on affirmative action in its public universities and government contracting in 2014.

Outside the confines of Washington, the spirit of cross-racial unity that attended Obama's election had been replaced by a deep pessimism and increased racial polarization. Black America's hopes that with Obama's election, the country would finally and fully confront its racial past, and white America's wish that Obama's rise would reduce or even remove the need to do so, had been equally dashed. Both liberals and conservatives looking for racial reconciliation in the election of the first black president were left unsatisfied. The country's interracial mood felt tense, and raw, ready to explode with each new police shooting, every presidential pronouncement, and with every confrontation between congressional Republicans and the White House, over everything from the budget to foreign policy.

An NBC News/*Wall Street Journal* poll taken in January 2015 found that few Americans believed that, to paraphrase Dr. King's speech at the March on Washington, "America is a nation where people are not judged by the color of their skin but by the content of their character." A scant 27 percent of white Americans strongly agreed with that sentiment, as did an even more dismal 16 percent of African Americans and Hispanics, while 70 percent of African Americans, 55 percent of Hispanics, and 39 percent of whites disagreed with the rosy assessment of America's racial progress. The country's population was more diverse than it ever had been, and yet there was precious little cross-racial faith in our system of justice and our political processes.

Our political divisions were essentially racial, with increasingly multiracial Democrats and increasingly monolithically white Republicans holding polar views on *everything*, from whether a movie, *12 Years a Slave,* should win an Academy Award (53 percent of Democrats versus 15 percent of Republicans saying it should) to whether disgraced NBA team owner Donald Sterling, caught on tape making racially inflammatory remarks, should be forced to sell his team (68 percent of Democrats saying he should versus 26 percent of Republicans).

As President Obama and his family stood on the Edmund Pettus Bridge in Selma on March 7, 2015, to mark the fiftieth anniversary of "Bloody Sunday," they were flanked by legends of the "heroic age" of civil rights: John Lewis; Amelia Boynton Robinson, who like Lewis was subjected to the baton blows of Sheriff Jim Clark's troops fifty years before; nearly a hundred members of Congress, just a handful of them Republicans, including Tim Scott, South Carolina's first black senator; his counterpart from Alabama, Jeff Sessions; one member of the Republican congressional leadership; former president George W. Bush, who signed the reauthorization of the Voting Rights Act in 2006, and his wife, Laura; and Rev. Al Sharpton.

More than forty thousand people descended on Selma, twice the population of the city, which fifty years after becoming a national pariah for its mistreatment of African Americans had fallen into economic despair. Selma's population had been cut by a third, after decades of white flight. Just 2 percent of its public school students were white, and nearly every white child in Selma was enrolled in private school. Nearly 4 in 10 residents were living in poverty. The town was bursting to capacity with the influx of people from around the country, including many who'd marched over the Edmund Pettus Bridge in 1965, and who now looked back on that era in wonder at what they'd been bold enough to do, in many cases as teenagers or even as children.

The commemoration weekend brought civil rights pioneers to Selma: Diane Nash, Bob Moses and Andrew Young, C. T. Vivian, Dick Gregory along with the daughters of Lyndon Johnson and even the daughter of George Wallace, the descendants of Rev. James Reeb, Viola Liuzzo, and Jimmie Lee Jackson, as well as Rev. Clark Olsen, a fellow white, Unitarian minister who was with Reeb when they and a third minister were beaten by white supremacists after having dinner at an integrated restaurant two days after Bloody Sunday, resulting in Reeb's death. Bernard Lafayette, who as a young SNCC organizer took charge of the Selma voter registration campaign after the national leadership declared Selma to be hopeless, was there, too, as was Jawana Jackson, who was just five years old in 1964 and 1965 when her parents, Dr. Sullivan "Sully" Jackson, a black dentist, and his wife, Richie Jean, a teacher, housed "Uncle Martin" Luther King Jr. and Ralph Bunche at their corner home in Selma, a house preserved as if in amber, down to the beds where the two Nobel laureates slept and the yellow throw-covered living room chairs where the Jacksons and Dr. King watched Lyndon Johnson's televised address announcing the Voting Rights Act.

Jesse Jackson came to Selma, too, as he did most years for the annual commemoration. But the well-worn and intractable rift with the White House, and a lesser-known breach with John Lewis over how to properly commemorate the events of 1965, had not healed. Jackson was featured prominently at events around Selma: on the second day of the bifurcated program organized by Representative Lewis and his Washington, D.C.–based committee for the members of Congress and the president for Saturday, March 7, as well as by local organizers whose annual jubilee had for forty years been held on the first Sunday in March, which this year fell on March 8. But the onetime protégé of Dr. King watched the historic convergence of Selma's tortured racial history and the country's first black president from the crowd. When, after his speech, Obama, the congressional delegation, and the civil rights luminaries gathered to traverse the bridge, with their symbolic crossing captured in iconic photos splashed across the front pages of newspapers around the country, Jackson and his family had already returned to the St. James Hotel, the antebellum relic with delicate lattice balcony railings that was once occupied by Union troops during the Civil War, and that still stood along the fading main drag of historic downtown Selma.

But Jackson and the other civil rights veterans, who had weathered the movement's darkest hours, hadn't come to Selma to commune with the president. They'd come to *hear* him, in hopes that he would find the words to place the nation's ugly racial past and its complicated present into a context that would bring most Americans into rare agreement. And this time, Barack Obama delivered.

Standing on the bridge emblazoned with the name of a notorious Ku Klux Klan leader, the looming iron edifice soaring above him, after being introduced by an emotional John Lewis, President Obama gave a speech that at long last lived up to the oratorical promise his supporters had long dreamed he would display as president.

Drawing from Dr. King but also from James Baldwin, and from biblical verse, the country's first black president made the case for an America that is evolving, and that at its best has the courage to acknowledge that its evolution is not complete:

> The Americans who crossed this bridge, they were not physically imposing. They gave courage to millions. They held no elected office. But they led a nation. They marched as Americans who had endured hundreds of years of brutal violence, countless daily indignities— but they didn't seek special treatment, just the equal treatment promised to them almost a century before.
>
> As we commemorate their achievement, we are well-served to remember that at the time of the marches, many in power condemned rather than praised them. Back then, they were called communists, or half-breeds,

or outside agitators, sexual and moral degenerates, and worse—they were called everything but the name their parents gave them. Their faith was questioned. Their lives were threatened. Their patriotism challenged. And yet, what could be more American than what happened in this place? What could more profoundly vindicate the idea of America than plain and humble people—unsung, the downtrodden, the dreamers not of high station, not born to wealth or privilege, not of one religious tradition but many, coming together to shape their country's course? What greater expression of faith in the American experiment than this, what greater form of patriotism is there than the belief that America is not yet finished, that we are strong enough to be self-critical, that each successive generation can look upon our imperfections and decide that it is in our power to remake this nation to more closely align with our highest ideals?

Obama acknowledged that the work of America is unfinished, that "the march is not yet over." As a small protest broke out among the crowd, led by demonstrators from Ferguson, he also acknowledged two just-released Justice Department reports. Though one report stated there was insufficient evidence to charge the now former officer Darren Wilson with civil rights violations in killing Michael Brown, noting there was inconsistent and insufficient evidence to prove the "hands-up" narrative of Brown's killing that had so animated protesters nationwide, the second report, on the patterns and practices of Wilson's former department, summarily condemned the long-standing city and municipal court–sanctioned practice in Ferguson of profiting off the systematic targeting of black residents for ticketing and fines and arrest. Such a practice had turned the relationship with police into one in which African American citizens were little more than ridiculed and disrespected sources of income for the city of Ferguson.

"Just this week, I was asked whether I thought the Department of Justice's Ferguson report shows that, with respect to race, little has changed in this country," Obama said. "And I understood the question; the report's narrative was sadly familiar. It evoked the kind of abuse and disregard for citizens that spawned the civil rights movement. But I rejected the notion that nothing's changed. What happened in Ferguson may not be unique, but it's no longer endemic. It's no longer sanctioned by law or by custom. And before the civil rights movement, it most surely was.

"We do a disservice to the cause of justice by intimating that bias and discrimination are immutable, that racial division is inherent to America," the president said. "If you think nothing's changed in the past fifty years, ask somebody who lived through the Selma or Chicago or Los Angeles of the 1950s."

The speech drew broad praise from historians and writers and even some Obama foes. (After pointing to "danger signs" and "wrongful interpretations of the American experiment," *National Review*'s Quin Hillyer admitted to its beautiful crafting, declaring the speech to be "for anyone who appreciates good writing . . . a masterpiece.") Charles Blow, one of five African American writers invited to travel with the president, his family, and members of his cabinet, including Valerie Jarrett, to Selma, noted in the *New York Times* afterward that Shelby County, whose lawsuit to overturn the preclearance requirement to change its voting laws had brought down Section 4 of the Voting Rights Act, was just an hour north of where the president spoke. Among those gathered at the base of the bridge, Blow wrote, there was, beyond the raw emotion of watching a black man embody the nation's highest office and speak to its highest principles, a sense of frustration in the air at what felt like a national retrogression; it was "a pessimism about a present and future riven by worsening racial understanding and interplay."

Still, the president seemed, at last, to have sounded the right notes.

Among those who were not in Selma were Bill and Hillary Clinton, who spent the weekend in Miami raising funds for the Clinton Global Initiative. The organizers of the competing Saturday and Sunday commemorations extended invitations to all of the living former presidents and their families, but the Clintons, along with Jimmy Carter, cited prior commitments, and former president George H. W. Bush was absent due to his health. And while local organizers in Selma had warm feelings toward the Clintons, who in the past had provided financial support for the annual pilgrimage to the Edmund Pettus Bridge, their absence drew notice from the national media, as did that of the panoply of potential Republican candidates for president.

One black writer, Michael H. Cottman, noted on Black America Web, an online outlet of Tom Joyner and other popular black radio hosts, that the Clintons had allied themselves closely with black America. Bill Clinton had been "affectionately known as America's 'first black president' before Obama actually filled that role." Hillary Clinton was poised to run for president, a prospect for which she would need substantial black turnout and support. Given all that, "it would only seem prudent" for Hillary "to show up in Selma, sit on the stage with the other dignitaries, and show her support for civil rights legislation and restoring the Voting Rights Act."

Some in the media speculated that the Clintons stayed away from Selma to avoid the inevitable questions about 2016, given the fact that the last time they and Barack Obama marched in Selma together was in 2007, when Hillary and Obama were competitors in the Democratic primary. Others cited the rift between John Lewis and local organizers, and the Clintons' desire to not get between friends; they remained close both to Lewis and to state senator Hank Sanders and his wife, Rose, the longtime organizers of the local yearly commemoration. Two weeks before the celebration, Bill Clinton personally telephoned Rose Sanders to explain his coming absence due to the couple's commitment in Miami, which he said was scheduled before he knew the date—Saturday or Sunday—when the commemoration would take place.

The Clintons weren't silent on Selma. From Miami on Saturday, the former secretary of state joined in the praise of President Obama's "superb speech," and called on the country to keep up the fight, for voting rights, for LGBT rights, and for women's equality. It was a signal that the coming Hillary Clinton presidential campaign would likely make gender the next great sociopolitical battleground, much as the enthusiasm for African American advancement had animated Barack Obama's victory over her in 2008. For his part, Bill Clinton shared on social media a video, produced by his foundation, in which he recalled growing up in the segregated South and "witnessing firsthand, the degrading consequences of segregation"; the former president lauded the events in Selma that "fifty years ago, became one of the most profound appeals to the founding principles and enduring conscience of our nation." In the video, Clinton spoke of the many marchers from 1965 who remained alive and in the struggle for civil rights, citing just three by name: "my friends John Lewis, and Hank and Rose Sanders," a pointed reference to the leading antagonists of Selma in 2015.

On Sunday, with the first family back in Washington along with most of the congressional delegation, it was the local Selma community's turn to commemorate its place in history, fifty years on, and to stage its own mass reenactment of the march over the Edmund Pettus Bridge. Several Obama cabinet secretaries arrived at historic Brown Chapel AME Church, where the

Bloody Sunday march was planned and launched, including Jeh Johnson, the country's African American director of homeland security. Then the church erupted in a standing ovation as Eric Holder entered, and he later rose to speak. Seated beside Holder and his wife was Loretta Lynch, who was poised to become Holder's successor and the first African American woman to be attorney general of the United States, but who was in the midst of the longest delay for confirmation vote ever imposed on an attorney general nominee by the Senate; more than four months had passed since the president had nominated her. On the dais were Jesse Jackson and Andrew Young, the heads of the NAACP and its Legal Defense Fund, Rev. Sharpton, and Martin Luther King III. Seated inside the packed sanctuary were many who had marched fifty years before.

When it was his turn to speak, King, known as "MLK III" to his friends and associates, told the congregation it was no time to celebrate, with access to the ballot under fire in multiple states. He said his father would want them to keep marching. Sharpton closed the service with a fiery sermon, telling the cheering congregation and those gathered outside the church watching on a giant screen that "people fought and bled and died for our voting rights, and we didn't come to Selma to give 'em back!" Members of Congress were vowing to return to Washington filled with the spirit of Selma, to push their Republican colleagues to restore the Voting Rights Act. But few believed House Speaker John Boehner or Senate Majority Leader Mitch McConnell would prioritize it. Even as a handful of Republicans publicly declared their support, a bill to restore Section 4 of the act stood languishing in the House. Even if it was ultimately brought forward, civil rights leaders like Wade Davis and Sherrilyn Ifill, leader of the NAACP Legal Defense Fund, openly worried that it would be festooned with hated provisions like a national version of voter ID.

A CNN poll released on March 6 found that while

three-quarters of African Americans believed the act was still necessary to secure the right to vote (a figure that rose to 82 percent for blacks in the South), just 48 percent of whites agreed. In that poll, 54 percent of black respondents, versus just 19 percent of white ones, said they believed black Americans were not given an equal chance to land jobs for which they were qualified. Three-quarters of blacks versus 42 percent of whites felt the criminal justice system favors white Americans. Forty-five percent of white respondents and 26 percent of blacks believed race relations had gotten worse during the Obama era, with just 15 percent overall, and just 20 percent of Democrats, believing they'd gotten better.

Given that polarized atmosphere, and with the headwinds of reflexive loathing battering him relentlessly from the Right, it remained to be seen whether Barack Obama, in his final two years in office, could marshal the national and congressional will, and summon the country's moral courage, to make Martin Luther King Jr. and Lyndon Johnson's triumph whole again; to "use the inspiration of Selma" to press for criminal justice reform and "spark a conversation around the continuing legacies in Jim Crow that led to impoverished and isolated communities," as he told the group of black journalists aboard Air Force One. It remained to be seen how hard he planned to try.

To do so would risk reopening the racial wounds that were exposed every time this president stepped into the chasm of America's racial history and present condition.

Six years into his presidency, and in the third jubilee year of the civil rights movement, whose pivotal years between 1963 and 1965 produced such monumental change, Barack Obama was presiding over a nation still strongly divided by region, political tribe, and race. He was preparing to bequeath to his Democratic successor—in all likelihood, Hillary Clinton—a party that in fifty years had gone from exclusionary on matters of race to embodying the nation's diverse future. He would bequeath to his successor in the White House a country that had a choice: to push further into the breach and fully confront its racial demons at last, so that a future black or brown or Asian president could speak freely about America's interracial triumphs and its challenges, or to retreat into a state of benign forgetfulness and conscious "unknowing," while a thousand Fergusons burn beneath the surface.

Epilogue

EVEN BEFORE THE CANDIDATE ANNOUNCED SHE WAS RUNNING, the campaign chose as its headquarters One Pierrepont Plaza in Brooklyn Heights, a bustling, downtown neighborhood that spoke to their determination to appeal to a modern, young electorate and to attract a dynamic team.

The offices were in biking distance of Manhattan and a short walk from the upscale bars and hipster cafes whose presence, along with a seemingly endless expanse of high-rise apartment and condo buildings, was part of Brooklyn's transformation from the troubled, ethnically segregated borough of the 1970s and '80s to the emblem of New York City's quickly gentrifying melting pot.

Hillary Clinton's name may have been vintage, but her campaign was determined not to be. A campaign memo leaked ahead of the announcement laid out the themes: The campaign would be "diverse, disciplined, and humble." Early hires were young, heavily female, drawn from Google, EMILY's List, and the previous Clinton, Obama, and Howard Dean campaigns. They included the architect of Michelle Obama's media tour through the living rooms of American women, from her much-publicized trips to Target to her comedic "mom dancing" skits with *The Tonight Show*'s host, Jimmy Fallon.

The official moniker of the campaign echoed Obama's 2008

run. It would be called "Hillary for America," and would seek to put less emphasis on the candidate and her sometimes tortured, quarter-century-long dance with the country and the media, and attempt to turn the focus outward, to Hillary's chosen bedrock issue: economic inequality. Campaign manager Robby Mook— poised to become the first openly gay manager of a presidential campaign and at thirty-five already a veteran of the 2004 Howard Dean and 2008 Hillary Clinton campaigns, as well as the successful gubernatorial bid of longtime Clinton friend and fundraiser Terry McAuliffe in Virginia—enjoined his staff to "take nothing for granted. . . . We are humble. . . . We are never afraid to lose, we always out-compete and fight for every vote we can win. We know this campaign will be won on the ground, in states."

Hillary made her formal announcement on April 12, 2015, via Twitter—a medium she has adapted to with surprising wit and ease. And then the campaign hit the road, literally, driving in a van dubbed the "Scooby-mobile," on a road trip from New York to Iowa. She traveled along Route 80 through Pennsylvania and Ohio to Iowa, a place where her staff hoped to bury the ghosts of her defeat there in 2008 and to start anew. Iowa was the first leg of the familiar Hillary Clinton operation: a listening tour, which would take the campaign in its early weeks along the golden primary and caucus trail, to New Hampshire, Nevada, and South Carolina. A listening tour was how she'd launched her successful Senate bid in New York in 2000, at a time when she was a soon-to-be former First Lady in the midst of rebranding and a new transplant from Washington, D.C., by way of Arkansas, by way of Illinois.

Now the Clintons were New Yorkers, ensconced in offices in Harlem, midtown, and Brooklyn, with a home in the town of Chappaqua. It seemed fitting that Hillary would base her presidential campaign in the state that had embraced her and her family, and where her daughter and granddaughter lived, with Chelsea working at the family's nonprofit enterprises, the Clinton Foundation and the Clinton Global Initiative.

Around the country, Hillary Clinton's friends and supporters had awaited the formal announcement of her campaign with nervous anticipation. Her second try for the White House had seemed a certainty to many of them from the moment she had lost the 2008 Democratic primary to Barack Obama, taking the shattered dreams of millions of women with her.

"I'm hopeful that a new Clinton era will look a lot like the old Clinton era," said Weldon Latham, an African American business leader and longtime friend of the Clintons, who recalled the Bill Clinton administration as an era of inclusion. "As an African American, I can say that I thought it was the best period of time I can remember in America, when we had a president who openly spoke about the advantages of diversity and was trying to move everybody up; moving people in poverty up to the middle class, and [moving] people in the middle class all the way up to being the millionaires. The Clinton years were some of the best years in my lifetime."

That Hillary would try again had a feeling of certainty to it, despite the seemingly endless delays in the formal announcement. People who had been allies of the Clintons from the beginning believed that even accepting the role of secretary of state in the Obama administration was a step along the path and was what one supporter called "a quid pro quo," adding: "I think it was pretty common knowledge among Hillary people that it was. And at that point everyone was just thinking, 'Well, she's gonna be secretary of state and then she's gonna be president.'"

The birth of Chelsea's daughter in September 2014 was the lone event that friends and longtime observers surmised could push Hillary off the road to the presidency. Instead, she began incorporating the baby into her stump speeches, often telling audiences during her increasingly frequent speaking events that as a newly minted grandmother, she wanted to see to it that her granddaughter grew up in the kind of America where women enjoyed full equality. Two days before the campaign announcement, the scrupulously private Chelsea appeared on the cover of *Elle,* opening up to the magazine about a pair of topics that would be highly germane to her mother's campaign: motherhood and women's rights.

The message was deliberate: Women's rights and ambitions were to be a touchstone of Hillary's candidacy this time, much the way the unfulfilled hopes of African Americans, and the dreams of many white Americans for cross-racial unity, were the currency of the Obama campaign in 2008. Hillary and her team had learned the lesson from the Obama victory over what had seemed like an inevitable Clinton romp to the nomination: that you cannot inspire a crucial base indirectly. You have to make a direct appeal to their hearts, minds, and souls.

In 2008, she had sought to make her gender incidental to her image as a strong leader and a credible commander in chief. But for 2016, Hillary would go to the well of dreams, and women would be objects of her embrace. A Gallup poll released on March 21 found that the number-one selling proposition among would-be voters for a potential Hillary Clinton presidency was her status as a potential first female president, with twice as many (18 percent) choosing that answer over her experience and foreign policy acumen (9 percent).

But if women's claim on the White House was the current coursing through the Hillary Clinton campaign, the direct message was borrowed from the Democratic Party's increasingly resurgent Left, which after decades in the political wilderness was driving the agenda in the Senate and in the House after the ranks of the "blue dogs" and New Democrats were depleted in the midterm elections of 2010 and 2014. The Obama era had seen the party move leftward, on issues from what Obama termed "middle-class economics" to gay rights, and its most visible leaders were liberals like Massachusetts senator and Wall Street nemesis Elizabeth Warren and Bill de Blasio, Hillary's onetime campaign manager who was now the very liberal mayor of New York City. To win the White House, Hillary Clinton, the New Democrat, would have to prove to the liberal base of the party that she was one of them.

The campaign was determined to do so through both its message and constant displays of the candidate's humility. Hillary didn't appear on camera until ninety seconds into her two-minute announcement video, naming her run for president as one among the many things ordinary Americans (in the video, mainly women) were preparing to do: buying a home, going back to school, or starting a family. Robby Mook told reporters in background briefings as the Hillary road trip sped toward Iowa that the purpose of her run for president was to "create a better economic future for all Americans." In Iowa, she met with small groups at coffee shops, at a community college annex in tiny Monticello, and at a family-owned fruit distribution business in Norwalk just outside Des Moines, hoping to create an intimate campaign that allowed Americans to meet Hillary, a public figure for a quarter century, all over again.

She told a student roundtable in Monticello that her quest for the White House was rooted in her late mother's struggles. "I've been fighting for children and families my entire adult life, probably because of my mother's example," she said.

> She had a really difficult childhood—was mistreated, neglected, but she never gave up. She had to basically be on her own at the time she was fourteen, and she just kept going. And my father, who was a small businessman and just believed that you had to work hard

to make your way and do whatever you had to do to be successful, and provided a good living for our family. And then I was thinking too about, you know, the lessons I learned from my church. You know, you're supposed to give back. You're supposed to do what you can to help others and that's what I've tried to do, and we'll have more time to talk about that as we go forward.

Hillary lamented the growing gap between the haves and the have-nots, saying she was running for president to be a champion for everyday Americans who've been left behind, as the rich have gotten richer during the economic recovery, while many Americans have been struggling to just maintain.

Would-be Iowa voters responded sometimes with enthusiasm. At Java Joe's, a bustling coffee shop in downtown Des Moines, a young woman in her thirties, an employee at a hunger-focused nonprofit, crowed that she had admired Hillary Clinton since age six, while a smiling grandmother who was Hillary's contemporary, gushed about the prospect of a female president. A high school principal in Monticello, who had caucused for Barack Obama in 2008 and even hosted the then candidate in his home—as Iowans, unique in all the country in their retail politics, sometimes got the chance to do—said he was open to Hillary this time, and enjoined her not to forget the small-town people and the issues she heard in Monticello.

Other times there was skepticism, about the Clintons' past and what specific policies Hillary planned to put on the table. At Joe's a pair of men playing Scrabble voiced that dichotomy, as the younger man, in his sixties, ranted about how thoroughly the Clintons had let down their generation, while his octogenarian playing-partner praised Hillary as experienced and ready to be commander in chief.

One running theme that repeated from Des Moines to Cedar

Rapids to the campaign's subsequent stop in Keane, New Hampshire, was clear, from supporters and detractors alike: If Hillary Clinton were to win and became the first female president, that would be something special indeed.

Still, some Democratic activists worried that it was all too easy, too neatly gift-wrapped. "It's unbelievable to me that in this day and age no other Democrat has stepped up to the plate to say the Democratic Party needs someone that doesn't have the last name Clinton to run," said a Florida Democratic leader. "And I'm loyal to the Clintons because that's who I am, but it still amazes me that she's being given an open runway."

And it was indeed an open runway. Polls consistently showed Hillary with a commanding lead over all other announced and potential challengers, including former Maryland governor Martin O'Malley; Senator Jim Webb of Virginia; Independent Senator Bernie Sanders; Joe Biden, Obama's loyal and jocular two-term vice president; and Elizabeth Warren, who progressives were practically begging to join the primary. All of them polled well below the former senator and secretary of state, rarely getting out of the single digits, while Warren repeatedly insisted that she had no intention of getting into the race. And while the polling against Republicans was close, an unremarkable feature of national politics in a heavily polarized country, the fact of Hillary's upcoming presidential candidacy, the overwhelming nature of her advantages, both inside the Democratic Party and in the coming general election campaign, was undeniable.

The next presidential election would take place on a demographic playing field heavily tilted in favor of Democrats, with the nonwhite share of the electorate projected to be higher than those who elected and reelected Barack Obama. The nonwhite percentage of the voting population had grown by 2 percent every four years for a generation, and if the trend continued, the Democratic nominee would face an electoral universe that was 30 percent nonwhite, meaning the Democrat could win the popular vote handily, even with fewer than 4 in 10 white voters siding with them. Women, who have voted at higher percentages than men since the 1960s, represented a tremendous opportunity for a candidate willing to make a direct appeal to them. Single women, who tend to disappear during midterm elections, held the potential to deliver the 2016 election, particularly to a first woman president.

Meanwhile, as a Pew Research Center survey—culled from twenty-five thousand interviews over the course of 2014 and released in April 2015—pointed out, younger voters gave Democrats a partisan advantage of 15 and 17 percent for younger millennials (ages 18 to 25) and millennials ages 26 to 33, as well as an 8 and 13 percent advantage for younger and older members of Generation X (ages 34 to 41 and 42 to 49). Even baby boomers, who formed the core of the tea party, continued to lean Democratic, by 5 to 8 percent in the Pew poll, leaving only the oldest voters, those ages 69 to 78 (the "silent generation") who gave Republicans a partisan advantage of 4 percent.

And though white millennials leaned more Republican than nonwhite young voters, the youngest cohorts of Americans contained far more minority members than their parents' or grandparents' generations did. In short, Hillary Clinton's Brooklyn campaign had ample potential targets. Where Republicans found the strongest advantage was among white evangelicals (a +46-point gap), Mormons (+48), white southerners (+21), and white men with some college education or less (+21). Among white voters overall, the GOP advantage held at just 9 percentage points, while Democrats enjoyed an advantage of 69 points with black voters, 42 points with Asian Americans, and 30 points with Hispanics.

And yet, the candidate did face potential pitfalls on the road to power. Despite the protestations of humility, the notion of inevitability and hubris would be a sword of Damocles over the campaign, since by all appearances Hillary had no serious

Democratic challengers. The media and the Right had a long history of skewering the Clintons, the latter in unbridled, sometimes hysterical fashion. As a woman, and a grandmother, Hillary could hardly hope to avoid the kind of sexist attacks that roiled her 2008 campaign, compounded by an undercurrent of age bias especially reserved for women. On the day she announced, the top Google search term related to the coming campaign was "how old is Hillary Clinton." And the head of the NRA, Wayne LaPierre, declared at the group's annual meeting the day before, "Eight years of one demographically symbolic president is enough," a side-swipe at Obama's race and Hillary's gender that offered a preview of the tone of the coming contest.

Republicans were promising to litigate not just Mrs. Clinton's time as secretary of state, but even Bill Clinton's personal, financial, and sexual affairs dating back to the 1990s. And Hillary was continuing to fend off a March media boomlet triggered by a *New York Times* story detailing her use of a private e-mail server while secretary of state and a Republican-controlled Congress determined to use the story to revive questions about the Benghazi attacks.

Skeptics of her prospects pointed to the fact that the last person to succeed a two-term president of their own party was George H. W. Bush, while Bill Clinton's two terms were followed by eight years of Republican George W. Bush, and Bush's two terms were followed by eight years of Barack Obama. The oscillation of executive power between two-term presidents of opposite parties had become an American habit. And despite the rebounding economy, the fact that the country remained at peace, and the enormous growth in the number of Americans with health insurance and thus access to health care, Obama's approval ratings remained modest, rising to 48 percent in a May NBC News/*Wall Street Journal* poll. He would be an asset on the campaign trail in wooing African Americans, but Republicans would surely try to use him as cudgel with white voters.

And Hillary faced the ever-present danger of leaning so far toward inspiring women that she appeared to take other key constituencies for granted, namely African Americans. She and Bill had opted out of the Selma commemoration, and they had taken their time responding to the events in Ferguson.

She responded more quickly to the death of Walter Scott, a fifty-year-old black man gunned down by a South Carolina police officer who then appeared to fabricate claims that he'd fought Scott over a Taser. The shooting was captured by a bystander on a cell phone camera and showed Scott running away from the officer, who shot at him eight times, hitting him four times in the back. "Praying for #WalterScott's family," Hillary tweeted on the day of Scott's April 11 funeral, which was attended by hundreds of mourners, including both South Carolina senators and Congressman Jim Clyburn. "Heartbreaking & too familiar. We can do better—rebuild trust, reform justice system, respect all lives," Mrs. Clinton wrote. But members of the Black Lives Matter movement made clear that they intended to hold Hillary to account, even threatening to protest at her events if she did not make clear her stand on police reform.

Hillary sought to do just that by making criminal justice reform the centerpiece of her first major public speech, which was held on April 29 at Columbia University's public policy center, named for former New York mayor David Dinkins. The speech came in the wake of yet another death of a black man at the hands of police: Freddie Gray, a twenty-five-year-old man from an impoverished Baltimore neighborhood known as Sandtown. He was arrested by bike patrol officers on April 12 and later that day was taken unconscious from the back of the police wagon. After lapsing into a coma, he died one week later. His spinal cord had been nearly severed at the neck.

The officers claimed Gray had a switchblade (a subsequent investigation found that he did not), and video of his arrest shows the police handling him roughly, before dragging a wailing Gray, his legs all but dangling, into the back of the transport wagon.

Gray's funeral on April 27 touched off a day of violent riots and looting in West Baltimore, drawing national attention to the city's dire poverty and its history of toxic policing. This includes the old and nationwide scattered practice of "rough rides," in which the poor, and often black, suspect is driven unbelted in the back of a police transport van, his body tossed around like a rag doll during a deliberately jarring trip. Baltimore—a city with a black female mayor and a black police commissioner—would be the latest American city to erupt in the national conflagration over the policing of black bodies.

At Columbia, Hillary Clinton said,

> What we've seen in Baltimore should, indeed does, tear at our soul. And from Ferguson to Staten Island to Baltimore, the patterns have become unmistakable and undeniable. Walter Scott shot in the back in Charleston, South Carolina. Unarmed. In debt. And terrified of spending more time in jail for child support payments he couldn't afford. . . . Tamir Rice shot in a park in Cleveland, Ohio. Unarmed and just twelve years old. . . . Eric Garner choked to death after being stopped for selling cigarettes on the streets of this city. And now Freddie Gray. His spine nearly severed while in police custody. Not only as a mother and a grandmother but as a citizen, a human being, my heart breaks for these young men and their families.

Hillary's staff had been hinting for days that this speech would be a centerpiece of her coming campaign, which became clear as she continued,

We have to come to terms with some hard truths about race and justice in America. There is something profoundly wrong when African American men are still far more likely to be stopped and searched by police, charged with crimes, and sentenced to longer prison terms than are meted out to their white counterparts. . . . There is something wrong when a third of all black men face the prospect of prison during their lifetimes. And an estimated one point five million black men are "missing" from their families and communities because of incarceration and premature death. . . . There is something wrong when more than one out of every three young black men in Baltimore can't find a job. . . . There is something wrong when trust between law enforcement and the communities they serve breaks down as far as it has in many of our communities. We have allowed our criminal justice system to get out of balance. And these recent tragedies should galvanize us to come together as a nation to find our balance again.

Two days after Mrs. Clinton spoke—on a Friday, the first day of May, following a week of marches and rallies that had spread to cities around the country, and as three thousand National Guard troops descended on Baltimore—six police officers were charged with crimes concerning Freddie Gray's death, including manslaughter and second-degree murder. Three of the officers were white; three were black. It was an unprecedented step, taken by a thirty-five-year-old African American woman named Marilyn Mosby. She had been elected just a hundred days earlier to be Baltimore's state attorney. The city's black residents, straining under a week-long curfew, erupted in jubilation.

As for Hillary Clinton, few doubted that if she became the Democratic nominee, she would win the lion's share of African

American votes. Indeed, a May 2015 NBC/*Wall Street Journal* poll showed her holding 90 percent of African American voters in a hypothetical matchup against Jeb Bush, compared to 66 percent if the Democrat facing Governor Bush was Joe Biden. But percentages don't count in elections if they're not backed up by volume.

"There can be no assumptions," said Bertha Lewis, head of the Brooklyn-based Black Institute, which she formed after the collapse of ACORN, the antipoverty organization that registered tens of thousands of minority voters. At its peak, ACORN boasted five hundred thousand members nationwide, only to be shuttered in 2010 when congressional Republicans pushed to strip the group of federal funds in the wake of a soon-discredited "investigation" by a pair of conservative activists linked to Breitbart.com. Breitbart.com was the same conservative media installation that went after Shirley Sherrod while Democrats stood silent and let the organization fall. Lewis declared herself an enthusiastic supporter of Hillary's candidacy but warned that the candidate couldn't afford to take minority voters for granted.

"She's got to go after this vote and go after it aggressively," Lewis said. "The challenge is: Can she produce the long lines that Barack Obama produced [at the polls] and have people saying it's my duty to go out and line up to vote?"

Still, Lewis and others found the prospect of a woman president tantalizing, as exciting in fundamental ways as Barack Obama's candidacy was in 2008.

"I'm quite ready for Hillary because I really do believe there was far more fear of a woman in 2008 than there was of a black male, since at least it was a male," said Lewis. "And I do want to see a woman in the highest office. It would just so fundamentally change the dynamic of domestic policy and foreign policy. It isn't just putting pink on it. I just think it's a whole different mind-set and a different lens of looking at issues."

Not everyone shared Lewis's enthusiasm. Liberal activists were gearing up to challenge Hillary on everything from her support for the Iraq War to her and her husband's ties to Wall Street to the Clinton Foundation's expansive list of foreign donors. Many hadn't forgotten that it was Bill Clinton's signature on the bill that ended the FDR-era separation of banking and investment speculation and opened the door to many of Wall Street's worst abuses, or that Bill Clinton's crime bill had unleashed some of the very police abuses the Black Lives Matter movement, and Hillary, were condemning. To mollify that base, Hillary Clinton would face enormous pressure to keep moving her message, and her campaign, to the left.

And she would have to carefully calibrate her embrace of the sitting president, since any significant movement away from Obama would risk bringing on the wrath (or worse, the apathy) of black voters, while too close an association put her in potential peril with the white working-class voters who had been the object of the Clinton–New Democrats' political project since the mid-1980s. Obama declared on Hillary's announcement day that she would make an excellent president, adding, "I'm not on the ballot." But in fundamental ways, he very much would be.

Still, whatever the doubts and discomfort among some Democrats, it seemed that nothing could stop the Hillary Clinton machine now that it was rolling toward 2016. There would be challengers, but none like Barack Obama with a claim on a large and passionate constituency, who could whisk the rug out from under the Clinton juggernaut. (Indeed, one of Hillary's challengers was Martin O'Malley, the former Maryland governor and onetime mayor of Baltimore, whose pursuit of "zero tolerance" policing was blamed by many of the city's black residents for the deteriorating relations with the police.)

The Clintons had been smarter this time and cleared the political decks of all potential strong rivals, including Senator

Warren. They began to lock down key black staffers and influencers early, and they hugged potential progressive allies like de Blasio close, even if de Blasio sometimes seemed to lean away from their embrace by declining to endorse Hillary on her announcement day or in the days immediately afterward, saying he first needed to hear what she planned to do as president. (Hillary's new campaign headquarters were just blocks from the de Blasios' home, and in the weeks before her announcement, she appeared side by side with New York City's First Lady, Chirlane McCray, to promote early childhood education.)

And while a chorus of Democrats worried about the lack of a truly contested primary, about whether a second Hillary Clinton campaign would be more disciplined and less contentious than the first, including whether Bill Clinton could be reined in and kept on message this time; whether issues of gender would prove to be as divisive as questions about race both during and after the campaign; and about how Hillary Clinton would choreograph her very public political dance with the first black president of the United States on her quest to make her own mark on history, the country was preparing for another battle of demography and destiny. And it promised to be a battle royal.

ACKNOWLEDGMENTS

WHAT A DAUNTING THING IT TURNS OUT TO BE, TO WRITE A BOOK. This one, which was more than a year in the making, would not have been possible without substantial help and support, starting with my family: Jason (who is beyond the best and most patient and supportive husband on earth), Winsome, Jmar, and Miles Reid, who put up with my long absences and travel, and my disconnection from everything around me as I buried myself in transcripts, interviews, and a monster manuscript that was followed by successive edits. You are invaluable and much loved.

In particular, I could not have gotten through this project without Winsome Reid. Winsome—who served as my personal assistant, research aide, and interview booker, taking a year off from college in the process—was my invaluable right-hand girl, travel buddy, and sidekick, and she is as responsible as anyone for the existence of this book. Thank you for making all of those phone calls, sending all of those e-mails, posting all of those calendar reminders, and being my "plus one" at every stop.

Which brings me to Henry Ferris, on whom I dumped the mother of all elongated manuscripts and who helped turn that heap of words into a book. I have been blessed throughout my writing career with terrific editors: Michael Bellas at Beverage Marketing Corporation, Joe Oglesby and Myriam "The Machete" Marquez at the *Miami Herald,* and Steve Kornacki and Joan Walsh at Salon.com. But Henry brought a particular patience, wit, expertise, and ruthlessness with the cut, without which there would have been no book at all. What a blessing to work with such a terrific editor, and such a wonderful person. Thank you to Henry and the entire team at HarperCollins.

These acknowledgments would not be complete without also including sincere and warm thanks to my team at WME: book agent extraordinaire Suzanne Gluck (the "not-tall" Suzanne); Suzanne Lyon (the "tall" Suzanne), a fabulous agent and an even more fabulous person; Henry Reisch (Henry 1.0), who is both my principal agent and my friend, and who makes my day with every phone conversation; and Eve Attermann, who helps keep me in great writing form. These agents, their assistants, and the entire WME team are simply the best.

Not to be forgotten: Melissa Harris Perry, for insisting that I write a book and holding me to it; Michael Eric Dyson, friendship, aid, and inspiration; Marcia Dyson, for wisdom; April Ryan, for epic advice on all things Washington; Chris Matthews, Joan Walsh, David Corn, Touré, and Jonathan Alter, for being my "how-to-be-an-author" Obi-Wan Kenobis; Desirée Tate, for helping me find all the best places to eat in Chicago and for endless patience even when it wasn't her day off; Clo Ewing, my friend from campaign days, for great meals in Chi-Town; Professor Charles Ogletree, for giving me an excuse to come back to Harvard and for being a great conversationalist; Lynn Sweet, for insights; Vernon Jordan, Julian Bond, and Bob Moses, for perspective on the civil rights era; Bob Shrum, for sharing his vast experience; Yvette Miley, for time off to write that was always right on time; Jonathan Capehart, Karen Finney, and Krystal

Ball, for filling in when I took that time and for being great friends; my MSNBC team—Meaghan O'Connor, Bridget Flanagan, Larry Epstein, Alexis Garrett-Stodghill, Stefanie Cargill, Michael Biette, Ayan Chatterjee, Michelle Brown, Meg Corzine, Amanda Ingersoll, John Flowers, and Omnika Thompson— for patience and forbearance during my absences, physical and sometimes mental; Frank Watkins, Howard Dean, Keith Boykin, Jamal Simmons, Marc Morial, and Wade Henderson, for civic wisdom; Representative Marcia Fudge and the Congressional Black Caucus; Angela Rye and Nina Turner, for sisterly advice; David Bositis and the staff of the Joint Center for Political and Economic Studies; Harold Lee Rush; Afoyemi Kirby; the Miller Center of Public Affairs at the University of Virginia; the Lyndon Baines Johnson Presidential Library; the Woodlawn Organization of Chicago; Rev. Al Sharpton and the amazing staff at the National Action Network; Rachel Noerdlinger and Tamika Mallory, for being inspirational; Johnny Wilkerson and Larry Nesmith of the Georgia NAACP; and all of the people, named and unnamed, who talked to me, e-mailed with me, shared stories, insights, and memories with me, and helped shape my understanding of a political party and its presidents.

NOTES

Chapter 1: 1964

3   *"I want to appoint these judges"* President Lyndon Johnson conversation
with Whitney Young, January 6, 1964, Lyndon B. Johnson White
House Recordings, Miller Center, University of Virginia.

    "[The] strategy is as simple" Theodore H. White, "The Negro Voter:
Can He Elect a President?" *Collier's,* August 17, 1956.

4   *By 1964 just 4 in 10* "Voter Participation in the National Election,
November 1964," U.S. Department of Commerce, Bureau of the
Census, October 25, 1965.

    "They say I'm an arm twister" President Lyndon Johnson conversation
with Roy Wilkins, January 6, 1964, Lyndon B. Johnson White House
Recordings, Miller Center, University of Virginia.

    He urged them to work Groups like the Congress on Racial Equality
had already begun massing protests outside Dirksen's state offices,
prompting him to complain loudly from the Senate floor, while civil
rights and labor groups were mounting a national pressure campaign
of letters and telegrams intended to win Republican support and keep
northern Democrats on board.

5   *"The races segregate themselves"* Mike Wallace interview with Senator
James Eastland, July 28, 1957, video and transcript from the Harry
Ransom Center, University of Texas at Austin.

7   *"The Democratic Party has encouraged lawlessness"* Senator Strom
    Thurmond, "Address to the People of South Carolina," September 16,
    1964.

8   *"I'm not inextricably bound"* The Papers of Martin Luther King, Jr.:
    Symbol of the Movement, edited by Peter Holloran, Ralph Luker, and
    Penny A. Russell (Berkeley: University of California Press, 2000).

9   *When Roosevelt was elected to a fourth term* "Trends in Party
    Identification," Joint Center for Political and Economic Studies, 2012,
    with data from the Pew Research Center, 2012.
    "By 1948, when Truman squeezed out" White, "The Negro Voter."
    Democrats held their overwhelming share Ibid.
    But when Eisenhower faced Stevenson again "Trends in Black Party
    Affiliation and the Black Vote, 1936–2012," Joint Center for Political
    and Economic Studies.

10 *And though Stevenson was now running* "Adlai 'Spanks' Manifesto
    Softly," NNPA news story as reprinted in *Washington Afro-American*,
    March 3, 1956.

11 National Review *publisher William Rusher* Martin S. Levine,
    "Magazine Publisher Says Goldwater Will Announce His Candidacy
    Soon: Rusher Sees 'Remarkable' Support," *Harvard Crimson*,
    December 10, 1963.

12 *Clinton would later write in her memoir* Hillary Rodham Clinton,
    Living History (New York: Simon & Schuster, 2003).

13 *But in 1964, Hillary was* Ibid.
    With weeks to go before the election Cabell Phillips, "U.S. Negro Voters
    Put at 5.5 Million," *New York Times*, October 13, 1964.
    On election day, they were proven right U.S. Census Bureau figures.
    "I have seen certain changes in the United States" Interview by Bob
    McKenzie with Rev. Martin Luther King Jr., *BBC World News
    America*, December 1964.

14 *By March, Johnson's approval ratings* Roper Center Public Opinion
    Archives, Roper Center for Public Opinion Research, University of
    Connecticut.
    After the telecast Margaret A. Blanchard, ed., *History of the Mass Media
    in the United States: An Encyclopedia* (New York: Routledge, 2013).

15 *"It was sending their sons"* Ibid.

16 *By 1966, Americans' disapproval* Per Gallup: "In 1963, King had a 41%

positive and a 37% negative rating; in 1964, it was 43% positive and 39% negative; in 1965, his rating was 45% positive and 45% negative; and in 1966—the last Gallup measure of King using this scalometer procedure—it was 32% positive and 63% negative." By the December Gallup list of the "Most Admired Americans," King had been off the list for two years, and George Wallace entered the list, at number eight.

17 *But the revered athletes Joe Louis* Shelia Curran Bernard, Steve Fayer, and Samuel D. Pollard, "Aint Gonna Shuffle No More (1964–72)," *Eyes on the Prize II: America at the Radical Crossroads (1965–1985)*, season 2, episode 5, directed by Shelia Curran Bernard and Samuel D. Pollard, aired February 15, 1990 (PBS Video, 2006), PBS series.

18 *But Robinson was also a military veteran* John Vernon, "Jim Crow, Meet Lieutenant Robinson: A 1944 Court-Martial," *Prologue* 40, no. 1 (Spring 2008).

Robinson was a fervent patriot Jackie Robinson letters, from *First Class Citizenship: The Civil Rights Letters of Jackie Robinson*, edited by Michael G. Long (New York: Times Books, 2007).

In May 1967 David Falkner, *Great Time Coming: The Life of Jackie Robinson from Baseball to Birmingham* (New York: Simon & Schuster, 1996).

19 *Black enlistees accounted for* Spencer C. Tucker, ed., *Encyclopedia of the Vietnam War: A Political, Social, and Military History* (Oxford: ABC-CLIO, 1998).

20 *The furious attacks on Ali in particular* Herman Graham, *The Brothers' Vietnam War: Black Power, Manhood, and the Military Experience* (Gainesville: University Press of Florida, 2003).

Hillary Rodham, then a junior JoAnn Bren Guernsey, *Hillary Rodham Clinton: Secretary of State* (Minneapolis: Lerner, 2010).

21 *Everett Dirksen, whose negotiating skills* Under pressure from LBJ, the House would pass the Fair Housing Act on April 10. Though he'd broken with King, the president wanted the bill signed before King's funeral. He signed it on April 11, 1968, two days after King was laid to rest. In announcing the bill's final passage, Johnson said: "I do not exaggerate when I say that the proudest moments of my presidency have been times such as this when I have signed into law the promises of a century."

22 *King's murder sparked riots* Christopher Chandler, "Shoot to Kill . . . Shoot to Maim," *Chicago Reader*, April 4, 2002.

23   *The ads were tagged* Transcript of Nixon campaign ad, "Vietnam," 1968.
    Phillips foresaw a day Review of Kevin Phillips, *The Emerging Republican Majority,* by Warren Weaver Jr., *New York Times,* September 21, 1969, BR3.

24   *As the nomination was announced* "A Brief History of Chicago's 1968 Democratic Convention," CNN.com. Sources: Norman Mailer's *Miami and the Siege of Chicago*; Facts on File, *CQ's Guide to U.S. Elections.*

25   *Humphrey, for his part* David S. Broder, "Nixon Wins with 290 Electoral Votes; Humphrey Joins Him in Call·for Unity," *Washington Post,* November 7, 1968.

Chapter 2: All in the Family

28   *Carroll O'Connor played the Queens native* TVHistory.tv, Nielsen Media Research.

29   *In January 1969* The founding members of the Congressional Black Caucus in 1971 were Representatives Shirley Chisholm (D-NY), William L. Clay Sr. (D-MO), George W. Collins (D-IL), John Conyers (D-MI), Ronald Dellums (D-CA), Augustus F. Hawkins (D-CA), Ralph Metcalfe (D-IL), Parren Mitchell (D-MD), Robert Nix (D-PA), Charles Rangel (D-NY), Louis Stokes (D-OH), and Walter Fauntroy (D-D.C. Delegate).

31   *"We come to Gary"* "The Gary Declaration: Black Politics at the Crossroads," National Black Political Convention, 1972; Dr. Quintard Taylor Jr., University of Washington, Department of History.
    "[b]oth parties have betrayed us" Ibid.

32   *The Gary Declaration asserted* Ibid.
    Instead she was calling for Shirley Chisholm, campaign announcement, transcribed from video of January 25, 1972, news broadcast, ABC News archives.

33   *The rejection disappointed* It would surface years later that Nixon operative G. Gordon Liddy, architect of the plan to break into Democratic National Committee headquarters, presented a plan to Nixon's attorney general and former campaign manager John Mitchell in 1972, to funnel money to the Chisholm presidential campaign to sow racial discord within Democratic ranks. Liddy dubbed the plan, with no apparent sense of irony, "Operation Coal." Mitchell turned it down.

34 *Even the selection of Missouri senator Thomas Eagleton* Eagleton would
    eventually be forced to resign from the campaign, which led to a member
    of the Kennedy family, Sargent Shriver, joining the doomed ticket.
    It instantly added more than 10 million new voters Connecticut was the
    first to ratify the Twenty-Sixth Amendment, lowering the national
    voting age to eighteen. North Carolina was the last. Eight states,
    including Florida, never did.

35 *With more than 55 percent* National exit polls, 1972 election.
    "The most pervasive factors" Eddie Williams, "Perspective," note
    in *Focus,* the newsletter of the Joint Center for Political Studies,
    December 1972.

36 *In March 1974* David S. Broder, "The Democrats' Dilemma: There
    Is Less to the Party's Prospects Than Meets the Eye," *The Atlantic
    Monthly,* March 1974.

37 *Carter made a major misstep* *Today,* April 6, 1976, NBC News
    archives.
    "I think Americans" Ibid.
    "seventeen black members of Congress" Ibid.
    "I think you have to assume" Ibid.

38 *And for the first time* Jordan was the first black woman to serve in the
    Texas legislature since 1883, a feat that earned her an invitation to the
    White House to preview Lyndon Johnson's 1967 civil rights address.

39 *On the campaign trail, Carter* "Carter Dogged by Church Incident,"
    United Press International, November 2, 1976.
    "If it was a country club" Ibid.
    But unlike McGovern Demographics of the 1976 Election, Roper
    Center for Public Opinion Research, University of Connecticut, based
    on a CBS News exit poll of 15,300 voters taken November 2, 1976.

41 *By the time Carter arrived in Miami* The Reagan administration later
    drastically cut those funds.

42 *In the South, the story morphed* Paul Krugman, "Republicans and
    Race," *New York Times,* November 19, 2007.

43 *It was Reagan who managed to field* Roper Center for Public Opinion
    Research.
    A Joint Center analysis noted Joint Center for Political Studies, analysis
    of the 1980 election.

47 *Even after millions of petition signatures* When the King Day bill

finally passed, 78 to 22, with 18 Republicans and 4 Democrats voting against it, Helms denounced the vote as a "tyranny of the majority." The bill was signed into law in November 1983. Arizona would become the last state to adopt the holiday in 1990.

49   *"That's all Hymie wants to talk about"* Gigi Anders, "'Hymietown' Revisited," interview with Milton Coleman, *American Journalism Review,* May 1999.

      "Do not forget that this entire nation" Mario Cuomo, keynote address to the Democratic National Convention, July 16, 1984, San Francisco.

50   *"Our flag is red"* Jesse Jackson, address to the 1984 Democratic National Convention.

      Jackson touted the country's ending Ibid.

52   *Jackson broadened his message* "For Jesse Jackson and His Campaign: Jesse Jackson Is a Serious Candidate for the Presidency," editorial, *The Nation,* April 16, 1988.

53   *He'd won nearly as many votes* E. J. Dionne Jr., "Jackson Share of Votes by Whites Triples in '88," *New York Times,* June 13, 1988.

      Where in 1984 Ibid.

Chapter 3: The Third Way

59   *"I like Mario, but once again"* Associated Press interview with Governor Bill Clinton by Ron Fournier, excerpted in Al From, *The New Democrats and the Return to Power* (New York: Palgrave Macmillan, 2003).

61   *Angry protests, even riots* Unlike in the 1980 Arthur McDuffie case, a police officer was convicted in the 1989 killings.

65   *"We are ready for any opportunity"* William Raspberry, "Will Jesse Jackson Limit His Ambition for the Good of the Democratic Cause?" *Philadelphia Inquirer,* May 2, 1992.

      "For all his brilliance" Ibid.

66   *"If black people kill black people"* David Mills, "Sister Souljah's Call to Arms," *Washington Post,* May 13, 1992, B1.

67   *"I do not know why he used this platform"* Sam Fulwood III, "Fool Me Once," TheRoot.com, February 28, 2008.

68   *"Clinton had given them"* Ibid.

      Sister Souljah quickly called Transcript of Sistah Souljah press conference, Rainbow/PUSH convention, June 1992, Rock Out Censorship online archive.

68   *"First of all, to imply"* "Clinton Rap a New Strategy?," compiled
      by staff writer Ron Goldwyn from reports by the Associated Press,
      Reuters, and other news services, *Philadelphia Inquirer,* June 16, 1992.
69   *Butts, pastor of the storied* Ibid.
72   *Thomas had triumphed* "Americans' Response to the Nomination of
      Clarence Thomas: At Every Point, The Public at Large, Women and
      Men, Blacks and Whites Backed Thomas' Confirmation," Roper
      Center for Public Opinion Research, University of Connecticut, *The
      Public Perspective*, November/December 1991. Thomas's nomination
      split the national NAACP, with its chief Washington hand, Wade
      Henderson, vehemently opposed, and other factions within the
      organization in support. It also roiled the black elite: black legal scholars
      like Harvard Law School professor Charles Ogletree, who represented
      Hill, denounced Thomas, while luminaries like author and poet Maya
      Angelou rose in support, with Angelou even penning an August *New
      York Times* op-ed entitled "I Dare to Hope," citing Thomas's childhood
      in poverty in rural Georgia as a reason to give him a chance.
      The forty-seven women Adam Clymer, "The 1992 Elections:
      Congress—The New Congress; Democrats Promise Quick Action on
      a Clinton Plan," *New York Times*, November 5, 1992.
73   *He tapped his friend Mike Espy* Herman would become the secretary of
      labor in the second Clinton administration.
76   *The attacks built to such a fury* President Bill Clinton, "Remarks on
      the Withdrawal of the Nomination of Lani Guinier to Be an Assistant
      Attorney General and an Exchange with Reporters," June 3, 1993.
77   *That Clinton would accept that characterization* A former White House
      staffer noted that Clinton was actually closer to Jocelyn Elders, his
      onetime Arkansas health secretary, whom he named as U.S. surgeon
      general, than he personally was to Guinier. But as the former aide
      noted, Clinton had no trouble cashiering Elders, too, in December
      1994, over a controversy involving Elders's statement during a Q&A
      following a speech on World AIDS Day, about perhaps teaching teens
      about masturbation as a way of curbing riskier sexual activity.
      New York congressman Charlie Rangel Clarence Page, "Who Says
      Congressional Blacks Have Nowhere to Go?" *Chicago Sun Times,* June
      18, 1993.
78   *When the crime bill passed* "Rare Bipartisanship Gives Clinton a
      Needed Victory," *Santa Cruz Sentinel,* August 26, 1994.

80   *Just 45 percent of eligible voters* U.S. Census Bureau.
      Now, for the first time, those voters Voter News Service, exit polls, 1994.
      Among white men and women U.S. Census Bureau.
      Just 37 percent of black voters Ibid.
      "Race was at the heart of this election" Isabel Wilkerson, "The 1994
      Elections: Voters Minorities; Many Blacks See Betrayal in This Year's
      Campaign," *New York Times*, November 10, 1994.
81   *"It was absolute disgust"* Ibid.

Chapter 4: The "First Black President"
82   *Going into the 1994 midterms* David A. Bositis, Ph.D., "Resegregation
      in Southern Politics?" Joint Center for Political and Economic
      Studies, November 2011.
84   *The president's January address* State of the Union address by President
      Bill Clinton, January 24, 1995, transcript.
86   *The bill handed federal welfare funds* Barbara Vobejda and Judith
      Havemann, "2 HHS Officials Quit Over Welfare Changes,"
      Washington Post, September 12, 1996, A01.
88   *Indeed, by the end of the president's second term* Center for American
      Progress.
      White House spokesman Joe Lockhart Thomas J. Brady, "Jesse Jackson
      to Be Roving Ambassador to Africa," *Philadelphia Inquirer*, October
      10, 1997.
91   *But Hall's idea unleashed* Michael A. Fletcher, "Slavery Apology Idea
      Sparks Criticism," *Moscow Times*, August 6, 1997.
92   *Even Jesse Jackson dismissed the idea* Ibid.
      "Any American, I hope, feels badly" Sam Fulwood III, "Gingrich Rejects
      Apology for Slavery," *Los Angeles Times*, June 14, 1997.
93   *"As an African American"* R. W. Apple Jr., "Clinton's Contrition," *New
      York Times*, April 1, 1998.
94   *After all, Clinton displays* Toni Morrison, "Clinton as the First Black
      President," *The New Yorker*, October 1998.
      "No matter how smart you are" Ibid.
102   *The First Lady spent considerable time* Moynihan and the Clintons
      shared a media consultant, Mandy Grunwald, who in addition to Bill
      Clinton's 1992 race had previously worked on the New York senator's
      campaigns.

104   *Soon, however, Hillary's campaign*   The Street Crimes Unit was disbanded one month later, on March 27, 1999, by then New York police commissioner Howard Safir, with the officers ordered back into uniform.

106   *"I know most people in America"*   "Diallo Case Draws More Scrutiny," Associated Press, March 5, 2000.

        "Even President Clinton, following"   Michael R. Blood, "Giuliani Says She Counts on Sharpton," *Daily News,* March 10, 2000.

        "The mayor knows that Hillary Clinton"   Ibid.

        Despite the reticence of her spokesman   "Mrs. Clinton Lambasts Giuliani," Associated Press, March 24, 2000.

        By April, polls showed voters   Adam Nagourney with Marjorie Connelly, "Giuliani's Ratings Drop over Actions in Dorismond Case," *New York Times,* April 7, 2000.

107   *Giuliani's rambling exit*   Elisabeth Bumiller, "Giuliani Quits Race for Senate, and G.O.P. Rallies Around Lazio," *New York Times,* May 20, 2000.

111   *"We have more in common"*   Ted Kleine, "Is Bobby Rush in Trouble?" *Chicago Reader,* March 17, 2000.

        Rush, along with the third candidate   Ibid.

113   *The soon-to-be senator's call*   Keynote speech by Illinois senate candidate Barack Obama, Democratic National Convention, July 27, 2004, transcript.

115   *"People are really hurting"*   "Illinois Senate Race Offers Historic Opportunity," *People's World,* February 27, 2004.

116   *"I want to be elected"*   Jack Germond and Jules Witcover, "Feeling Left Out in Massachusetts," *Chicago Tribune,* September 1, 1978.

Chapter 5: Kanye

120   *Myers later told* GQ *magazine*   Chris Heath, "Mike Myers's Comeback Is Groovy, Baby," *GQ,* June 2014.

121   *"We associate a person charging racism"*   John McWhorter, "Kanye West: Bard or Bully?" *The New Republic,* November 16, 2010.

122   *He was traveling overseas*   Lynne Sweet, "To Obama, Tragedy More About Class than Race," *Chicago Sun-Times,* September 5, 2005.

123   *No, the failed federal response*   Ibid.

        Obama told Sweet that Katrina   Ibid.

123   *"What I think is that we as a society"* Ibid.

124   *In every sense, it was clear* "Blacks Blast Bush for Katrina Response,"
      Gallup News Service, September 14, 2005.

125   *Bush's approval ratings* Dan Froomkin, "Was Kanye West Right?"
      White House Watch blog, washingtonpost.com, September 13, 2005.
      In many of the races National exit poll, 2006.
      Surging black turnout David A. Bositis, "Blacks and the 2006
      Midterm Elections," Joint Center for Political and Economic Studies.
      Nationally, Democrats triumphed National exit polls, 2002 and 2006.

126   *"some Republicans gave up on winning"* Mike Allen, "RNC Chief to
      Say It Was 'Wrong' to Exploit Racial Conflict for Votes," *Washington
      Post,* July 14, 2005.
      Steele, the affable Maryland lieutenant governor Ibid.

127   *And brochures distributed in several states* In December 2006, the
      Bush administration would fire seven U.S. attorneys, and allegations
      would arise that many of them were dismissed for insufficient vigor in
      finding and bringing cases of voter fraud.
      An October 2006 Pew poll found Pew Research poll, October 11, 2006.

131   *"The question is, is Barack Obama"* Denise Watson Batts, "Tavis
      Smiley to Hold Annual 'State of the Black Union 2007' This
      Weekend," *Virginian-Pilot,* February 6, 2007.

132   *Chisholm had positioned herself* Shirley Chisholm, campaign
      announcement, transcribed from video of January 25, 1972, news
      broadcast, ABC News archives.

133   *The decision followed the publication* Benjamin Wallace Wells,
      "Destiny's Child: The Radical Roots of Barack Obama," *Rolling Stone,*
      February 22, 2007.

134   *"The question is: Will this generation"* Peter Wallsten, "Would Obama
      Be 'Black President'?" *Los Angeles Times,* February 10, 2007.

137   *"It's a slim possibility"* David Miller, "2 Key Black Politicians Endorse
      Clinton," Associated Press, February 13, 2007.
      "I'm a gambling man" Ibid.
      "Black Americans in the South" Perry Bacon Jr., "Can Obama Count
      on the Black Vote?" *Time,* January 23, 2007.

138   *On CNN, weeks after the State of the Black Union* Tony Harris
      interview with Radio One founder Cathy Hughes, CNN, February 23,
      2007, transcript.

139   *"Can't have a black man"* John Dickerson, "Obama's South Carolina Debut: Feeling the Love in Columbia," *Slate,* February 17, 2007.

142   *"If I were a candidate"* Roddie A. Burns, "Jackson Slams Obama for 'Acting White,'" *State,* September 19, 2007.

        Jackson later reiterated his support Ibid.

        Jackson took another, more veiled swipe "Jesse Jackson: For Obama, but Maybe Also Clinton," interview with *Los Angeles Times* editorial board, October 8, 2007.

        "I've said I would vote for Barack" Ibid.

143   *Afterward, Obama headed for a fund-raiser* Jason Horowitz, "Obama, Celeb Supporters, Upstage 'White Lady' Hillary in Harlem," *New York Observer,* November 30, 2007.

        The two events couldn't have been Ibid.

144   *"You'd be really embarrassed"* Ibid.

Chapter 6: Hope and Change

146   *"We can't have false hopes"* Claudia Parsons, "After Obama Win, Clinton Warns of 'False Hopes,'" Reuters, January 4, 2008.

147   *"I would," Senator Clinton said* Major Garrett interview with Senator Hillary Rodham Clinton, January 7, 2008, Nashua, New Hampshire, Fox News, transcribed by the author.

149   *"[S]ince you raised the judgment issue"* Bill Clinton town hall at Dartmouth College, January 7, 2008, transcribed by the author from video courtesy of ABC News.

        "It's wrong that Obama" Ibid.

        Clinton ended his tirade Ibid.

150   *"It's not easy"* Hillary Clinton campaign event in Portsmouth, New Hampshire, January 7, 2011. Transcribed by the author from video courtesy of ABC News and Talking Points Memo.

        "This is very personal for me" Ibid.

        New York Times columnist Maureen Dowd Maureen Dowd, "Can Hillary Cry Her Way Back to the White House?" *New York Times,* January 9, 2008.

151   *"When we've been told we're not ready"* Senator Barack Obama, New Hampshire Primary concession speech, January 8, 2008, Nashua, New Hampshire, transcript from American Rhetoric.

        He derided the spectacle Bob Herbert, "Of Hope and Politics," *New York Times,* January 12, 2008.

153   *"We have to be very, very careful"* Carl Hulse, "Civil Rights Tone
       Prompts Talk of an Endorsement," *New York Times,* January 11,
       2008.
       "To call that dream a fairy tale" Ibid.
       The campaign quickly scheduled "Aftermath: Clinton's 'Unfortunate'
       MLK Remark," Associated Press TV package by Ted Shaffrey, January
       14, 2008.
154   *"There's nothing fairy tale"* Katharine Q. Seelye and Kate Phillips, "Bill
       Clinton Tries to Tamp Down 'Fairy-Tale' Remark About Obama,"
       Caucus blog, newyorktimes.com, January 11, 2008.
       A memo went out Sam Stein, "Obama Camp's Memo on Clinton's
       Politicizing Race," *Huffington Post,* January 12, 2008.
155   *Texas congresswoman Sheila Jackson Lee* Ibid.
       "But I also said that" Ibid.
156   *The attempts at damage control* Katharine Q. Seelye, "BET Founder
       Slams Obama in South Carolina," Caucus blog, newyorktimes.com,
       January 13, 2008.
       "We may differ on minor matters" Patrick Healy, "Clinton and Obama Call
       for Truce Over Dr. King Dispute," *New York Times,* January 15, 2008.
157   *"How race got into this thing"* Interview with Representative Charlie Rangel
       by Dominic Carter, NY1, *Inside City Hall,* January 14, 2008, transcript.
       "Our party and our nation is bigger" "Statement of Hillary Rodham
       Clinton," January 14, 2008, American Presidency Project, University
       of California, Santa Barbara.
       "I don't want the campaign at this stage" Jeff Zeleny, "Obama Tries to
       Stop the 'Silliness,'" *New York Times,* January 14, 2008.
       Obama called the Clintons Ibid.
158   *"There are still two people around"* CNN correspondent Jessica Yellin
       interview with President Bill Clinton, Charleston, South Carolina,
       January 23, 2008, transcript.
159   *Asked if he was proud* Jake Tapper and Jennifer Parker interview with
       Bill Clinton, Columbia, South Carolina, January 28, 2008, ABC
       News, transcript.
       "That's just bait" Ibid.
164   *"In recent days, there is a sense"* Jeff Zeleny and Patrick Healey, "Black
       Leader, a Clinton Ally, Tilts to Obama," *New York Times,* February 15,
       2008.

164   *Lewis made it official*   Statement from the office of Congressman John Lewis, February 27, 2008.

165   *"It was easier to walk across that bridge"*   "John Lewis Switches Support to Obama," interview with reporter Monica Pearson, WSB-TV 2, Atlanta, February 28, 2008.
       "To me, there's a historical consideration"   Quote from Representative John Conyers in Noam Scheiber, "The Morning After," *The New Republic,* February 27, 2008.

167   *During that time, a steady stream*   Factcheck.org.

173   *Smiley questioned*   Joy-Ann Reid, "Smiley Takes On Obama at Florida Memorial," *South Florida Times,* March 15, 2008.

174   *"If you're asking for black folks' support"*   Ibid.

175   *"I have already condemned"*   "A More Perfect Union," speech by Senator Barack Obama, March 18, 2008.
       Obama called Wright's words   Ibid.
       "I can no more disown him"   Ibid.

176   *"These people are a part of me"*   Ibid.

Chapter 7: Father's Day

180   *"We're not electing him to be"*   Perry Bacon Jr., "Jackson Incident Revives Some Blacks' Concerns About Obama," *Washington Post,* July 11, 2008.

181   *"By choosing that moment to castigate"*   "Eric Easter of *Ebony/Jet* magazines on Jackson's Obama remarks," Deadline USA blog, *Guardian,* July 10, 2008.
       "On father's day [sic], when Barack Obama"   Michael Eric Dyson, "Obama's Rebuke of Absentee Black Fathers May Score Politically, but It Won't Help Solve the Problem," *Time,* June 19, 2008.

182   *one of two black students*   The second student, James Hood, left the University of Alabama two months after the dramatic standoff, citing "a complete mental and physical breakdown" brought on by racist abuse and isolation. He returned to earn his doctorate in 1997.

184   *Sharpton did the interview*   Interview with Rev. Al Sharpton on *Hannity & Colmes,* Fox News, July 9, 2008, transcript.

189   *That night, Bill Clinton lauded*   "Democratic Convention: Extracts from Bill Clinton's Speech," *Telegraph,* August 28, 2008.

192   *And the Clintons, Bill Clinton in particular*   U.S. Census Bureau.

194   *He got just 10 percent* "Election 2008: Did Southern Whites Vote for Obama?" Institute for Southern Studies, *Facing South,* November 10, 2008.

195   *Indeed, in the four years since* U.S. Census Bureau, 2008.
       Obama's campaign also benefited Exit poll data from Edison Media Research/Mitofsky International for the National Election Pool, including NBC News, ABC News, CBS News, Associated Press, CNN, and Fox News.
       And despite all of the hand-wringing "The Gender Gap: Voting Choices in Presidential Elections (1980–2012)," Center for the American Woman and Politics, Eagleton Institute of Politics, Rutgers University, December 2012.

Chapter 8: Post-Racial

206   *"our ticket to coming back"* Michael Grunwald, *The New New Deal: The Hidden Story of Change in the Obama Era* (New York: Simon & Schuster, 2012).

207   *"That boy's finger"* Caucus blog, newyorktimes.com, April 14, 2008.
       "All the hunters gather up" Joseph Duarte, "Longhorn's Expulsion Shows Need for Caution on Facebook," *Houston Chronicle,* November 11, 2008.

208   *Even Mrs. Obama's mother* Greg Toppo, "In-laws in White House May Add New Meaning to Domestic Policy," *USA Today,* December 4, 2008.

210   *"we, average Americans"* Attorney General Eric Holder, speech at the Department of Justice African American History Month Program, February 18, 2009.

211   *Asked about Holder's comments* Helene Cooper, "Attorney General Chided for Language on Race," *New York Times,* March 7, 2009.

214   *"Now, I don't know"* Obama prime-time news conference, July 22, 2009, CQ transcriptions.

216   *The Pew poll also found* "Section 2: Henry Louis Gates Jr.'s Arrest," Pew Research Center for People and the Press, July 30, 2009.

218   *Back in February, radio host* *The Rush Limbaugh Show,* February 22, 2010, Media Matters for America.
       On September 9, President Obama Nielsen Media Research.

218   *But as the president sought* Dana Milbank, "Washington Sketch:
       Republicans Behaving Badly at Obama Speech," *Washington Post,*
       September 10, 2009.

219   *On the balconies overhead* Philip Rucker, "Lawmakers Concerned as
       Health-Care Overhaul Foes Resort to Violence," *Washington Post,*
       March 25, 2010.

220   *Barney Frank of Massachusetts* Ibid.
       When a brick was through into Ibid.
       "You're dead. We know where you live" Ibid.

221   *"Violence and threats are unacceptable"* Statement by House Minority
       Leader John Boehner, March 24, 2010.

Chapter 9: Backlash

225   *"I'm here like most of you"* Ta-Nehisi Coates, "The Trials of Benjamin
       Jealous," *The Nation,* July 1, 2009.

227   *"I think he [Obama] was very clear"* Michael A. Fletcher, "Obama,
       Civil Rights Leaders Discuss Improving Conditions for Black
       America," *Washington Post,* February 10, 2010.

233   *The fact that Congress* Sam Youngman, "White House Unloads Anger
       over Criticism from 'Professional Left,'" *Hill,* August 10, 2010.

234   *"We are the ones that must stand"* Kate Zernike, "Where Dr. King
       Stood, Tea Party Claims His Mantle," *New York Times,* August 27,
       2010.
       "a lot of people may not be feeling" Remarks by President Barack
       Obama at the Congressional Black Caucus Foundation Phoenix
       Awards Dinner, September 18, 2010.

235   *"the 46-year transition"* David A. Bositis, "Resegregation of Southern
       Politics?" Joint Center for Political and Economic Studies, Civic
       Engagement and Government Institute, November 2011.

236   *"Republicans in control"* Ibid.

238   *It was a bizarre* Melissa Harris-Perry, "Cornel West v. Barack
       Obama," *The Nation,* May 17, 2011.

240   *"Take off your bedroom slippers"* "Obama Tells Congressional Black
       Caucus to 'Stop Complaining,'" Associated Press, September 25, 2011.
       That reticence rankled Frederick C. Harris, "The Price of a Black
       President," *New York Times,* October 27, 2012.

245   *"If I had a son"* Remarks by the President on the Nomination of Dr.
       Jim Kim for World Bank President, Rose Garden, White House,
       September 23, 2012, transcript.

Chapter 10: Victory

248   *Polls showed African Americans* TheGrio.com/NBC/*Wall Street
       Journal* poll, November 7, 2011.
       And there was the math Ronald Brownstein, "Obama Needs 80% of
       Minority Vote to Win 2012 Presidential Election," *National Journal,*
       August 24, 2012.
258   *On the podium, Obama launched* Obama Commencement Speech at
       Morehouse College, May 19, 2013, as prepared for delivery.
259   *"the scold of black America"* Ta-Nehisi Coates, "How the Obama
       Administration Talks to Black America," *The Atlantic,* May 20, 2013.
260   *"To expect the president to introduce"* Jonathan Capehart, "Obama
       Can't Win with Some Black Critics," *Washington Post,* May 21, 2013.
261   *In August 2013, conservative writer* Ross Douthat, "Republicans,
       White Voters and Racial Polarization," Evaluations blog, *New York
       Times,* August 6, 2013.
262   *By 2010, researchers at Brown University* Thomas B. Edsall, "The
       Persistence of Racial Resentment," Opinionator blog, newyorktimes
       .com, February 6, 2013.
264   *"Our country has changed"* Opinion of the Court in *Shelby County v.
       Holder,* June 25, 2013.
       Civil rights groups also noted John G. Roberts Jr., Supreme Court
       Nominee Profile, National Council of Jewish Women, September 2005.
       In dissent, Justice Ruth Bader Ginsburg Dissenting Opinion in *Shelby
       County v. Holder,* June 25, 2013.
265   *"Throwing out preclearance"* Ibid.
266   *"We will not allow"* Statement from the U.S. Department of Justice on
       the filing of lawsuit regarding Texas Voter ID law, August 22, 2013.
       Texas governor Rick Perry accused Hilary Hylton, "Eric Holder Takes
       the Fight for Voting Rights to Texas," *Time,* July 27, 2013.
       "Once again, Perry said" Ibid.
267   *Perry was joined by Texas senator* Senator John Cornyn, "Voter ID
       Protects Voter Equality," op-ed, *Austin American-Statesman,* August 8,
       2013.

267 *Greg Abbott, the state's attorney general* Attorney General Abbott Statement on DOJ Lawsuits Challenging Texas Voter ID and Redistricting Laws, August 22, 2013.

"respect the call for calm reflection" Statement by the President on the George Zimmerman verdict, White House, Office of the Press Secretary, July 14, 2013.

268 *Michelle Alexander, a law professor* Michelle Alexander interview, *Democracy Now!*, July 17, 2013.

Civil rights leaders, including Interview with Jesse Jackson, CNN, July 18, 2013.

"an opportunity for us not to kick the can" Edward-Isaac Dovere, "President Obama Keeps Quiet on Race—Again," *Politico,* July 16, 2013.

269 *"On multiple occasions, Obama has"* Janet Langhart Cohen, "After Zimmerman Verdict, Obama Needs to Speak About Racism," op-ed, *Washington Post,* July 16, 2013.

Three days after the verdict Text of Attorney General Eric Holder's Address to the NAACP Annual Convention, July 16, 2013, Orlando, Florida.

271 *"You know, when Trayvon Martin"* Remarks by the President on Trayvon Martin, James S. Brady Press Briefing Room, White House, July 19, 2003.

272 *"For those who resist that idea"* Ibid.

273 *"He represents the same damn stuff"* The Rush Limbaugh Show, July 22, 2013, transcript.

274 *Polls, meanwhile, showed the repeat* "Big Racial Divide over Zimmerman Verdict," Pew Research poll, July 22, 2013.

Chapter 11: Fracture

278 *Five years later, in 1998* B. Drummond Ayres Jr., "Political Briefing; Black Voters Exiting This Campaign Bus," *New York Times,* July 13, 1998.

279 *On Tuesday, as protests continued* Statement from President Obama on the death of Michael Brown, White House, August 12, 2014.

282 *"To be clear, I didn't have"* Marc Lamont Hill, "Obama, Can't You See Black Anger in Ferguson?" CNN, August 15, 2014.

The president may have disappointed members Jamie Schram and Bob Fredericks, "Law-Enforcement Head Criticizes Obama for Ferguson Response," *New York Post,* August 15, 2014.

286 *"Fuck the White House"* Alexander Bolton, "Ferguson Protesters Say Obama Needs to Take Charge," *Hill*, August 20, 2014.

288 *"Imagine what we would feel* Maggie Haberman and Katie Glueck, "Hillary Clinton Makes First Ferguson Remarks," *Politico*, August 28, 2014.

289 *"By siding with the black Gates"* Jamelle Bouie, "Why Did Obama Say So Little About Ferguson?" *Slate*, August 18, 2014.

"twice as good and half as black" Ta-Nehisi Coates, "Fear of a Black President," *The Atlantic*, August 22, 2012.

290 *"This decision seems to underscore"* Congressional Black Caucus statement on the grand jury's decision in the case of Officer Darren Wilson in Ferguson, Missouri, November 25, 2014.

"Which elected official disappointed" Jarvis DeBerry, "Ferguson Response Shows How Barack Obama Struggles to Be Black and President," NOLA.com, November 28, 2014.

297 *A scant 27 percent of white Americans* NBC/*Wall Street Journal* poll, January 14–17, 2015.

Our political divisions were essentially racial Michael Tesler, "Donald Sterling Shows the Separate Realities of Democrats and Republicans About Race," Monkey Cage blog, washingtonpost.com, May 1, 2014.

298 *More than forty thousand people descended* Casey Toner, "As 'Selma' Wows Hollywood Critics, White Flight and Poverty Haunt Selma," AL.com, January 7, 2015.

300 *"The Americans who crossed this bridge"* "Remarks by the President at the 50th Anniversary of the Selma to Montgomery Marches," Selma, Alabama, March 7, 2015, White House, Office of the Press Secretary.

302 *"Just this week, I was asked"* Ibid.

The speech drew broad praise Quin Hillyer, "Obama at Selma: A Beautifully Crafted Speech," Corner blog, nationalreview.com, March 9, 2015.

303 *"a pessimism about a present"* Charles Blow, "Race, History, a President, a Bridge: Obama and Selma: The Meaning of 'Bloody Sunday,'" *New York Times*, March 8, 2015.

One black writer, Michael H. Cottman Michael H. Cottman, "Hillary Clinton Wants Our Vote—So Why Wasn't She in Selma?" BlackAmericaWeb.com, March 10, 2015.

304 *Several Obama cabinet secretaries* Ironically, local organizers had broken with Congressman Lewis, who organized the annual pilgrimage to Selma, over the date of the major celebration and the president's visit. Lewis insisted that the main event be held on Saturday, the actual fifty-year anniversary of "Bloody Sunday," while the local organizing committee wanted to keep the celebration on the first Sunday in March, as it had always been. The result was dual celebrations, and a great deal of acrimony between the two sides.

305 *A CNN poll released on March 6* CNN/ORC International poll conducted by telephone, February 12–15, 2015, among a random sample of 1,027 adult Americans; released on March 6, 2015.

306 *"use the inspiration of Selma"* Zerlina Maxwell, "Flying with President Obama to Witness History in Selma," *Essence,* March 8, 2015.

Epilogue

309 *"take nothing for granted"* Annie Karni, "Clinton Campaign Memo: No Drama This Time," *Politico,* April 11, 2015.

311 *A Gallup poll released on March 21* Frank Newport, "Clinton's Top Selling Point in 2016: First Female President," report on March 15–16 Gallup poll (released March 21, 2015).

315 *by 5 to 8 percent in the Pew Poll* Pew Research Poll, "A Deep Dive into Party Affiliation," April 7, 2015.

INDEX